'NO GUTS N[O...]'

Bob the Bike

(Travels on a Pushbike)

ISBN 13: 978-1512368116
ISBN 10: 1512368113

http://arkpublishing.co.uk/

Robert Winstanley
Linda Swinford

Copyright © 2015 Ark Publishing UK. All rights reserved. No portion of this book may be reproduced, mechanically, electronically, or by any other means, including photocopying, without written permission of the author.

CONTENTS

Publisher's Note 9

Foreword by Linda Swinford 10

'Bob the Bike' Introduction 11

MEMORIES

I first rode a bike with no wheels 13

The Prequel 17

Childhood 20

Schooldays 26

Work and the Army 29

In a Foreign Country 33

Army Capers 37

Locked Up 40

Catching Up 42

Bob the Bike and Bromyard 49

CHAPTERS

1. Bob the Bike - Portugal 51

2. The Continuing Account 54

3. Bob the Bike Returns 58

4. Bob the Bike in Central America (1) 62

5. Bob the Bike in Central America (2) 66

Cycling on to Belize

6. Bob the Bike Reaches 71
Guatemala and Honduras

7. Nicaragua to Costa Rica 76

8. COSTA RICA 82
As I was saying

9. Here am I in Panama 85

10. And there's more 88

11. No guts, no story 91

12. Into Mexico 94

13. Cycling through Mexico 98

14. Cordoba and Beyond 101

15. Into America 104

16. Through Texas on a Pushbike 108

17. The Alamo and the Billy the Kid Museum 111

18. Into Louisiana 117

19. Mississippi, Alabama, on to Florida 119

20. The Crazy American Lifestyle 121

21. In Central America once more 128

22. Belize to Birmingham 131

23. India 135

24. The Taj Mahal and Holy Cows 137

25. Nepal and a Chicken Dinner 141

26. Isn't it? 146

27. The End of the Trek, and Over to Thailand 152

28. The Bridge Over the River Kwai 155

29. You famous man 159

30. Thai islands 163

31. Pineapple Trouble 166

32. From Thailand into Malaysia 169

33. Christmas on the Road 175

34. Happy New Year 179

35. You one are? 183

36. A Flat-Headed Tarmac Snake 186

37. A Gift and some Bees 189

38. A Visit to Singapore 191

39. Mooching in Malacca 195

40. Into Indonesia 198

41. A Chain Smoker and a Tattooed Lady 201

42. Several Deaths 204

43. A Moment With Cendra 207

44. A Stag Party and a Pelting 212

45. Trouble with Eggs Again 213

46. Over to Java 222

47. The Rambo of the Village 224

48. Only Five Knives 228

49. Smelly Hotels and a Beautiful Temple 231

50. Bicycle Saddle – Horse Saddle 235

51. A Broken Bone in Bali 238

52. From Bali to Birmingham 241

53. In South America Again – Rio and Onward 247

54. Fame in Brazil 251

55. Locked in the Lavatory 253

56. Close Encounters of the Dog Kind 256

57. Superfit Athletes 259

58. Snakes or Not 262

59. Towards the Borders 266

60. In Paraguay 271

61. A Bicycle in Bolivia 275

62. Through the Barricades 279

63. The High Plains 282

64. An Abduction Attempt 289

65. Into Peru 290

66. Lima, a Desert Robbery and the End of the Journey 293

67. Man on a Saddle in Vietnam 296

68. Swapping Stories 300

69. Rocks, Rain and Mr Pompous 302

70. Da Lat 306

71. Vung Tau and Veterans 309

72. Love En Route and a Robbery 312

73. In Cambodia 315

74. In Thailand 319

75. The Real Thailand 321

76. Smiles and a Punch 324

77. Village Life 327

78. Stop Me and Buy One 329

79. The Drunk on the Floor 332

80. Injuries and Idyllic Times Together 336

81. A Stuck Pig 344

82. My Machete Proves Useful 347

83. Back in Bangkok 351

84. Welcome to Bangladesh 354

85. Forrest Gump and his Followers 358

86. Bangladesh is Part of the World 361

87. Bangladesh – India – Nepal 36

88. A Holy Mess 370

89. An Aston Villa Fan in Nepal 377

90. Biscuits for Rhinos 378

91. Language Problems 382

92. Hanging on the Back of a Lorry 385

93. Welcome to Greece (Not) 387

94. Moussaka or Beer? 391

95. Easter Goes On and On 394

96. Pedalling Like Mad 397

97. Ups and Downs in Austria 400

98. One Beer in a Brewery 403

99. The Green Green Grass of Home 407

100. Epilogue – Sirima 411

101. Wanderlust Returns 414

102. What About Sirima 416

Publisher's Note

After hearing from the locals about 'Bob the Bike' and requested by Linda Swinford to publish his book, I first met Robert Winstanley one Friday evening on May 8th 2015 in Bromyard's local public house, The King's Arms. Bob was sat with a familiar acquaintance, Bob Craddock, who was the one who first put me on the track and privilege of finally publishing Bob the Bike's many accounts of his cycling world travels. We shook hands vigorously and talked over a few drinks. The rugged and healthy looking eighty year old man had clearly the story of his travels written on his face as lines of experience. I asked when he had arrived in the UK. He replied:

'Today, from Birmingham Airport (a distance of over 50 miles).'
'How? I asked,
'By bike,' was his reply.
'And your luggage?
'In my bike's pannier bags.

Bernard Paul Badham

Ark Publishing UK

Foreword by Linda Swinford

An old-ish man propped a pushbike against the window of the Tourist Office in Bromyard, Herefordshire and came in for a chat and some leaflets. I was doing a stint behind the counter and that's how I met Robert Winstanley, 'Bob the Bike.'

He said he liked the town; he often made it the starting point of his long-distance cycling holidays. I said he should write this down because Bromyard people would enjoy reading it in our local magazine. Bob didn't fancy the idea, he said he hadn't the education. So I told him not to worry, I'd type it up for him. I found a handwritten piece shoved under the door next morning and I began helping Bob to tell his story. The words are all his, just the full stops and capital letters are mine.

I kept on typing because I liked his style of writing and his story, funny, touching, modest, true. When the amazing travel section ended I got him to write an autobiographical prequel about the lad from Stetchford, Birmingham, who loved long-distance cycling all his life and decided in his sixties to go thousands of miles alone with just a map.

This book follows Bob's journeys through many countries in Asia and South America. Sheer slog, plus narrow escapes, interesting encounters, heroism, thefts and romances, mixed with humour and thoughtfulness.

As Bob says, 'No guts, no story.'

Linda Swinford

'Bob the Bike'
Introduction

Bob Winstanley was born and brought up in Stetchford, Birmingham during the 1930's and '40s. At that time a lovely country lane ran through Chelmsley Woods to Coleshill and on to Maxstoke, where Bob and his gang rode every day in the long summer holidays to play on the disused railway track or in the river catching sticklebacks in old wine bottles lifted empty from the local off-license.

At eleven years old and very small, he had got hold of a Hercules Roadster wreck with 28' wheels, which he rode with his legs through the triangle. On his first journey to school a pedal fell off and try as he might, he couldn't screw it back on. A passing stranger explained about the left-hand thread.

His love of long-distance cycling began around 1950 when a friend suggested they cycle to Wales. Scraping every penny together to make 25 shillings, the two teenagers set off with emergency ration coupons for their big adventure. In a week, they went 500 miles to Pwllheli and back and amazed at the distance they had covered, a passion was born.

Bob bought a bright blue Hercules Falcon with the six shillings a week he earned delivering papers through Britain's worst winter in 1947. Later, on two years military service in Germany he drew a bike from stores on his first day, setting out to explore with the other guys shouting, 'You must be mad! The Germans will kill you!' When he returned they clapped him on the back and said how brave he was.

Back in Civvy Street he met the girl he was to spend 38 years with, and although he rode a bike every day to work he withdrew from the longer rides. One day he realized how much he missed them and he told his wife he must cycle again. She was in agreement, but soon found he planned to be away for several weeks at a time in Spain and Portugal!

Bob bought a Claud Butler bike and later a Dawes Super Galaxy. He continued his cycling pastime until tragedy came along when after a terrible illness his wife died at only 57. It took him two years to pull himself together and decide to have a crack at the world. He was then sixty-two years old.

In the next four years he rode 40,000 miles through 32 countries, completely alone. No back-up vehicles, no computers or telephones, he travelled through every country in Central America, Mexico, Peru, Paraguay, Brazil and Bolivia. Then India, Nepal, Bangladesh and more... Armed with a tent he slept free anywhere.

Reaching Thailand he became aware that at sixty-four he didn't want to grow old alone. He met and married Sirima and is now based in Thailand, returning to England yearly to visit family and friends. England is an ideal place after all to start his current cycling trips, such as touring through Spain, as he did this summer. He was ending this tour when he met up with Solihull Cycling Club members.

At home in Thailand he leads a group of ex-pat Sunday cyclists and regularly goes out for a ride of eighty miles or more. Bob is now an incredible seventy-eight year old.

Bob's whole story at time of writing is currently being edited and put together for possible publication. It makes amazing reading.

Linda Swinford

MEMORIES

I first rode a bike with no wheels

My very first contraption was an old Hercules with a 28-inch frame and 28-inch wheels, a roadster, the type that big, solid policeman used to ride. Not long back from the war, my father worked as a dustman and he brought this wreck of a bike home. It had many parts missing but over a few months he found bits and pieces that people had cast out, and we codged a bike together.

I was only eleven years old and very small – I had to ride with my legs through the triangle. On my first day riding the bike to school a pedal came off, and try as I might I couldn't screw it back on. I didn't know that one pedal has a left hand thread. Those were the days when the school bike-sheds were full of bikes, the places where the boys sneaked a cigarette and learned about sex. Now they just watch television to learn about sex.

From where I lived in Stetchford, Birmingham, there was a lovely country lane that ran through Chelmsley Woods to Coleshill and then on to Maxstoke. Now it is covered in massive housing estates. It was further on then to Maxstoke, because now the roads have been straightened out and fresh short cuts added. My local gang and I used to ride there every day in the long summer holidays and play in the river or on the disused railway track, occasionally sleeping in abandoned railway wagons. We had no money; we took a bottle of water each and a sandwich if we were lucky.

We caught sticklebacks by breaking a hole in the bottom of a wine bottle, the type with a funnel in the base, lifted empty from our local off-license. Then, tying a length of string round the neck and putting a few breadcrumbs inside, we threw the bottle in the river. The fish swam in through the hole in the centre of the base but when they tried to swim out they were trapped against the sides of the bottle. Many times I walked home alone with flat tyres – we had no equipment, but they were the happiest days of my childhood.

Came the time when I was old enough to deliver newspapers (well, not quite, but nobody was counting). I was paid six shillings a week and saved every penny, trudging through Britain's worst ever winter in 1947. I bought a bright blue Hercules Falcon with the six shillings a week and that bike brought me the pleasure I still enjoy today. It was the bike that first introduced me to long distance cycling and it was mine after fifty payments.

Military service came along, and I served two years in Germany, starting in 1953. None of us lads had ever been abroad before and this was the first time I encountered people's fear of being in another country. On the first day there, I had to explore, so I drew a bicycle out of the store – a sit up and beg Raleigh, rod brakes, no gears and olive drab green army colours. I set off with all the guys shouting, 'You must be mad! The Germans will kill you!' When I returned they clapped me on the back and said how brave I was. During my two years I used this bike time after time.

Returning to Civvy Street I gradually withdrew from the long rides. Girls had entered my life and I met the girl that I was to spend 38 years with. I still rode a long distance to work every day for years – sometimes to Worcester and back and so I remained very fit.

Many times I reflected on the pleasures I used to enjoy and finally I told my wife that I must cycle again. She was in agreement but thought it might be just an hour or two at the weekend. She wasn't pleased when I set off for a week at a time in England, and then as time went by for several weeks in Spain or Portugal.

I bought a Claud Butler; they used to be considered the Rolls Royce of bicycles and then a Dawes Super Galaxy. Expensive bikes, but they were both stolen from my garage at the top of the garden.

I bought another Galaxy and continued my cycling pastime, but tragedy came along and after a terrible illness my wife died at the age of only fifty-seven. It took me two years to pull myself together and I decided to have a crack at the world. For the marathon ride that I managed I used only two bicycles. I would have used only one except that my Galaxy was stolen in the deserts of Peru.

I replaced it with a Thorn Nomad road bike. This is an excellent machine and it's the one I still have although all that remains of the original is the frame, the spokes and the hubs. Everything else has been replaced, some several times, handlebars, mudguards, pedal chains at least four times, chain set, rear block and hangers several times, saddle three times, pump twice, brake levers and brake blocks many times, tyres and inner tubes dozens of times. The wheels have been rebuilt at least four times, but the spokes and hubs don't wear out. The punishment these two bikes coped with was colossal.

I never used to package my bike although I was told at Birmingham Airport in 2012 that it must now be boxed or bubble wrapped. Of course there's a fancy charge for doing this plus a charge for carrying the bicycle.

I don't ever recall being asked to pay airfare for my bicycle. It was regarded as my luggage. I let the tyres down as instructed, removed the pedals and turned the handlebars parallel with the frame. Sometimes I wrapped the chain. One time when I couldn't release the handlebars and so I needed a hammer to give the bolt a tap. The nearest thing to a hammer was a policeman's revolver but he refused to lend it to me.

As for equipment and clothing for my adventures, I carried a minimum, reasoning that it would be cheap to buy new as I went along. So I had three shirts, one pullover, spare shoes, three pairs of underpants and socks, long trousers, a waterproof jacket, a towel, a tent and a sleeping bag. I had a small stove with little blocks of fuel, a small saucepan and a bag of oats to make porridge to get me going in the morning. I kept one of my water bottles filled with toffees.

I had spare inner tubes, two spare tyres that I kept coiled and fixed to my front pannier rack, a spare chain, chain rings, spokes, brake blocks and spanners including a link remover, all sorts of useful bric-a-brac. I learned early to keep it all in plastic bags so that it kept dry and I could see it straight away. When you want something you have to search through bag after bag to find it and it's always in the last bag, so I purchased some strong sizeable plastic bags. Of course I carried loads of maps. Armed with maps I just set off. I made no plans. It amuses me how people spend two years preparing, especially wimps on motorbikes. So I still ride the Thorn Nomad. When my wife Sirima has time we ride together. I also have two excellent Dahon folding bikes that we take in the car when we tour. How great to park up and ride a bike.

The Prequel

A sharp slap, a voice says, 'It's a boy,' and here I am.

I already have a brother and a sister and following on from me my mother produces another six. It is June 1935. I am born in Lancashire. When I am nine months old my father takes us to Birmingham in search of work. Depressions are not a new thing.

My first real recollection is of sitting on the top stair crying for my mother who for some reason is in the back bedroom with a nurse. A baby cries. Shortly afterwards midwife Shakespeare places my three year-old self beside my mother. I don't know where that little pink face called Edith has come from.

As I get older I become used to midwife Shakespeare visiting our house and leaving a baby behind. On the back of her bicycle is a black rectangular box. Mom tells me she brings the babies in that box. Many times I try to pluck up courage to raise the lid and see for myself. Three of the babies die. Roy and David, had pneumonia and diphtheria respectively; Vera? I don't know. It's a blessing, still six children and two adults to feed; on not much more than pennies.

I grew up during the Second World War. I don't remember feeling fear; too young to understand. I just thought, 'This is life.' Mom's daily parting words to us going to school were, 'Don't forget your gas masks.' The policeman crossing us over the road wore a gun in a white holster, in case some German had been forced to parachute.

At times, if the air raid warning was early enough, we threw the youngest in the pram and joined hundreds of others in the headlong rush through blacked-out streets seeking the comparative safety of a communal shelter. Stetchford swimming baths now stand on the site that was our nearest public shelter. Close by was an underground command post (After the war these places were sealed up, but we Bash Street kids soon got in and made them our dens. The command post still had equipment inside, including an air conditioning system. In the darkness we played kiss-catch. I recall the girls didn't run very fast.)

Other times in the air raids we would crawl into the corrugated iron Anderson shelter that the government supplied. One such night I slipped and gashed my face on the front fascia. The corrugated iron penetrated my cheek. I suppose I should have claimed a pension for a war wound. We crouched in the entrance and watched the searchlights trying to pinpoint the German aircraft for the anti-aircraft guns. We listened to the whistle that the bombs made as they fell.

On the way to school we sometimes saw people working frantically, searching through rubble for trapped victims. Sheila, the little girl who shared my desk, didn't turn up one day. I had passed the ruins of her house. She never turned up again. An incendiary bomb fell through the school roof and the damage meant serious loss of education. Children were being evacuated, but it's the old story, only those with money. The government paid two-thirds of the cost, the parents' one-third. Our family could not afford this. None of the families in our road could afford it.

I have no good memories of my Dad. He always had money for beer and cigarettes while we kids had no shoes. He was called up and for eleven weeks Mom received no allowance. With the help of a more worldly-wise neighbour, who contacted the authorities, she finally got monthly payments from a Dad who couldn't be bothered to fill in a form.

When I got older I discovered that he spent his home leaves back in Lancashire getting drunk with his brother. He was sent away to fight in Egypt, Italy and Germany and it was years before I saw him again.

As the war came to a close a day arrived when I was travelling on a tram from the Bull Ring and a soldier sat in front of me. We alighted at the same stop and I walked behind him. Only when he opened the gate to my house I realized he was my father. He died at the age of forty-nine. By this time I was in uniform myself. His funeral cost £40 and I had to borrow the money from a neighbour to pay for it. There was a lighter note to a sombre occasion. I had been writing to a girl who worked in the flower shop and a note came with the wreaths. So my two weeks compassionate leave turned into two weeks passionate leave.

Childhood

In our road most families were large. You were a sissy if you had fewer than three siblings. Most of us grew up poor, but I don't recall being envious. Once again I just thought this was life.

My house was in a road near Stetchford railway station. Many Lancashire people had disembarked there and they became our neighbours. The rent was fifteen shillings a week. In some of the houses two families shared to halve the cost. I remember coming home from school one day to find Mom and Dad jubilant because a distant uncle of Mom's that she couldn't even remember had died and she had received a share of his will, £11. That would have paid a lot of weeks' rent, but Dad had a better use for it and Mom never saw a penny.

Mom's twin sister had married and remained in Lancashire. She only produced one child. With her husband she opened a fish and chip shop in Liverpool. To us they were rich people. As her son grew out of his clothes Auntie Sarah would post them to Mom. They all smelt strongly of fish and chips. My teacher looked round the class and shouted, 'Who has brought fish and chips to school?' and my classmates pointed at me.

My mother broke her false teeth and Auntie Sarah sent one of her old sets. I shouldn't really have said it but I did, 'Mom, you look like a horse.'

A humiliation I experienced many times at school still scars me. At times an outing was arranged, maybe to the zoo or Cheddar Gorge. Each child paid a few shillings for the trip, but I couldn't do that. Placed in another class for the day I suffered the mocking of the kids there. More still when my classmates returned.

On arrival in Stetchford Dad secured a job at Parkinson's, opposite the railway station. They made gas cookers, water heaters, fires and so on. With the coming of war they had to produce arms and so became a target for German bombers. The worst bombing raid Birmingham suffered destroyed the water mains. If the Germans had come again the next night Birmingham would have burnt to the ground, no water to douse the fires. It was a long time before water was restored to our houses and we either walked a few miles to fill buckets from the River Cole or queued at the emergency tankers.

To the delight of many women the Americans arrived. Neighbours gathered at the gate or leaned on the garden wall, all dressed in turbans and wraparound pinnies and talked about Mrs So-and-So and Mrs Thingummybob. I couldn't see anything wrong with inviting a Yankee soldier in for a cup of tea.

We kids ran like mad behind the troop carriers shouting, 'Give us some gum, chum,' and the Yanks threw chewing gum into the road. German and Italian prisoners of war were allowed to work on the roads and farms. They wore jackets with POW stencilled on the back. They were also invited in for a cup of tea. Everything was rationed and in short supply. Our family had plenty of ration coupons, but no money. The rich people had the money, but they were short of coupons, so we sold them our coupons or exchanged them for goods. My mother sent me to the butcher's with a load of clothing coupons and he asked, 'Do you want meat or money?'

'Mom told me to ask for a pound of whale meat and leave the head on for the cat.'

Petrol was reserved mainly for commercial vehicles. Only a small allowance was given for the few private cars. Fuel for commercial vehicles was pink, so when the police stopped private vehicles and inspected the petrol they knew if it was pink it was stolen or black market.

One day my school received a parcel of sweets from America. What a treat! Shared out we got one each.

Everyone had an open fire, that's if you had money for coal. Many a time we all huddled in the kitchen seeking warmth from a gas ring and praying the penny wouldn't run out. Out of desperation my older brother and I went out in the dead of night with the pram. He scaled the wall of Parkinson's and filled a bucket with coke. I emptied it into the pram and we ran hell for leather back home through blacked-out streets.

Gas lamps lined the road. The bigger boys shinned up them to impress the girls by lighting a cigarette from the pilot light. The ornamental lamp tops were removed to be stored until the bombing finished, so we lived in the dark for a long time.

To make a little pocket money we searched everywhere for pop bottles, even knocking on doors, to collect the few pennies deposit. We climbed over a large gate at the back of Cox's Off-Licence to help ourselves from the crates of empty beer bottles. Then we returned the bottles to the off-licence to put a few coppers in our pockets. We bought an orange box for four pence and broke it up to make two buckets of firewood, sold them for four pence each and repeated the exercise. With a little money we could go to the pictures and see Flash Gordon and the Clay Men, Dagwood Bumstead and later, Ma and Pa Kettle. No sweets in the shops so we bought a packet of sweetened cocoa each and sat in the stalls dipping a wet finger into the box and transferring the cocoa to our mouths. We emerged from the cinema looking like Al Jolson. Two films were shown and between the films the Home Guard appeared on stage and demonstrated their drill capabilities. We kept our gas masks with us all the time. Toddlers' gas masks looked like Mickey Mouse and for babes in arms they resembled oxygen tents. Children could get into the cinema for more adult films only if accompanied by an adult. Scores of kids gathered on the forecourt pleading, 'Will you take one in, mister?' usually successfully.

My young sister Margaret injured her foot while paddling in the River Cole and needed to visit the doctor. We were all brought up to be frightened of the doctor, because before 1948 you had to pay, impossible for Mother to do. If any of us was ill she would threaten, 'If you don't get better you'll have to go to the doctor's.' This forceful statement put us in fear of what the doctor might do, to this day I fear the doctor. Mom nursed us herself, but an injury was different. The doctor refused to believe there was anything wrong with Margaret, saying she was malingering to avoid school. She suffered two weeks of agony until a shard of glass passed through her foot and emerged on top. Then, 'Bless my soul,' said the doctor.

The whole population was urged to dig for victory. Along with growing vegetables people bred chickens and even pigs. People disposed of what few scraps were left over by putting them in bins placed in the streets and council workers collected the contents to help feed pigs on farms. In our road two men sent home from the war suffered badly from shell shock. They wandered aimlessly around the streets and scavenged the slops in the bins. Not understanding, we kids used to tease Bodger and Todger, as we called them. Many times in the night the clang awoke me of the bin lid hitting the road and from my window I could see local men stealing the pig food to give to their own pigs. These were not the only opportunists. Horses and carts delivered most things, like bread, milk and coal. The horses twigged there was food to be had and they soon learned to nudge the lid off the pig bin.

The Richmond pub in Stetchford let people shelter in the cellars during air raids. It turned out lucky for those living in the semi-detached houses next door. They were flattened by a direct hit. These council houses were rebuilt after the war to match the houses still standing, except that the roofs were tiled with different tiles. On house roofs in the road now called the Meadway, which leaves Station Road next to the police station and shortly reaches the crossroads at Queen's Road, are large patches of different coloured tiles. I remember going to look at the gaping holes caused when a bomb landed at the crossroads and blasted off parts of the roofs. In a daylight raid, shoppers at Glebe Farm, a short distance away, were machine gunned by a German plane.

With the end of the war came huge celebrations, triumphant marches round the streets carrying effigies of Hitler, Goering and Goebbels. After the parade people hanged the effigies on pre-erected gallows and burned them to oblivion on huge bonfires. Fences ripped up the whole length of the road provided fuel for the fires. We each received two tickets, one for a drink and one for a cake or an ice-cream. My eldest sister Nora won a hundred yards race and was presented with a hairbrush. I was so proud of her.

Dad came home. His health was gone, but he still managed to sire the ninth baby, Edward. I have often wondered how many the family would have numbered if there hadn't been a war, there was a six year gap between Margaret and Edward and only a couple of years between the rest of us. In the eight years he had left to live, Dad had several jobs. One was as a carpenter's mate. He came home one evening with a Yale lock, which he fitted to the front door. But back at work somebody had squealed and he was told, 'Return that lock or else.' He returned the lock, so now we had a 1¼ inch hole in the front door at shoulder height. Nobody who knocked the door could resist looking through that hole. Responding to a caller meant walking along the hall with an eye staring at you. Nora and I had a contest guessing whose eye it was.

Goods must have become more available, but I hardly noticed. We still couldn't buy fish and chips unless we had our own newspaper to wrap them in, we had to use treacle to sweeten our tea and we cut out pieces of cardboard to fit over the holes in our shoes. Anderson shelters were in big demand, re-erected as workshops and garages. The kids in the road assembled in one of these door-less structures, a sort of gang hut. One day Margaret Plimmer, a big girl, jumped up and held onto a hanging piece of corrugated iron. The whole garage collapsed trapping ten of us inside. Nobody was seriously injured, and I was the last brought out, with a gash in my leg. As the blood ran into my shoe I thought, 'Oh well, it'll run out of the hole in the sole.'

My pal Billy Gittins, one of ten children, came home to find his mother resting her head on a cushion. She was lying on the kitchen floor and her head was in the gas oven. The family was re-housed but a few years later, Mr Gittins full of remorse chose the same way out. My mother and Mrs Gittins used to help each other out. If we had tea and no margarine, I would be sent with half a packet of tea to swap for half a packet of margarine, and so on.

By this time I was at senior school. I assembled a bicycle with bits my Dad brought home from his job as dustman at the time. A boy was killed in a road accident. I didn't know him, in fact I doubt if many people knew him. His funeral cortege drove past our school and all the children stood along the pavement to pay our respects. Afterwards we went back to our classes. These days somebody would insist we all needed counselling. The large Co-Operative shop was the site of one of our pranks. They used to spread sawdust over the floor, sweeping up the dirty sawdust at the end of the day and replacing it for the morning. The mischief we got up to was to hold up the letterbox flap (very carefully, strong spring) and aiming with the other hand to see who could pee the furthest mark in the sawdust. Johnny Plimmer always won. He had a couple of inches start on the rest of us.

We still played cowboys and Indians, pretending to gallop horses round the streets, slapping our rumps and shooting cap pistols that we acquired from Woolworth's one way or another. It was getting dark one night and outside my house I could hear my pals. Grabbing my cap gun I rushed out to join what must be a cowboy game. What a disappointment! Several lads clustered next to a tall overgrown privet hedge in a dark corner of our cul-de-sac. They were taking it in turns to fumble with Dorothy Ollerenshaw and Peggy and Annie Schofield. I went home.

They never wanted to play cowboys again.

Schooldays

'Why weren't you at school yesterday?' asked the teacher.
'I had no shoes, sir,' I replied.

Mom and I had spent most of the day before in an enormous queue at Steelhouse Lane police station where clothing and footwear were being distributed courtesy of the Daily Mail. I received a pair of Daily Mail boots, easily recognisable, which made me the subject of much taunting. In my house we didn't go to bed until most of us were home, because with only the odd blanket we needed everybody's coat on the two beds that six of us shared. In my final year at junior school my teacher Miss Evans had told me I had top marks in most subjects.

'You would pass for the grammar school,' she said.

But Dad had spoken. 'Who do you think you are? We can't afford uniforms and we can't afford you spending extra years at school. Grammar school is for posh kids. Remember your place. You'll have to get to work as soon as possible.'

A black boy from Jamaica joined our school. He amazed us, the first black person we had ever seen in the flesh. We made him very welcome and everybody wanted to be his friend. Most of our sports heroes were black, such as Joe Louis the heavyweight boxer and McDonald Bailey the runner, so we expected this boy to be able to run like the wind and swim like a dolphin. But of course, he was just like the rest of us. My oldest sister Nora and her best friend Jean Lewis had started going to dances, and Jean used to come to our house to get ready. She made Marilyn Monroe look like a man and she used to tease me unmercifully, smothering my twelve-year old face with kisses and leaving it as red as her lipstick. She was in the Land Army and I can see her now in her jodhpurs, riding a bike with her blonde hair streaming behind her.

The two girls sent me to the park to gather a small bag of sand. They wetted their legs before rubbing the sand all over. They pencilled a thin black line down the backs of their legs so that without close inspection they looked as if they could afford nylons.

When Nora finally met the man who became her husband it was winter and she was wearing the only shoes she possessed, a pair of ankle-length fur boots. Spring and summer came and she still had to turn up on dates wearing those boots. Years later I lost several girlfriends because I turned up in appalling weather with no overcoat. They thought there wasn't much prospect with this guy.

A group of us was heading for the park to play football when Jean's sister Pauline emerged from the house. She didn't have Jean's looks but the material of her blouse was at breaking point.

'Austin,' she called to a lad she had a fancy for, 'there's nobody in.'
'I'm going to play football,' was the reply he stunned me with.
Pauline dragged her blouse open to reveal an amazing super-structure.
'There's nobody in,' she repeated.

We all went to play football, including Austin, but I couldn't keep my mind on the game.

Following the fatal road accident our lessons included road safety, eventually leading to a test. Michael Peach and I were the only pupils who produced the correct answer to every question. We each received a road safety certificate and a ticket to Billy Smart's circus. That's the only certificate I've ever had on my wall.

With the shortage of labour the government allowed boys over thirteen to work on the farms. We piled into the open lorries that transported us to the fruit or potato picking. It meant loss of education, but it also meant earning ten pence an hour (five pence in today's money). I handed the money over to Mom. During lunch breaks we rolled around in the hay stored in a barn. One of the lads set fire to the hay while smoking a cigarette. The barn burned down and the farmer was not pleased.

Weekends and holidays a little gang of us pedalled off into the countryside beyond Coleshill, about twelve miles east of Birmingham. A super-highway has now replaced the winding country lanes. I rode a huge sit-up-and-beg bike that my father had stolen from outside a pub only a mile from home. I had to ride with my legs through the triangle because if I sat on the saddle I couldn't reach the pedals. We took a bottle of water and a sandwich if we were lucky, and we played on a disused railway track. I started a paper round. I lied about my age as I was only twelve, but the newsagent wasn't much bothered. Twice a day, for six days and Sunday mornings, six shillings a week. Mom let me keep the money and for six shillings a week I bought a bright blue Hercules dropped handlebar road bike. Now the real cycling began. Every chance I got I was off.

My school was in two parts, one for boys and the other for girls. Girls left ten minutes before boys so that they wouldn't be pestered. The headmaster got it the wrong way round.

I learned to swim at Green Lane Baths. There had been two pools, first and second class, but first class got bombed so it was girls one day and boys the next in second class. The reason was that there were no changing cubicles, only a shelf fixed round the walls.

Three of us went shoplifting in Woolworth's. Two staged a fight, wrestling on the floor. While shoppers crowded round the third grabbed torches, marbles, fountain pens, water pistols and so on to sell at school. Honesty was a luxury we couldn't afford.

At fourteen years old I was the only boy in the fourth year wearing short trousers. When my older brother Eric joined the army I had the trousers he left behind. The thigh of the right leg had a small hole where he had burned it with a cigarette. Mother darned it but the place was still visible. I developed the habit of holding my hand over the patch, and I did this for so long that even when I acquired patch-free trousers I still stood or walked with my hand covering my thigh. I couldn't conceal the patch all the time. My tormentors soon spotted it.

Work and the Army

1947 – the worst British weather on record. Thirteen weeks of snow and ice. People had primitive heating methods; most only heated the living room. The same winter would seem nowhere near as bad now. Everybody has central heating, open the door of any shop and heat pours out. Snowploughs are abundant and we can cope better.

As a paperboy I struggled through drifts of snow taller than me. The 'Mail' must go through. Most of the other lads didn't turn up, but I needed the six shillings for my Hercules bike.

With the snow gone we had a glorious summer and I happily delivered my papers over a large area still blessed at that time with fields and farms. I passed Blakesley Hall, boarded up after bomb damage but restored later. I used to dream about how nice it would be to build a bungalow here, silly dreams for a young boy, but I looked at various sites and carried on dreaming. Gradually the city spread and the land got taken up, but for some reason one plot was fenced round and left untouched.

For years and years I checked on this plot. When I got married I bought a new terraced house on mortgage for the staggering amount of £2,000. I was earning £11 a week and I paid £11 a month mortgage for thirty years. Thirty years after dreaming of buying the plot I realised that with the equity on my little house it was actually a possibility. The council informed me that they owned the plot and had completely overlooked it. So I bought it and built a bungalow. I called the bungalow 'My Way.'

My sister Nora worked at Southall's Alum Rock. Many women in our road worked there. The factory produced women's sanitary goods. The materials came to the factory in muslin sacks and the women brought the sacks home to use as net curtains. The sacks had black stencils every few inches and my mother boiled and boiled the muslin to remove the brand before dyeing and hanging them. Nobody else bothered, they just hung them up. To walk down our road was to see primitive net curtains branded with the name Southall's.

When I left school Dad got me a job painting lamp-posts. I refused the job and started with a small building and decorating firm. War damage work was priority, and permits to buy materials were issued for it. This didn't affect the rich people, who claimed that work needed doing on their business premises and then used the materials to spruce up their elegant houses.

One of my first jobs was in Small Heath, replacing slates that were full of shrapnel holes.

I was doing more cycling. Not only did I find it enjoyable, and still do, but it was also an affordable pastime. Geoffrey Colman suggested we spend a week's holiday riding in Wales. After some persuasion I was hooked. I spent a year saving every penny I could get, resorting once again to selling firewood and collecting bottles. My wages were seven pence an hour, or £1-5s-0d a week. I handed them over to Mom and she gave me back 3s-6d a week for myself.

That first serious cycle ride hooked me for life. We covered five hundred miles in one week. We stayed at youth hostels and had to obtain emergency ration cards to buy meat. We had a tremendous time.

For the next three years I rode out a good distance every fourth weekend, I couldn't afford to do it every week. I was usually alone because Geoff played rugby for Dunlop's. In 1953 we set out together to ride to Land's End. We got there on Coronation Day and saw countless people enjoying street parties despite the rain. I didn't think then that I would be riding round sixty years later enjoying the street celebrations laid on for the Queen's Jubilee, in the pouring rain again.

I was at Hartington Hall in Dovedale Valley when the announcement came on the radio saying that men my age must register for National Service. The announcements were made fortnightly. I presented myself with hundreds of other men at Oozells Street for documentation and a thorough medical examination.

A nurse took details and told me to join a very long queue. 'To save time,' she suggested, 'remove your clothing. If you have no underpants you can leave your trousers on.' I put my clothes on a shelf and stood in line. Many more men were wearing trousers than underpants. My first ever underpants were Army issue. Description: Drawers, cellular, green.

After a touch your toes examination the doctor pronounced me Grade One fit. He added, 'You're a small fellow.' He wasn't referring to my height. Over the years being a small fellow has never given me any big problems. Rephrase that, has never given me any small problems.

Every two weeks the call-up gave you a three-month wait before you actually enlisted. Teddy Tudor had a religious mother and declared himself a conscientious objector. He went into the medical corps. Roy Howarth worked at the Rover car plant. He was imprisoned for raping a girl in the park. The newspaper headlines said about him, 'Nineteen pounds a week at age nineteen.' This was a colossal wage then. I was earning £7 a week, £5 for Mom and £2 for me.

Hughie Megetigan died very young from a heart attack. Colin Nicholls failed his medical, to the huge disappointment of his father, who had been my own dad's sergeant major and had lived for the day his son would be in uniform. Eventually Colin was accepted into the police force and became a motorbike cop. His dad was over the moon, but three months later Colin crashed into a telegraph pole. He was buried in uniform.

Gideon Williams' mother took him back to Wales. She didn't want him in the army, too dangerous. If you worked down the mines you were exempt from military service. Gideon was crushed between two coal trucks and he lived, but ......

I got to know Jack Ferdinando, an older man who had been a professional soldier. Shortly after the outbreak of war his entire unit was captured and spent the whole war in captivity. Jack was the Regimental Sergeant in charge of discipline. 'As long as we behaved there were no problems,' he told me. 'Could have done with more food but we had enough.'

Under supervision they worked on farms and in factories, content to wait the war out. 'We'll be free soon.' Over such a long period of time they formed friendships with guards and exchanged family news. They wept in each other's arms when they heard about the bombing of their respective towns.

When at last the allies swept across the country the Germans moved the prisoners deeper into Germany. Jack instructed his men to keep together. 'We'll be free soon. Don't make a break for it just so you can boast you escaped. You'll be shot.'

Gradually the Germans lost interest in the prisoners and began to scatter. The allies surrounded them and set up tables for short interviews. Some of the Germans who could now speak good English tried to pass themselves off as English in the hope of going to England. (Well, the girls are lovelier.)

With RSM Ferdinando at his side the commanding officer set about his task. 'Point out any German who has treated prisoners badly and he will be dispatched immediately.'

Jack told me, 'We didn't need to point out a single one.'

In a Foreign Country

Two years of military service ahead, hundreds of us were herded onto the train like sheep. I was more than a little frightened. The other recruits seemed much more worldly-wise than me, setting up card schools, practically all smoking and every other word an obscenity. When we reached London I couldn't understand why so many young women were standing around. They must have been waiting for a pop star.

In quarters at the barracks I selected a bed from the thirty available. 'Strip to the waist,' was the order and we marched away to collect our uniforms. On return all money had been removed from our jackets. Discipline was brutal, in those days they could get away with it. We had to serve our time like it or not.

We received £1-8s a week. I sent seven shillings a week home to my mother and spent most of the rest on cleaning materials. The floor had to be polished with black boot polish, then it was covered with our bed blankets, nobody must walk on the floor. The pot-bellied stove shone like a full moon, it was never used. Nobody put coal in the coal bucket, but every man spent ten minutes a day polishing the darned thing.

The clothes in our lockers had to be placed in a particular order, showing a one-inch strip to the front. To achieve this effect we inserted pieces of cardboard in the garments. There had to be thirteen studs in our boots. We were issued with a plate and a mug. As we queued in a long column a ponced-up commissioned officer walked up and down the line, demanding here and there to see the crockery. Without fail he smashed it on the floor, shouted 'Filthy! Now pick up the pieces!' and walked on.

I reported that my greatcoat had been stolen. The sergeant gave me a blistering telling-off. 'I'm not your mother. You're in the army now. Just make sure you have a greatcoat at the next inspection.' I had to steal one from another barrack room.

After eight weeks of training I came home on embarkation leave. I was being sent to Germany. 'What an adventure,' I thought.

Dad was more or less bedridden. We had a terrible row when he insisted on seeing me off at the station. I thought it would look sissy to be seen off by my Dad. I nearly missed the train because he could hardly walk. He knew he was dying and I didn't. We shook hands and I boarded the train. That was the last time I saw him alive.

From the barracks in Harwich I was the mug who had to march in front of a column of soldiers with a sign saying 'Soldiers Marching'. I felt a complete fool. We were on our way to board ship. Many of the lads were very sea sick. We docked at the Hook of Holland. Again crowds of young ladies at the docks, the pop star must have been appearing there as well.

We reached Munchen Gladbach by train and here I spent almost two years. I was so excited at being in a foreign country that I marched up to the guard post to sign out. I got a plastering from the sergeant. Apparently I was a disgrace to my country; the crease in my trousers wasn't good enough. Back to barracks, trousers pressed, I was allowed out. Months later guys said how brave they thought I was. The majority served their two years frightened to leave the camp. I drew a bicycle from stores and explored the countryside, I went on outings by coach, I just loved to get about.

I lost my virginity in Amsterdam. Regular coach trips took soldiers to Holland and they came back with thought-provoking tales. So there I was with two pals taking in the sights and Lordy, Lordy what sights! Three women took charge of us. We entered the same house and climbed the stairs. We each took a bedroom.

'You have money for me, darling,' spoke the maiden.
'How much?'
'One pound,' she said.

I objected. Taffy Hopkins had just told us he paid ten shillings. She shouted down the corridor to check with the other maidens, but my pals must have had money to burn.

'No,' she said, 'they agree to one pound. But I take all my clothes off.'

That clinched it, and I found all was in working order.

I was determined to learn German and I got pretty good. I met Marta and we had some pleasant times together. I got jealous one day when a German youth got too chatty with her and we finished by squaring up outside. I landed some solid punches and was enjoying myself until he started hitting me back. Marta's brother stepped in and called it off, thank goodness.

I did better with a Scots guy, Jock McQuillan. He was a self-styled tough with a little band of followers. He repeatedly bullied assorted victims and swaggered about, bragging what he and his boys could do. I was working shifts in battery section, no work, just supervising the German workers. I returned from shift and fell asleep in a flash. Our room had ten beds, so it had the most space to congregate in. Jock and his cronies entered, making a hell of a row boasting about how they had just roughed up a couple of blokes from another company.

I was flaming mad at being woken up. 'Shut up and get out of our room.' Silence descended. The guys not on shift sat up. Nobody talked like that to Jock McQuillan. Jock found his voice.
'See if you can shut me up.'

I swung my feet out of bed and put on my shoes. Jock was describing what he was going to do to me. I stepped round the bunch of other Scotsmen and hit Jock in the face as hard as I could. As the blood spread across his face everybody gazed at me in disbelief that somebody had struck hard man McQuillan.

I should have followed it up, but I stood back. He came at me like a battering ram and I backpedalled down the room. I came to a stop with my rump against the card table. I went back on the card table as the Scotsman gripped my hips and held me down. But my hands were free. I punched him insensible and his cronies dragged him away.

'Get him out of our room and don't come in here again.' I didn't have a mark on me.

A damaged McQuillan stood at attention for muster inspection. Sergeant major said not a word, fights were encouraged. From that day on guys spoke very politely to me.

Army Capers

17 Vehicle Battalion, Ayrshire Barrack was my address. Now the Munchen Gladbach football ground, it had been an airfield during the war. Excellent quarters, the only largish room was battery section. The rest mostly contained two beds so they were easy to keep clean and tidy with your best pal.

Christmas came along. I bought a chicken and the cookhouse sergeant had it roasted for me complete with roast potatoes and vegetables. The others ridiculed me because I wouldn't have a drink. I blamed the poverty our family endured on my father's drinking and smoking habits, and to this day I have never smoked a cigarette. Later in life I realised there was nothing wrong with having a drink, providing the family came first, and my family wanted for nothing within reason.

I was dead set on not drinking and at age nineteen I still drank orange pop. One night on prowler guard, spruced up and carrying a rifle (no ammunition), it was hot and I slipped into the NAAFI to grab a quick drink. They'd stopped serving soft drinks in the restaurant and I had to enter the bar. A huge cheer went up as my already inebriated comrades pulled me to their table and placed a pint of beer in front of me. After much badgering I drank it, followed by two more. I was taking a risk drinking on guard duty. My mates pushed me outside. I staggered round, found my way back to the guardhouse and with the other guards looking at me in amazement I threw myself on the bed and passed out. I think it was only because I was known as the guy who belted Jock McQuillan that nobody reported me. So I blame the NAAFI for my long time habit of drinking beer instead of sticking to orange pop.

Two years passed very slowly. We weren't allowed to work, only to supervise the German Service Organisation. What a waste of manpower, over a thousand men at our camp and we could have been put to good use clearing bomb damage and rebuilding.

I took a job as a waiter in the sergeants' mess. I thought I looked handsome in my white jacket and black trousers, and some of the sergeants had teenage daughters. Those men who shouted orders at us every day lost any respect I had for them. They got hopelessly drunk every night, but I wasn't about to look a gift horse in the mouth, they never counted their change. At the end of the night glasses of drinks were left over. I kept several trays of drinks and sandwiches outside the back door. Sometimes the sergeants complained they hadn't enough sandwiches, but they didn't look outside the back door. Loaded up I returned to my block (several journeys necessary) and woke the lads for their midnight feast.

Coupons were issued to buy cigarettes, a shilling for twenty. I sold mine to the Germans for one shilling and eight pence for twenty. On battery section we had tea and sugar supplied, much more than we used. I sold the surplus.

Bored with doing nothing I applied for protective clothing to work with the Germans among the batteries. I was moved to tyre section. The bonus here was that almost every day a truckload of used tyres got taken miles away to a salvage depot. I supervised the German driver, a huge man being supervised by a little skinny man. He had a girlfriend along the way and I sat helpless in the cab while he sampled some sauerkraut. I got to know him quite well as my German improved, so when he asked me if I'd like to make some money I didn't refuse. It was easy to load a few brand new tyres underneath the worn ones. A glance inside the lorry at the guardhouse showed them nothing and Wolfgang and I drove to a dropping-off point he was well aware of. I suppose the army was lucky I didn't get a job in the armoury, I could have re-armed Germany and started World War Three.

I got involved in all sorts of things that could have caused me serious trouble. One of the escapades was when the lads broke into the NAAFI in the early hours, pushed out a two foot square panel in the suspended ceiling and hid cigarettes, lighters, watches and other attractive goods while the prowler guard was persuaded to prowl elsewhere. The search of barracks that followed was fruitless.

The major trouble I found myself in was eight weeks from demob. It started when two of our lads returned to camp badly beaten by some German youths. They ran round the rooms, assembled a group totalling twenty-eight, and we all set off down town for a revenge attack. At the pub we challenged the youths to come outside and all hell broke loose. Pitched battles erupted as hundreds of Germans poured out of the houses. Paving stones were ripped up and thrown at us or else through the windows of British businesses that had been set up. Snatch squads dragged some of the lads away in cars. Twenty-eight against that mob was useless and we ran in the direction of camp fighting all the way but swamped and badly beaten.

I ran past a man thinking he was one of ours. He tripped me up, he was one of theirs. I laid into him and punched him to the ground, but then I was surrounded. I was on the floor. I saw feet coming in and I entered oblivion.

I came round in a German's house. People were patching up my face and my roommate and best friend Mick Pointon had come back for me. Once I was patched up the Germans pushed us outside. They didn't want repercussions. Outside was still a raging mob. Redcaps roared in with jeeps, lined us up and marched us out between two lines of bloodthirsty people. With all the bravado we could muster we pointed at the sky shouting 'Heil Hitler!' I was under arrest.

Locked Up

We all got locked up. Days of inspection parades began identity parades and interrogations by the Special Investigation Branch. Some of the badly hurt Germans were in hospital. The SIB put it down as an anti-British riot and left us to the mercy of the Regimental Sergeant Major. We were confined to barracks under open arrest, normally not too severe, but the RSM was in a flaming temper. The regimental police had orders to make things as tough as possible, we would be given the worst duties available and marched all over the camp at the double. Army police positioned a hundred yards apart each took over marching us until eventually we dropped to our knees.

One thousand men all wearing the same uniform lined up along the disused airstrip for an identity parade. A group of Germans moved slowly along the line, but I wasn't singled out even with my head heavily bandaged. Any man pointed out was ordered to step forward, but the pub owner pushed him back immediately, 'Nein! Nein'. He didn't want anybody punished. We had always behaved well, even taking presents to his four-year old twin sons. He knew we had been reacting to the behaviour of the German youths.

After yet another parade in front of the commanding officer the RSM blew his top. We had upset his cosy routine because instead of sitting comfortably in the mess nursing a beer he was organising parade after parade. At maybe fifty years of age he still stood out as some strong looking guy. He had fought all over the world during the war and he spelled it out to us.

'So you think you're tough, do you? I'll take each one of you on. Who's going to be first?'

The twenty-eight men included several boxers, one of them Barney Beale, British middleweight champion. But nobody stepped forward.

Civilian clothes could have simplified the identity parades, because we all wore Teddy boy gear, drainpipe trousers, bootlace ties and crepe-soled brothel creepers. Leaving the camp in civilian clothes necessitated a pass, and no way would the OC hand out a pass for our apparel, so between us we bought a grey flannel lounge suit and took turns to wear it when we applied for a pass. I wonder how many times he saw that suit? The camp perimeter had a chain link fence surrounding it, topped with barbed wire. Before open arrest the fence had never stopped us from staying out all night in town. If we booked out we had to sign back in at ten pm, so we just threw half a dozen blankets on top of the fence and over we went. Now we had to report spruced up every two hours of the day and night.

I still kept in contact with Marta, touching fingers through the chain link fence. I hadn't told her that my service days were nearly up and I ignored her questions of 'Will we live in England or in Germany when we are married?' No way was this twenty-year old thinking of marriage.

The guard sergeant received a phone call from the military hospital. A Welsh guardsman who had gone berserk was in a barred room there and they needed three guards and a lance corporal. Weary of reporting every two hours and fed up of all the worst duties, my two associates and I stepped forward. The first lance corporal that came in sight had no choice, but to volunteer. He was only a little chap and he knew what actions we had been involved in. We looked a bit fearsome with our shaven heads and assorted abrasions, and he listened when I said, 'Don't phone for the relief they are promising after twenty-four hours.'

Completely forgotten we took it in turns to guard the Welshman and enjoyed a great four-day break with excellent food and a bar. A big, big man, he sat up in bed naked to the waist, his arm muscles like huge knots. He had gone crazy in the NAAFI. An assailant had held him down and gouged his chest with the prongs of a fork. Gashes crisscrossed his body. He was on hunger strike and the orderly told him that the little corporal and I would force-feed him. The giant of a man looked at us and grinned.

'Perhaps he's not hungry,' I said in a subdued voice.

Catching Up

After guarding the big Welshman we were back at camp only a few days before the end of our eight weeks' punishment. On the last day I told the guard sergeant, 'I won't be reporting tomorrow. I'm going back to England for demob.'

His jaw dropped. He thought I was a green recruit. 'Two years in the army and you're still in trouble?'

'No,' I corrected, 'two years in the army and only in trouble the last eight weeks.'

At Feltham Barracks, England, a week to departure. Jock Warren and I had started our two-year stint together on October 1st 1953, and been through many adventures. When it got dark we went over the wall and made our way to London. We spent four days having a whale of a time mooching round pub after pub till closing time, hanging round the all-night cafe, sleeping on Victoria Station and on snooker tables in the Union Jack Club.

We boarded a bus back to camp and sat upstairs on a deck empty except for three regular soldiers. There was always animosity between regulars and national servicemen. Jock sat in the front seat next to a regular. I sat behind them and the other two regulars were in the seat behind me. One of the regulars was a corporal, who started insulting us and ridiculing the soldier next to Jock.

'How can you sit next to National Service scum?'

We had been in a lot of scuffles in our time and I knew as soon as the insults started Jock would be straight there. By the time the bus stopped outside the camp and we all stumbled off they didn't want to fight any more, but the corporal kept shouting, 'Stand to attention.'

At the guardhouse he tried to get the sergeant to lock us up. We wore lanyards on our shoulders indicating that we only had days to serve. The sergeant knew we had skipped out but he wasn't going to the trouble of any paperwork. Away from the guardhouse Jock challenged the three to continue. They ran. We laughed ourselves to sleep.

Jock and I stood side by side on our last parade. He owed me £10 (three weeks' wages) and I would most likely never see him again. 'Brummie,' he said out of the side of his mouth and he slipped me a £10 note.

So I came back home to Birmingham. 'Where have all the trams gone? And what's all this television?'

I spent a year with the lads, drinking too much and trying to pick up with a girl. Even if I got lucky enough to walk one home there was nothing doing. It was such a stigma for an unmarried girl to become pregnant or live with a man. Oh my word, that made her a helluva scarlet woman.

I made the mistake of going back to my old job with a family building and decorating business. They were a good family, but while they got rich I stayed poor. Although I started back full of confidence that I could work anywhere, somehow my confidence disappeared and I remained there several years.

I met Hilda, only four feet eleven inches tall, but tall enough to reach my heart. We scraped together every penny for four years to put a deposit on a house when we got married. Frustrating years for us both, because it was, 'NO! Not till there's a band of gold on my finger.'

We got married and moved into a brand new terraced house that cost £2,000. I earned £11 a week and Hilda earned £3. We could manage if we were careful. We had curtains only in the living room and one bedroom, nothing on the floors, no TV. Apart from the mortgage we owed nothing and I've kept it that way all my life.

The years went by. I worked every weekend as well as my weekday job. I could turn out a good decorating job and I gained lots of customers. Unfortunately decorating isn't a job that commands much money so it took a long time to build up some capital.

We deliberately avoided Hilda getting pregnant for six years. We had both endured a poor childhood and early adulthood until we got married and pooled our wages, plus what I made on side jobs. We could finally afford to live better, so we did. We bought a new Austin 1100 priced £550-12s-6d. I paid cash. Eventually we joined the throngs of people heading on holiday to Spain.

Our son Clive was born in Marston Green Maternity Hospital. We had no telephone so a policeman came to our house and I rushed to see them both in intensive care. 'You must come and see the baby first, every time you come,' advised the matron, because if there was bad news it was up to me to tell my wife. She was also very ill and didn't even see the baby for several days. I thought I was going to lose one or both of them. They both recovered, but it was a long time before Hilda regained herself. We stuck at one child.

I had been working for several years now for Birmingham City Estates Department. I wasn't happy with the waste of manpower and materials. It was a lie-down of a job. I doubt if anybody worked more than one-third of the day. The union kept getting the hours shortened and I felt like a kid doing school hours. In previous jobs I had worked eleven hours a day every day.

A lot of the men didn't like finishing early. 'It means we have to hang about too long waiting for the pubs to open,' they complained.

I managed to get onto some of the best council work, the police houses. An inspector came to pass your work so you had to turn out a good job. After I had completed the decorating work on three staircases the inspector started phoning the depot to ask who had done the work on the particular jobs. I was pleased to be told that when the inspector found out it was my work he said, 'There's no need for me to come out.'

I had some tempting offers in those police houses. It seemed to me that police wives were rather turned on. They mostly wanted to show me pornographic photos, no doubt confiscated. I never took it further.

I decided to become self-employed, but many a time I thought, 'What have I done?' So many things are against the self-employed man, especially in my trade of painter and decorator. It's a job many people can turn their hand to and be satisfied even if they don't produce a tip-top result.In other words they can do the job more cheaply themselves. So I concentrated on getting work from people who didn't do it themselves, doctors, solicitors, accountants, who didn't do manual work. My son has carried on my business forty-five years after I started it. We never advertised, we just worked from word of mouth recommendations. I never made much money, but I did a lot better than working for somebody else.

I resumed serious cycling when I was about forty and enjoyed hours of pleasure riding alone or with a CTC club, and most of all with two great friends Peter Wesley and Mick Brown. We are friends to this day. We rode thousands of miles in Spain and Portugal as well as in England.

There came the day when the doctors told me my wife was terminally ill, then the devastating ordeal of nursing her for seven months. When she died it was the end of thirty-eight years together. She was fifty-seven. I was in pieces and it took me two years to pull myself together. Peter and Mick were a huge support, and they rode out with me many Sundays.

So the idea came to me at the age of sixty-two to see how far I could ride round the world, no phones, no computers, no preparations, keeping no contacts.

Now seventy-eight I live in Thailand with my second wife, who is Thai. The move was financed by the sale of my house in England. I have built a house here, costing £8,000 ten years ago, with a swimming pool and four acres of surrounding land. I have two cars, two motorbikes and best of all four bicycles. I still cycle fair distances, in 2012 I covered 2,800 miles in England and Spain.

It's a far cry from when my mother took her brood of kids to the park so the ducks could feed us.

Bob the Bike and Bromyard

Bob the Bike is Robert Winstanley, who has earned his nickname from a lifetime of long-distance cycling. His link with Bromyard goes back to the many times when he cycled through on his travels, stopped off at a shop or a café and enjoyed the friendliness of our town. Nowadays he stays here with friends when he is in the area, friends he actually met far away in Thailand and who run a shop in Broad Street.

On one of his stays in 2011, Bob got into conversation with Linda, a volunteer at the Tourist Office. Amazed at his story, she told him he must write an article for Off the Record because Bromyard people would be interested to read about him, his round-the-world travels, and how he loves being in Bromyard.

At first, Bob said that he didn't think he could write anything, but he changed his mind and jotted down some lines that got published in OtR. More articles followed and Bob the Bike's incredible story began to unfold.

It's a story that includes humour, courage, robberies, generosities, and thousands of miles on a pushbike. It is entertaining and truly amazing to read, you can follow it in Off the Record and now also on bromyard.info

Bob the Bike

It is with the encouragement of Linda, the lady at Bromyard Tourist Office, that I write a very condensed account of the happenings in my life.

A great deal of my life is connected with long-distance cycling, which began around 1950 when a friend suggested we cycle to Wales. Still struggling after the war, most people round about my home in Stetchford, Birmingham were in a very impoverished state. From a family of nine children, at the age of fifteen I had never seen the sea, never been more than thirty miles from home, and never ridden in a car.

With great excitement my friend and I began to scrape every penny together, knocking on doors and asking for bottles to take back, buying orange boxes for four pence and chopping them up to make two buckets of firewood which sold for four pence each, to then repeat the exercise.

We slowly built up twenty-five shillings each and set off complete with emergency ration coupons, for our big adventure.

Clun Youth Hostel was our first night's stop after leaving Birmingham, a shilling a night. Clun remains one of the loveliest places I have experienced and only recently I spent another night at Clun Hostel (2nd October 2011), sixty years since my first visit. I have been there many times and still experience great pleasure as I pedal through Clun Valley.

Back in those days the hostel had no water. We washed in a stream and trundled a large drum on a trolley to fill at a village pump, I believe called Little Hospital.

In a week we covered five hundred miles there and back, our turn round point was Pwllheli. I remember being amazed at the distance that could be covered on a bicycle and the passion was born.

Over the years I passed through Bromyard many times, but it is in the last ten years that I have spent a lot of time here. And how did that start? Well, skipping a lot of stories I will explain.

Sadly, my wife who shared my life for thirty-eight years died and it took me two years to get to grips with myself. I was now sixty-two years old and decided to jump on my bike and see the world. In four years I rode through thirty-two countries around forty thousand miles completely alone, none of this wimpy back-up, computers or telephones, none of this sitting on a motor-bike turning a throttle!

I travelled through every country in Central America, Mexico, Peru, Paraguay, Brazil and Bolivia. Then India, Nepal, Bangladesh and so on. Armed with a tent I slept free anywhere and despite being robbed several times I was never physically hurt.

Where does Bromyard come in? Well, I reached Thailand and was very aware that I was sixty-six years old and I didn't want to grow old alone. I met a Thai woman and we have now been married ten years. She has a Thai friend who is married to a Bromyard man and we have all become good friends.

My wife and I live in Thailand, but visit Bromyard often. I love being here, all the people are so pleasant, the staff in the bank, the library, Age Concern, the bakery, the pubs, everywhere, couldn't be better. My Bromyard friend and his wife visit us whenever they can.

Best wishes

Bob the Bike

More from Bob the Bike...Hello Bromyard

Perhaps readers would be interested or amused at some of the many incidents that have occurred on my long distance bicycle rides...

Well, yesterday (28th October) I returned to Bromyard having completed my tour of England and part of northern Spain. After much touring of England (and now aged 76) I rode from Bromyard to Plymouth to catch the ferry to Santander, to date I have cycled 2,000 miles in five weeks.

An incident happened close to home on the Bromyard road as I headed for Worcester. On a countryside stretch I had a puncture and found as I prepared to repair it that my pump was broken! I then had to push my heavily laden bike two miles before I found an occupied house, 'The Vineyard'.

The couple there could not have been more helpful and the lady drove me and the bike about six miles to Worcester, where a bike shop soon had me back on the road. As I left 'The Vineyard' the gentleman even asked me if I needed any money, just one incident from dozens of acts of friendship and hospitality I have received on my travels. Very often they have been from people who had nothing.

I have pitched my tent in many unexpected places, in cemeteries, the edge of a golf course or a bowling green, Thai temples, petrol station forecourts, schools, the viewing platform of the Iguazu waterfalls in Brazil, in jungles and deserts. In the desert in Peru my bicycle was stolen.

I have seen many wonders of the world: the Taj Mahal, Machu Picchu, Iguazu Waterfalls, Cu Chi Tunnels, Angkor Wat, Lake Titicaca and many more. Erected on the shore of Lake Titicaca is a sign saying, 'Michael Palin visited here on his round the world trip'. I wrote underneath, 'Not on a bike he didn't!'

So, I had my bicycle stolen in Peru, and I've had my tent stolen in Vietnam, shoes stolen in Thailand, money stolen many times and several life-threatening occasions. But if nothing happened there would be no excitement in life and you might as well walk round the supermarket!

On 7th November I return to Thailand but I will be back to Bromyard.

Yours,

Bob the Bike

CHAPTER 1

Bob the Bike - Portugal

The start of Bob the Bike's four-year adventure: incidents, generosities, robberies, accidents, escapes from abduction, and more than a few romances

Oh, and Bob says, 'If you have to correct my spelling or grammar, my excuse is that the Germans bombed my school.'

It was on 26th September 1995 that although still grieving the death of my dear wife I set out to take a mammoth bicycle ride. I had decided to ride from Birmingham to Cabo Sao Vicente, Portugal, the Land's End of Europe, and then back. This was to be my test to see if I would be capable of tackling a large part of the world. Eventually at the end of my travels I had experienced over thirty countries and covered forty thousand miles. What stopped me? A woman.

On this first tour I did not carry a tent, which made sleeping very expensive. On the rest of my journeys I did, and it became a cheap way to travel. The bike carried me through and although I slept in some dodgy places (even coming under attack several times) fear never conquered me.

My first night was to be a youth hostel near Wantage and on the way there my glasses fell apart at Moreton-in-Marsh. A passer-by with my hand on his shoulder guided me to an optician. Searching for food I entered a pub at 2.05 pm, no food after two o'clock. A village shopkeeper blew the dust off two pork pies and I introduced myself to the taste of brake block material.

Youth hostels attract some eccentric characters. I found myself sharing a dorm with a backpacker, who earlier had stood eating a sandwich in the pouring rain rather than share shelter with others. At one a.m. he roused himself to take a noisy shower. At four a.m. he made a pot of tea and sat crunching digestive biscuits.

'I live alone, these are my habits,' he explained.

Once I was in a hostel where a Jewish couple refused to enter the kitchen, they couldn't cope with the smell of bacon. On a recent trip in England a guy in Stow-on-the-Wold swore he was going to end it all that night. He phoned a priest on his mobile and with a large audience poured out all his problems.

'My partner's left me; the bailiffs have taken my car.'
The audience drifted away.
'I want to buy a cup of tea but I only have 80p and tea is £1,' he carried on to his only listener.
'Have a drink on me, fella,' I said and gave him two teabags.

Day two: the sun shone, the bike skimmed along. The King's Head, Alton, was my lunch stop. They served dark mild, my all-time favourite and I am comfortable with three pints. It was two pints past two and I decided to move off at three pints past two.

(One of my cycling friends, knowing I wouldn't like the beer in France, once advised me to drink wine while I was there. Bad advice, three pints of wine make the bike wobble.)

'How are you finding time for this?' a young man in his twenties asked me. I saw his hopeless faraway look and red-rimmed eyes, for eleven months I had been looking at the same face in my mirror.

I informed him, 'I've been nursing my wife and since she died I can't stay in the house.'

'I know the feeling. I've just had to slip out, my eighteen-month-old daughter has only a week to live, leukaemia,' came the heart-breaking reply. I gripped his shoulder. What use are words?

Riding away I wanted it to rain, it would have camouflaged my tears.

I arrived at Portsmouth, France tomorrow. The tasty blonde at the ticket office listened to my cycling plans. She clapped her hands to her head.

'I couldn't think of a worse thing to do,' she exclaimed.

Crossing to Cherbourg the captain steered up all the one in sixes and I didn't like the descents either. Off the boat I headed south.

Each mile was better as I became accustomed to the road system. I passed many lovely stone cottages, all topped off with a rusty corrugated iron roof. Many things incorporated corrugated iron, there were even little cars trundling about like mobile Anderson shelters. Do the French have a fetish for this material? Do the women wear sexy black corrugated iron underwear?

'Is there any chance of finding out?' I wondered.

I drank coffee with an English couple. They told me they bred bulldogs. Dabbing her eyes the lady talked about her favourite.

'We only had him eighteen months when he had a stroke and died,' she sniffed.

'If he only had one stroke in eighteen months he didn't get much fuss,' I muttered.

An eleven-year-old lad gave me directions to a village. 'But it's too far on a bike, it's over twelve kilometres,' he said. On the map I showed him my starting place that morning, over one hundred kilometres behind me. I replaced Superman as his hero.

CHAPTER 2

The Continuing Account

The continuing account of Bob the Bike's travels. You will remember that he set out at the age of 62 in September 1995 to cycle to the tip of Portugal, to test himself for a possible even longer journey. Last time we left him in France and now he has reached Spain.

I reached Toro in Spain on 10th October, having covered 1,900 kilometres in two weeks. I rode through the fertile land of France alongside the glorious River Loire and enjoyed the tremendous scenery of the Basque country both French and Spanish. Now I rode across great plains of ochre-coloured soil that stretched further than the eye could see, while waiting mountains watched my progress.

I left magnificent Toro in blazing sunshine (better than August, said the Spaniards) and headed for the border village of Fermoselle, from which I entered Portugal at Bemposta. It was a great ride with a long plunge to a lake, but the struggle up the other side wiped the smile off my face. I stood in the path of a lawn sprinkler until I was well soaked, one of several such soakings as the sun daily increased its output.

In Portugal I would be struggling with language again. I am competent in Spanish, but that's all. I only know two words of French, Brigitte and Bardot.

This north-eastern area of Portugal holds the dubious honour of being its poorest region. I saw shepherds with so few animals that each was on a lead! Children were being delivered to school in mule carts. The main crop in the area is mountains; these grow everywhere and need no attendance. I was riding up or down (mostly up) and it was so hot that I was hard pressed to cover sixty miles a day. Over the years I have cycled thousands of miles in France, Spain and Portugal and apart from one incident I have never been threatened, though I have many stories of dangers I experienced when I broadened my horizons.

The incident I refer to happened in northern Spain at a time when the European Cup was being played. I am happy to boast that I have never watched a football match except once, when I was on military service. We were marched to the field and ordered by the sergeant major to cheer the team he pointed out. I was staying in a village where I was studying Spanish. One evening I was sitting in a bar that I had made my headquarters and I was reading my books. A tall Spaniard entered and walked to the counter with tears streaming down his face, England had just beaten Spain. The other customers teased him, but one pointed at me and said, 'He's English'.

The pathetic man threw a glass at me and it shattered on the wall above my head. I may not be a fan, but I'm as proud as anyone at an English victory. I strode up to the man and said, 'Inglaterra Sobre Todo,' England Over All. If the other guys hadn't grabbed his arms I think he would have ripped my head off.

I was riding in a barren area and was unable to get food. I entered a shack bar just as a woman put two meals on the table for herself and her husband.

'We have no food to sell,' he informed me, then on second thoughts he sold me his wife's dinner. Chauvinist that I am, I accepted it. Continuing my ride in Portugal I found the country changing, more palm trees, oranges, bird of paradise flowers. 16th October produced my longest ride of 120 miles. I met a group of car-carried Americans intent on seeing Europe in a week, they thought I was some kind of a nut. My route took me through Monchique, a really beautiful place. A few years ago I was seated outside a café there with a trusty cycling pal when an Englishman asked for our help. He informed us that his companions, including his wife, were trying to murder him. He accused them of trying to push him out of the car and make him fall down the mountain. His distressed wife explained that he had flipped his lid. We waited for an ambulance sent by the British Embassy, but the man refused to get in and it drove away. 'The attendants are part of the plot,' he insisted. We rode away, but we have often wondered if he shouted out, 'Those bloody Englishmen wouldn't listen,' as he was pushed over the cliff.

Reaching the Cape I felt somewhat exhilarated: 1,800 miles in 22 days. I spent the night in Sagres, the starting point of many great explorers. Tomorrow I would start the return journey.

I was riding in a furnace. Locals said they'd had hardly any rain in four years. It was 20th October and the metal on my bike was too hot to touch. I chose to ride some very minor roads and when my road petered out at a tiny village the rather bewildered villagers declared they had never seen an Englishman before. They pointed across a wasteland and I carried on, with the knowledge that there was a town six miles away. I stumbled and dragged the bike over ground too rough to ride and I paddled across two rivers running low. I arrived in Campo covered in dust and stepped into a café where to the amusement of the locals I stripped to my underpants and washed myself in the hand basin alongside the door.

I spent my last night in Portugal at Elvas, a fascinating town of cobbled streets, aqueducts and old buildings. I obtained a room but was only halfway up the stairs when a clatter of heels brought two gorgeous young Filipina girls offering their services, Bambi and Grace. That evening I dined out with Bambi, I must describe her as having doe eyes. Back at the digs as the day drew to a close Bambi suggested £100. I showed her the door.

'Bambi, you are too DEER', I said.

I crossed into Spain riding through the terrible city of Badajoz clogged with traffic, the resulting stench assailing my nostrils. On I went and as I rode I recalled the time in 1993 when I toured La Sierra de Gredos. I rode to Navalguijo, the isolated village that featured in the TV programme Disappearing World. The women wear a badge of status on their straw hats, a red square if married, black if widowed, green if single and looking for a husband.

It was in these mountains that I first encountered refugees. A man told me they were Palestinians from Beirut. The thirty or so could speak no Spanish and they held up pieces of cardboard on which some helpful person had written WE ARE HUNGRY - WE HAVE CHILDREN – WE HAVE NOTHING. I handed over what food and water I carried and with troubled mind I left them.

CHAPTER 3

Bob the Bike Returns

In this episode of Bob the Bike's true adventures, our hero cycles home from the tip of Portugal, encounters eccentricities along the way and finally, eats a big lunch...

I was travelling along the most glorious route of all, even surpassing the route to Avilla, seventy-five miles with only tiny villages dotted here and there. The road ran alongside El Rio Pedrosa, the Stony River, a joy as it leapfrogged the boulders in its haste to join El Rio Duero. The forests were aflame with yellow, orange and red leaves that delighted the eyes, a forest fire without the damage. Mile after mile the countryside was at its best.

There should also have been a huge man-made lake caused when a valley was flooded, immersing the village of Mansilla, but at the moment it was almost dry. After fifty years underwater the village could be seen again and three brothers all in their early seventies stood with a comforting arm round each other's shoulders as they gazed back in time to where they were born and schooled. Now after three years of minimal rain they could once more see the church where they were married.

My previous night's stop had been in a spartan room in the drab town of Sale de los Infantes. I was still feeling depressed over the death of my wife and memories spanning thirty-eight years crowded my head. Now, the glorious day's ride ended at Najera and turned into fifteen miles of terrible traffic. During the day I passed through a valley that has been home to vultures since forever. The story is that they all disappeared in 1914 and were not seen again until 1918 when they returned bloated from the battlefields of France.

A road sign proclaimed that I was riding part of La Ruta de Santiago. This starts in France and finishes in Galicia, north-western Spain. Many years ago a saint walked what wouldn't even be goat tracks, but now are main roads teeming with traffic. The trail is marked with large concrete seashells and thousands of people tackle it to pay homage to Santiago de Compostela. I would rather ride blindfold the wrong way up the M1. People prepared to do this walk are allowed to sleep and eat free at monasteries. This appealed to me but when I presented myself at a monastery I was asked if I was a real pilgrim.

'No,' I replied, 'but I know all the words to All Things Bright and Beautiful.' The monk sent me on my way and I lodged in Logrono.

It was a pleasant evening. I chatted with three buskers, two male Spaniards who played flutes and a German girl sitting in a pram and tapping a Turkish drum. They all slept in the woods under a plastic sheet. If I could have had a place next to the girl I would have joined the band with my bicycle bell. I strolled away to get some food for their three-legged dog and returned with a roast chicken, a load of chips and peppers plus a can of beer each. The meat and beer were refused.

'WE are vegetarians and teetotallers,' said these can-afford-to-be-particular beggars. To my surprise the pram now contained an eighteen-month-old baby.

'Some passer-by took him away to be washed,' explained the unconcerned mother.

I saw a bad road accident, car and lorry head-on. The car looked like a crumpled ball of paper. In Portugal I had already come on a scene where a coach had struck the mountain on a spiral road and turned over, causing death and injuries. The police urged me past as they struggled to extricate the hapless people.

A car containing three young women slowed as it drew level and they all laughed and shouted words I wasn't taught in my Spanish classes. The car stopped a hundred yards further on, the giggling girls got out and stood in a line. As I drew near they hoisted their skirts, squatted and peed in unison. Very red-faced, I cycled past. Ah well, girls will be girls.

At the end of October after four weeks of great weather I got very heavy rain. Despite this I was riding well but as usual concerned about getting a bed out of season when a good many places close down. I found a run-down hotel in Sore. In fact it was closed down but the owners were not going to miss the chance to make money. It took ages to get a room ready and there must have been two inches of dust on the floor, the bus shelter across the road took on 4-star qualities. With no food available I had to set off in the storm on pitch-black roads and managed to buy a meal with the last of my French money.

Next day in the nearest large town I found the banks closed on Monday. At that time I still hadn't started using the new-fangled ATM cards.

'There must be somewhere to change money,' I thought.

I approached several French people who couldn't or wouldn't understand me. The French don't like the English. They have never forgiven us for inventing the sit-on flush toilet; they prefer the hole in the floor. I spotted a language school and there a teacher told me that the post office changed money. I bought three small inedible cakes for £3.50. In Spain I had bought apples, a can of pop, four cakes and a hefty bunch of grapes - £1.40.

Tuesday started with dense fog that cleared to sunshine. Wednesday – rode hard, legs strong, body weak, not eating enough. Thursday - an expensive night in Becon-les-Granits. Cheapest on the menu was £12 but 'Only at lunchtime,' they told me. The other choices were £16.50 or £22. They were shocked when I walked out. I bought two currant buns and ate them in a bar.

Friday – this morning was a real change of scenery, the fields and trees were coated in frost. The roads were ice-free and I was warm with hat and gloves added to my attire. For my last night in France I settled on St Hilaire du Harcouet, it turned out to be the friendliest place I had stayed in this country.

I began my ride to Cherbourg in lovely sunshine. The thought was passing through my head that apart from two punctures I had enjoyed a trouble free journey. Just as I was thinking this, the rear mechanism broke apart and sprang into my back wheel. I dragged the bike to a farm gate, removed the mangled apparatus, shortened the chain and made do with a single gear for the rest of my journey. I reached Cherbourg after a horrendous traffic-filled road and the worst ride of my life.

The ferry sailed at 11pm. I was first aboard. Four times I went round the buffet and was back at 5am for an English breakfast, after a night of suffering drunks who only stopped drinking when the bar ran out of beer. I was first off the ship at 6.30am. I rode through the still, dark streets of Portsmouth, then to my delight I saw my achievement acknowledged! They had named a street after me, Winstanley Road. Straight into a pub at opening time for roast beef, Yorkshire pudding, three veg, two helpings of treacle sponge and custard. They can keep their foreign muck. Half an hour later I was feeling unwell, my stomach protesting. I slept in a bus shelter for an hour.

My night's stop was Wantage. The manager was pleasant but he expected me to leave my bike in the open yard. Every night my bike had shared my room. When his back was turned my bike shared my room again. I reached home on Monday 6th November. I had spent 42 days on the road and never taken a day's rest. I had covered 3,410 miles. YES, I can tackle the world. Central America, here I come!

CHAPTER 4

Bob the Bike in Central America (1)

At Cancun Airport, Mexico, I waited for my magic carpet. A porter wheeled it to me and my adventures began. This was to be the biggest bike ride of my life, destination Panama Canal, starting here in Mexico and passing through Belize, Guatemala, Honduras, Nicaragua, and Costa Rica on the way.

After a night in a guest house I set off, these bustling chrome and glass tourist resorts usually score no points, but I passed a poster proclaiming 'Ten gorgeous girls dancing naked every night' so maybe Cancun did have something going for it.

I cycled through jungle where butterflies of many hues fluttered in coloured confusion, brightly coloured birds went about their business, black vultures perched in the trees and gangs of men wielding three-foot poles hacked at the undergrowth. Now and then a dwelling built of slender poles and roofed with palm leaves, I was told the longest lasting roofs were made from leaves gathered under a full moon. A pinch of salt story. I encountered roadblocks manned by surly soldiers in sandbagged positions. Now I was travelling with camping gear not only to make the escapade more comfortable, but because I knew that I would be in isolated areas with no chance of accommodation. With darkness approaching I needed a spot to camp. Impenetrable jungle on each side, but finally I came upon a small clearing. Before it got dark, several groups of Mexicans passed by. I approached each group with extended hand. They expressed surprise, but said I would be safe. Sleep came easily and I had no fear. Twelve hours until daylight and from the screeching and chattering of animals they too welcomed the dawn.

Mayan Temples - Chichen Itza

My destination was the Mayan temples at Chichen Itza and I stayed two nights in the village of Piste. It is swarming with souvenir sellers. The woodcarvings all smell of creosote as they are carved out of old railway sleepers. I spent time with a couple of London lads who said how unsettling it was travelling on buses with civilians cradling a gun in their lap.

'We're taking a ship skirting Belize and Guatemala. We've heard it's too dangerous. Come with us,' they advised.

'I'm going to Panama and I'm riding every country,' I replied.

I climbed the temples and then visited the Balankanche caves with their amazing rock formations hanging from the roof and rising from the floor (If I remember right, transvestites hang down and transsexuals rise up.)

I had made friends with Raoul who offered free coffee to attract customers to his shop. 'Soon be Christmas. Stay here and I'll get you two young girls.'

'That would be the best Christmas present I've ever unwrapped, but I'll be long gone by then.'

I reached Peto, a dirty filthy town. I refused the first stinking room and entered the only other hotel; it was no better, a disgusting room with ensuite sewer. Heavy rain was falling so I took the room and promptly erected my tent on the bed (my tent is clean). I prowled this dump of a town constantly hustled by unsavoury characters trying to hem me in. Unwisely I went into a cantina and there I learned an essential survival lesson. In the bar were eight men who became instantly hostile and the big fat barman told me not politely to go and have intercourse with a pig. One man ran past me to the door, bolted it and reinforced it with a three-foot wooden bar. The eight men turned on me fists raised and backed me into a corner shouting obscenities directed at Americans. I always carry a small Union Jack and with great haste I produced this flag. It took all my ability with the language to convince them I was English.

This was the first of several such incidents in Central America and later on in other countries. The men now shook my hand and bought me a beer. I drank it very quickly and then as I walked out into the night unscathed I thought to myself, 'They were lucky I didn't lose my temper.' Thus I learned that from now on I must declare to all that I am not American.

Morning and on again. Thick jungle with howler monkeys scampering above, with a very frightening noise like King Kong. And always birds, butterflies and flowers competing to display the most vibrant colours. My favourite butterflies were large electric blue with a black-tipped four-inch wingspan. They fluttered in clouds about my face and cooled me in this stifling heat. I named them Patricians after a lovely woman I spent some time with before I came away. 'Just friends,' she said, and as is my custom I made up a few lines:

'Just friends you said and I sadly agreed
So we talked and we laughed both ignoring the need
The need to hold someone near to help weather the storm
Apart in the night instead of close up and warm
Yet what a pleasure it was your space to share
Lovely independent girl who needs no lasting care
Touching hearts never to be
Though perhaps at times a thought just for me
My machine carries me now in search of adventures new
I will return, return to what, return to whom.'

I left the road and pushed the bike deep into an orange grove. It swarmed with mosquitoes that drew blood on all exposed flesh. The repellent I used had no effect on them, but it was certainly keeping the women away.

CHAPTER 5

Bob the Bike in Central America (2)

Cycling on to Belize

I was in the town of Chetumal, clean, clean, clean.

I spent a few hours with a 21-year-old Dutchman and soon lost any feelings of friendship I had for him. He had been living in Acapulco for several months with a Mexican girl. When she told him she was pregnant he was out of there on the next bus. Not my kind of guy.

I had been hearing stories of robbery and violence. The Dutchman had been a victim himself a few days before. Two gunmen boarded his bus Jesse James style and forced passengers at gunpoint to part with what little they had. He was robbed, but he jumped off the bus and ran to a police station only a hundred yards away. The policeman on duty outside armed with a machine gun would not leave his post and the other police officers ignored the situation, too. But then how high have your wages got to be to risk a bullet?

Now I was riding alongside a palm-fringed Caribbean sea about to begin my story of Belize. I passed through border control with ease. Many times all sorts of reasons are invented to part you from your money. Every border in the world has a sign saying 'Welcome' but this has never been explained to the officials, who are all surely ex-Gestapo.

'How long will you be staying in Belize?' enquired Miss Vinegar-Face.
'Depends how friendly the women are.' No response.
'If they are all as lovely as you, the rest of my life.'
'Next!' shouted Miss Vinegar-Face.

Belize is a delight. Pedalling on the left, English dominates, shops stocked with Quaker Oats, Heinz beans and Cherry Blossom. I drank an orange juice and chatted with Aludia, a lovely Belizian girl with legs that ended several metres above sea level. I have had plasters on my finger wider than her skirt.

I stopped at Orange Walk town and the whole happy atmosphere gripped me. Throngs of people called out and welcomed me. I rode through a forest of waving arms and a sea of smiling faces, and at night I slept in a blanket of peace. To think this was the country that those two London lads in Mexico were afraid to enter. But two nasty-looking dreadlocked men sitting in a battered car began asking me questions after expressing surprise at how fast I had arrived from the border.

'Where are you going? Which way are you going? How long are you staying here?' Too many questions. Too easy to ambush me.

'I'm staying here,' was my guarded reply.

I carried on to Orange Rock River and set my tent on the bank.

'Yes, you can swim here. The crocodiles keep away, they don't like the sound of the traffic crossing the bridge,' advised a pleasant local boy. I plunged into the water. It seemed an eternity before a vehicle passed over the bridge.

A Mayan Indian demonstrated his fishing method. Mix flour and water, put the dough on the hook then every few minutes pull a protesting fish from the water. He explained survival techniques to me: plants that grow high in the trees collect water that often contains frogs, thus providing food and drink. Chicle trees from which chewing gum is made also have an edible fruit, and you can extract the heart from palm trees. When a branch from a particular bush is broken and allowed to hang, its leaves form a distinctive fan-shape, and you can mark your trail through the dense forest.

Morning, and thirty miles by boat along this magnificent river. A crocodile skulked under an overhanging branch. King birds no bigger than a blackbird fight any intruder that invades their territory, even a vulture. Snail kites' prey is the apple snails that float up from the bottom to lay their offspring and then can't sink for two days. Colonies of insect bats flew in clouds as our boat disturbed them. Jacaranda birds fly hardly any distance and appear to walk on water, hence the nickname 'Jesus Christ birds,' in fact they walk on the lily pads.

I reached the dusty temple ruins of Lamanai. I absorbed the history only to forget it ten minutes later. Back at the jetty I met a Creole Indian who revelled in the name Crocodile Jack When killing crocodiles became illegal he turned to fishing to make a living. That evening another new friend took me round the girlie bars and I settled on a maiden from El Salvador. This was the only Central American country I didn't visit, but at least I experienced its hospitality.

Crocodile Jack - Creole Indian

Crocodile Jack's Houuse

Crocodile Jack's Toilet

Trees forming a solid wall on either side I rounded a bend and rode into a squad of British soldiers, faces blacked up and dressed in camouflage uniforms. Their mouths dropped open. They were on a jungle survival exercise and had convinced themselves that they were in dangerous situations, 'wait till we get home and tell the folks what we had to go through'. An old Englishman on a bike destroyed that illusion.

'Aren't you frightened?' asked a young officer. I grinned and told them to watch out for Jap snipers.

The only thing I didn't like in Belize was Bellinke beer, the British soldiers call it Belly-Ache.

CHAPTER 6

Bob the Bike Reaches Guatemala and Honduras

Cratered, unsurfaced roads and clouds of dust from passing vehicles as I rode into Guatemala.

I had learned how to find a settlement, so I followed a path to look for a camping spot. The people themselves have difficulty finding where they live, so every now and then they fasten an item to a tree, a bottle, a tyre, a piece of cloth. Each item indicates a narrow path to a village. The Creole Indians were perplexed, delighted and amused to have an overnight guest. While the men sat talking in the darkness of the primitive village I soon slipped into sleep.

Awoken sharply by gunfire and the sound of bullets hitting the trees alongside my tent, I was startled at first, but settled to sleep to the sound of the Indians' laughter. Men who had sprayed the ground with ant killer before I erected my tent wouldn't hurt me.

Moving on through the grubby Isla de Flores I took an appalling earth road, virtually impossible to ride. (Drivers use whichever side of the road is smoother.) Part walking, part in the saddle, I had managed forty miles when Oscar, a Quechua Indian, stopped his pickup and I accepted a lift. Within two hundred yards a tyre went flat and right on the edge of a deep gorge the two of us worked perilously to change the wheel.

Twenty miles on we stopped at his ramshackle house. He pointed to a camp bed swarming with gruesome bugs, turned the bed on its side and gave it a couple of kicks.

'You can sleep there,' he said. Reluctantly I settled. The bugs returned throughout the night.

My next stop, Rio Dulce, was a gathering place for backpackers, each with the Lonely Planet Guide in one hand and a bottle of water in the other. I spent the evening with youngsters having a contest to see who could come up with the best chat-up line.

'Come on, Bob, you're in this,' the girls encouraged.
'Did you hurt yourself when you fell from heaven?' I contributed.
'You win,' they sighed.

I met Camilla, an attractive Canadian divorcee. She asked, 'Are you going to Livingston?' a town on the edge of the Caribbean, reached by water, a Rastafarian town where Bob Marley music plays all day. Later, when Camilla declared she wanted a shower, as there was no lock on the door, would I stand outside? I thought it would be better if I stood inside with my foot against the door but she didn't think much of that idea.

Next day we boarded a launch. 'I usually spend my evenings reading, but perhaps you will escort me tonight,' she suggested. (I had stopped using the insect/woman repellent.)

We dined together, and strolled to look at the sea. We stood on the landing stage, surrounded by the inky blackness of the sweet river, remarking on the clarity of the stars and the brightness of the moon, a night for lovers. We sat close together on the boat back to Rio Dulce, but then we went our separate ways. Badly scarred from her divorce Camilla confessed, 'The pain in my heart won't let anyone else in.'

A late start, but forty miles passed under my wheels before I pitched tent in Juan's garden. At one in the morning I was woken by hundreds of ants swarming all over my face, they had chewed through the groundsheet under my head. In oppressive heat, pitch dark and pouring rain I crouched naked, slapping the army of insects crawling over my body.

The next night in Zapaca I shared a bed with a few hundred fleas. Variety is the spice of life.

Helped by a swim in a pool I made it in blinding heat to Esquipulas, where worshippers flock by the thousands to a magnificent white church with armed guards and crowd control barriers. Inside they have Jesus on the cross, nothing unusual about that, except some entrepreneur has painted it black, so the multitude flock there.

I don't wish to offend readers, but I find it impossible to digest religion. I stood in this vast church and watched families drop to their knees, crossing themselves and banging their heads on the floor. These poverty stricken people left the church crawling backwards fearful of taking their eyes off a shaped lump of plaster painted black, and returned to sleeping and begging on the streets.

Petty officialdom at the Honduras border, plus after a few miles police demanded to see my cycle permit. Of course, there's no such thing, but who can argue? Ten dollars sent them on their way.

Mad and dangerous to ride in this heat, so I booked into a hotel, where the two barmaids had a shotgun within easy reach at the back of the bar. Leaving at six to try and cover ground before the heat, I found that Honduras was going to provide some of the toughest terrain ever, mountains too steep to ride, so I walked three hours dragging very heavy equipment. I made it to Santa Rosa de Copan and strolled through town gazing into workshops where rows of women sat rolling leaves into cigars, but not on their inner thighs as I had been led to believe. Off again at six, heavy going but sixty miles on the clock. Honduran people ran to shake my hand and ask me dozens of questions. I camped with them, and we all swam and washed in the Chamelecon River next morning.

When my shoes needed mending I paid forty pence and was told I should have paid only twenty-five! A television crew covering a cycle race filmed and interviewed me, the first of many TV and newspaper interviews. No choice of food along the road, only rice, black beans and tortillas. I was dreaming of the kind of bread you buy in an English bakery, but it's easier to buy a girl than a loaf, girls are on offer in most villages.

One day I met two young American cyclists who had been attacked in Mexico by three men with machetes. Everything was stolen, but the brave lads re-equipped themselves and carried on. They had camped in an isolated spot, this is wrong. Not only are you always seen, but also if you have trouble there is nobody to help you. I found it best to find a village and camp in the main square. Many times men holding machetes stopped me on the road. I reasoned with myself that these were their work tools. They just had not put them down, because they always wanted to wish me well.

So I reached Tegucigalpa, the capital city of Honduras, and devoured a filet mignon smothered in onions. The next year Hurricane Mitch struck this area with 180mph winds and torrential rain. Mountains collapsed and in massive flooding nearly six thousand Honduran people died. The capital city turned into an open sewer buried in mud. Malaria and dengue fever broke out; rats carried diseases that caused kidney failure and death. The mayor was killed surveying the damage from a helicopter.

Shabby, squalid Choluteca, roads paved with rotten fruit, masses of souls scraping a living. Beggars, thieves and worse, hemming me in and tugging my bike luggage.

'Do you want a hotel? A girl? A boy?'

I leaned my bike, assumed authority, pushed and kicked these unsavoury characters. Used to being underdogs they backed away.

I met a young Texan John Wayne lookalike, a 6ft 4in Baptist missionary wandering the restaurant, putting out fliers promoting his version of Christianity.

'They're all Catholics, isn't that enough?' I asked.
'That's the wrong religion,' was his reply.

My last day in Honduras and the poverty was striking. At the side of the road ragged barefoot kids stood beside piles of oranges that you can buy for any price you offer. These kids also sell lizards and armadillos, again for whatever price you offer.

I bought two lizards and released them into the wild.

Man selling live lizards and armadillos

CHAPTER 7

Nicaragua to Costa Rica

A windy day in Nicaragua

At Nicaragua the worst border corruption. I was sent from desk to desk and each official found reason to charge me ten dollars.

Outside, swarms of men latched on like leeches. I shook them off and some fast riding brought me to another filthy town, Chinandega. Every tourist is presumed to be American and Americans are hated. Four men picked up rocks as I approached, impossible to avoid and I rode straight up to them.

'Soy de Inglaterra,' I informed them.

They dropped the rocks, shook my hand and warned me, 'Be careful, there are some bad men round here.'

Having already established that it's safer to camp near people I knocked on the door of a shack. Soon my tent was on the veranda, the three children fascinated and the women cooing over a photo of my second grandson, only a few weeks old.

'We have a bathroom,' they offered. In a few minutes I stood in a contraption of four stakes wrapped round by sacking, with a bucket of water drawn from a well inside the house. Leaving these delightful people, some strong riding brought me to Masachapa, and ten minutes after taking a room I was swimming in the warm Pacific Ocean that lapped the shore a hundred yards away. The sea was alive with fish, local people working in pairs used lengths of cloth to scoop out schools of them while hundreds of birds also took their fill. Two nights at Masachapa gave me a full day walking along stretches of deserted beach, where Robinson Crusoe would have been hard pressed to find a footprint.

In a busy market two men wrestled on the ground while a crowd urged them on. They got to their feet hurling insults and one produced a long knife. My blood chilled, then the knifeman reached forward and gripped the other man's vest, at the same time lunging with the knife. There was a roar of laughter as he sliced through a shoulder strap. The man with the off-the-shoulder vest joined in the merriment.

On my departure day I woke with one eye almost closed and my cheek puffed up. No pain, but some bug had bitten me. Riding with only one good eye I battled against a tremendous wind and several times was thrown to the ground. The border crossing to Costa Rica was a nightmare, six hours in blazing heat, hundreds of people pushing and shoving. Most can't write and touts charge them a few dollars to fill in forms, usually incorrectly, so they are directed to the back of the shambles of a queue. The strip of No Man's Land declared that the countryside was mined. I didn't think it wise to drive in a few tent pegs.

In La Cruz I met up again with Terry, the Texan evangelist. We climbed a hill to watch the sun setting, from the same vantage point where Costa Ricans had watched Nicaraguan planes bomb their own people in a recent civil war. Back at the hotel at eight in the evening this 6ft 4in man told me he was going to bed to read his Bible. He was aghast when I said I was strolling into town for a beer.

He begged me not to. 'You'll be killed,' he said.

In town later I thought my arm would fall off from the number of people who shook my hand.

On a superb beach I spent the day with pelicans and only twenty people. When I told my landlady she said, 'I told you to go on a weekday, it's not so crowded.'

Christmas Eve dawned and I headed for a campsite at La Fortuna, an inland tourist resort. Restaurants promised in the brochure were all closed, so my Christmas meal was half a packet of biscuits, an orange and a can of pop. Toucans flew freely, spider monkeys frolicked and cheeky racoons begged for food. A few miles away Volcano Arenal announced its presence at intervals with a loud boom as it spewed another river of hot lava, a spectacular sight in the dark.

I joined a group from the campsite for the toughest grade jungle trek.

'No-one over sixty,' they said.

'I've cycled here from Mexico and you tell me I can't go for a walk?' I got a place on the trek.

In a travel agent's window I saw a sign in English: 'Travel with us to see the volcano. As you go through the countryside you will be able to see the unusual craps.' I slipped into the shop to advise on their spelling.

Costa Rica - wild and beautiful

Local Man

Boxing Day and a thrilling adventure: white water rafting on Penas Blancas River. For two hours we bounced from rock to rock. The guide overbalanced and I rolled onto my knees and managed to grab the paddle still in his hands. I pulled him back on board, where he resumed command.

Moving on I caught up with a young Belgian cyclist. There is an instant bond between long-distance cyclists; after all they are virtually the only real travellers. They learn survival; they touch the earth, causing no pollution as they silently roll along. The Belgian was carrying a tent and with me for company he had the courage to use it. We pitched together on the side of a lake, but he confessed in the morning that he had lain awake in his tent jumping at the slightest noise.

Separate ways in the morning and I camped later beside the Pacific. I sat in the dark and watched the bobbing lights of night fishing boats cast untidy patterns on the water. The stars were glittering diamonds embedded in a black velvet cushion and fireflies with their split-second brilliance like the on/off lights from a Christmas tree.

*Fireflies flicker like fairy lights
Stars shine cold on warmest nights
Silver seas sweep clean the shore
The man in silence dreams some more
Nut-laden palms lean over the sand
As lovers stroll each holds a hand
Sea birds call and wheel
Is this paradise is it real?
Mountains valleys flowers trees
All things that the eyes do please
Each day nature's beauties unfold
Though smiles on faces are worth more than gold.'*

As I passed San Jose Airport I saw a notice on the grass verge, saying that the 292 trees planted here represented the number of deaths on this stretch of road in one year. Hope they weren't all cyclists.

CHAPTER 8

COSTA RICA

As I was saying

In a guesthouse in San Jose I enjoyed a much-needed shower after six days under canvas. I made an early start, expecting a tough climb. It began comfortably then turned into thirty miles of steep descent. The rainforest was determined to live up to its name, the rain was the most ferocious I'd ever seen and it lasted for thirty hours. At dangerous speed I could hardly see through the rain stabbing my eyes.

A small restaurant provided cover for me to renew my brake-blocks, worn down to the metal. Now the road ran flat and I had covered a hundred miles when I reached Limon.

I stood in an ever-increasing pool at the hotel reception desk as water drained off me. The owner insisted on money in advance and in my room I became aware of the problems that the deluge had caused. Water had seeped into my panniers and bar bag, so maps, passport, visa card and dollars were soaked and stained. The maps fell apart, but I could replace them, the Visa card was my biggest concern. Luckily my smudged signature dried out well enough but later on, a lot of my dollars were refused at banks.

After a stroll round town I was soon asleep, to be woken at midnight by a knock on the door. Two young girls, fourteen and eleven years with knowing smiles, stood in the hallway. The elder one with the body of a woman made various remarks involving the bed. I gave them a bunch of grapes and shut the door.

Everything was still soaking wet when next morning I set off for the remote paradise of Puerto Viejo, riding on roads strewn with coconuts. At Puerto Viejo the black sand runs down to the Caribbean and it's a pleasure to sit under the palm trees, watching countless crabs scuttling over the rocks as the sun turns blood red and gradually extinguishes itself in the sparkling sea.

I met an Englishwoman called Mary. 'I came for one year and stayed twenty-two,' she informed me. 'This place grows on you. Stay a week and you'll stay forever,' she encouraged. But still after a brief stop I moved on.

I pitched tent on a tatty campsite occupied mainly by hippies of all nationalities. They spent their time swinging in hammocks, a bottle of rum in one hand and a dubious cigarette in the other, all with the same gormless glazed expression.

Just as I had finished my evening meal there was a power cut accompanied by loud groans. Three hours later a mighty roar of approval as light returned, 11.30 pm on New Year's Eve.

Morning meant joining a mixed queue of people each clutching a piece of paper, waiting to use a bucket inside a primitive four-sided six-feet tall roofless corrugated structure. I left this site with its fifty dropouts and realised not one of them had spoken to me, perhaps being twice their age they thought I was a drugs inspector.

Just before the Panama border I stopped for lunch. A permanent drunk of about 27, who would have passed for 50, made obvious suggestions and offered his woman.

'She won't cost much,' he said as she dutifully sat beside me.

'You are very lovely, goodbye and good luck,' I said to the eighteen-year old, and I moved away to the rotting gapped plank bridge that spanned the river forming the border. Still on the Costa Rican side stood eight very fed-up people. 'We've been here three hours,' they complained. 'The official is dead drunk lying across his desk. We can't pass over.'

'I'm going to try,' I said and strode over to the Panama office. A large uniformed woman insisted I needed an exit stamp from Costa Rica. 'I've been waiting three hours,' I lied. 'I have the man's name and I'm going to report him to the government.'

She stamped my passport, and now I must write the Panamanian story.

CHAPTER 9

Here am I in Panama

So here I am in Panama and my ears are ringing from shouts of 'Where are you from? Safe journey!'

This country was to have been my destination, but the travel bug bites deep and I knew I must move on, see what was round the next bend, meet more of the world's people. I had to experience danger and the feeling of invincibility at escaping unhurt. And many more women must be in need of TLC (Tender Loving Cyclist).

I had been told there was no road link to the next countries, Columbia and Venezuela and I decided not to try. I thought of my kid sister in Florida, I wondered could I ride to Florida from here. But thinking of the Pan-American Highway that I had already ridden with death thundering past my elbow, I decided instead to fly to Guatemala, start again and ride the length of Mexico to Texas and every state round the Gulf of Mexico.

First I must spend time in Panama. In the town of Changuinola I found a patch of grass to erect my tent, spent the night, and woke up lying in two inches of rainwater. The road now led to Almirante, sea one side and jungle the other, finishing at the dock where a boat continues, sailing through Bocas del Toro to Chiriqui Grande. A policeman on board asked me if England was bigger than the United States.

I made friends with a wonderful young German couple who took it upon themselves to cosset this old man. They insisted they should take me out of Chiriqui Grande in their Range Rover, because the Lonely Planet guidebook warns of danger. This always amuses me, if I took notice of all the danger warnings I'd be riding round my local park. We parked and slept out of town behind a petrol station. Dorothee put sunburn cream on my nose and said I must clean my teeth (she was a dentist). Next morning I was soon glad I had accepted their offer to drive me over the mountain, which rose thirteen thousand feet and provided the most impressive scenery out of all seven countries I had travelled. We said goodbye at the summit, Dorothee handing over the tube of suncream with strict orders to use it and Norman offering a sunhat. What a lovely couple.

Easy now, as I sped down to the Pacific Ocean. Choosing a place for the night where scores of families bedded down on the beach I joined the happy throng in the sea. Plenty of food was being cooked but I had a special treat, a tin of Spam, four bread rolls and a can of pop.

Another day riding the very dangerous Pan-Am highway, a night at San Carlos and on January 7th I reached the Panama Canal. I viewed this colossal engineering feat, and then rode out of town until I found a police station. The police were amused at my request to sleep there. In a taped-off area eight handcuffed men squatted on the floor, with three more chained to the wall inside while several armed police kept them under observation.

Panama Canal 7th January 1998

At sunset the flag must be shown respect, so on a sharp blast from a whistle the eight squatting men were kicked to their feet. 'You stand, too!' I was ordered. Two more whistle blasts and the men resumed squatting. Women folk and other relations gathered in a rowdy group shouting for their men to be released. The police tolerated them for ten minutes before they set about swinging riot sticks and cracking heads. The mob dispersed quickly.

I was flying next morning to Guatemala. The police escorted me the five miles to the airport driving behind me with lights flashing. Once there I unrolled my sleeping bag on the floor. Two guys boasted to me that they had driven motorbikes from Mexico to Panama, but were deflated when I told them I had done the same on a pedal bike and intended doing a lot more. I stripped naked in the men's toilets and had a good wash. I forgot that the women cleaners mop the floor whether or not the room is occupied. Tomorrow I land in Guatemala.

CHAPTER 10

And there's more

I booked a flight to land me in daylight so that I could find a camping spot, but the plane was delayed eight hours. When I explained to Copa Airlines staff how difficult this would be in the dark, the young lady said with a beaming smile, 'We'll have a taxi at the airport to take you to a hotel.'

I was transported to the five-star Camino Real, the best hotel in Guatemala City, sheer luxury. On every square yard of carpet stood a flunkey eager to assist. The commissionaire resplendent in his uniform carried my bike to the lift. The room was the plushest I'd ever been in, refrigerated bar, television, computer, giant-sized bed, ensuite bathroom with soaps, perfumes, toothbrushes, after-shave lotions, all rather overwhelming for a guy brought up in Stetchford, Birmingham. I bet it was the first and last time a bike was re-assembled in that hotel.

I strolled out and wandered the streets, took a meal and wandered some more. Then I became aware of two men behind me. One was a very big guy who came close to my left side and clamped his right arm around me. He lifted me off my feet and carried on walking. My toes were dragging on the ground. Any second now I would be feeling his left fist.

In my best Spanish I said, 'You are the first friend I've made in Guatemala and I need someone to show me round. You will be well looked after.'

He put me on my feet. 'I am Paco. We go drink beer,' he said.

'Not tonight, I'm very tired. I'll see you tomorrow,' I told him. He seemed satisfied and walked away. I'd be gone in the morning.

My next resting place was Antigua Guatemala, described as an architectural gem. I secured a room for a dollar and a quarter. At last night's hotel a room was over two hundred dollars, this one was more my cup of tea. The guesthouse had the usual collection of backpackers, but a rather odd-looking person approached me.

'People don't really understand me,' said the person, 'but I'm loving and kind and I'm a good listener. I could come to your room and we could talk. You see, I used to be a man, but I'm a woman now.'

I made my exit.

I spent two days exploring the fascinating old city with its Spanish style buildings. It was a pleasure to mix with the colourfully clad Indians who thronged the streets. Thousands sleep on the floor in whatever place they happen to be when it gets dark. You often have to step over sleeping bodies to enter a restaurant. Those not asleep crowd round the doors and as soon as you put down your knife and fork they rush in and snatch any leftovers.

In my third floor room I was violently shaken awake at 2.30am by an earth tremor that pushed my bed away from the wall. I lay for a while aware that there had been an earthquake and I could hear people shouting and screaming in the streets.

'It's not much,' I thought, and went back to sleep. When I moved off next day I was shocked to see the collapsed houses and people searching for missing neighbours.

The road now took me over the highest mountains in Guatemala. The ride took two days and covered almost a hundred miles in bitter cold. I had given away my jacket to a woman living on the pavement; the poor soul had nothing, so at night I lay in my tent wearing all the clothing I was carrying.

This lady needed my jacket more than I did

On the high road I looked back at the path I had taken. I could see other roads like ribbons scattered on the floor, all these roads led somewhere, led to someone, and I thought of the brief friendship I'd had with Patricia.

'If the ribbon road I ride threads its way up to a star
I will ride that ribbon road and look down to where you are.
If the road I ride bridges the deep blue sea
I will ride that road to have you next to me.
If the road stretches a thousand miles and even thousands more
I will ride that road to see what lies in store.
And if that road leads nowhere and circles back to me
I will happily ride that ribbon road if that's what's meant to be.'

CHAPTER 11

No guts, no story

In Solola, a night in a primitive shed with polythene walls. The town is on the edge of Lake Atitlan, ringed by volcanoes, a beautiful and impressive sight improved even further by their reflection in the lake.

Another day of gruelling climbing and Quezaltenango became my overnight quarters. 'Tenango' means 'place of' so I was in the place of quetzals. These beautiful birds are in danger of becoming extinct, their exotic long blue-green tails sought after for fashion accessories. At my evening meal I met Thomas from Honduras. From a poor background and father of fourteen children he had struggled hard to educate himself. Now as boss of a road gang, the only one who could read and write, he earned £25 a day and the crew earned £2.

We talked about the shortages of so many things during World War Two, and he remembered the rapturous reception he and his brother experienced as members of the ship's crew that brought the first bananas to banana-starved Britain after the war. There was even a song, 'Yes, we have no bananas, we have no bananas today.' In today's stocked supermarkets I joke with the checkout girls, 'All these oranges and I haven't got a green ration book.' They just look blank. Thomas pointed out that Guatemala's 36-year civil war had only ended twelve months ago. 'You couldn't have ridden then as you can now,' he said. 'It was commonplace to pass bodies on my way to work.' It was still an uneasy place with many armed men. At the shops you were served through iron bars, a shotgun within easy reach of the shopkeeper. But I never research anything; never have prior contact with anyone, no guts, no story.

In the morning thick frost coated the land. I rode up to a derelict building to don more clothing and was immediately surrounded by a crowd of down-and-outs who had been sleeping inside. They meant no harm and I cracked a few jokes. They waved and cheered as I rode off.

Now came miles and miles of downhill riding with the pleasure of looking back at the mountains and that great feeling of achievement that only riding a bicycle can bring. I rode through wonderful scenery, stopping to listen to children singing at a school. How glorious they sounded, even the birds seemed to have fallen silent, they knew they were no match.

Today was a day for meeting other cyclists, a young Swiss couple who had already ridden seven thousand miles from Alaska, then Sean, a fine young American from Colorado who had set out to ride the world with his two friends. The friends had given up after two weeks and I heard later that Sean gave up when he found out his dog had cancer. We got along famously together and talked a long time. He gave me his girlfriend's address. 'If you get to Florida, you can stay with her,' he said.

'You've just insulted me,' I replied. 'If I were a younger man, there'd be no such invitation.' We laughed, and in weeks to come I enjoyed this hospitality.

The conversation took on a serious note when Sean asked if I had heard about the atrocity in Mexico. I hadn't. Sean had met three English girls in San Cristobal who had produced a report of a terrible action that took place in Chiapas, a notorious region where at least eight groups of bandits terrorised the people. (I would soon be entering Chiapas.) These girls were doing their best to tell the world in the hope that something would be done to protect the poor Indians, people that the Mexican government mostly ignored.

This was the report:

'At 11am on December 22nd 1997, sixty men dressed in blue and with their faces hidden by red scarves surrounded an Indian refugee centre in Chenalho, Chiapas. At a church, nine men, twenty-one women and fifteen children were slaughtered and many more were injured. Four of the women were pregnant. The police did nothing, although they had been warned of the impending attack. The forewarned Indians had sent three men to seek protection from the police, all three were detained until after the attack. Two of the pregnant woman were mutilated after the attack and foetuses held aloft as trophies. The camp was put to the torch. The group responsible is known as Red Mask. They are known to be strong government supporters. It is estimated that over seven thousand Indians have fled to the mountains in the past twelve months in an attempt to escape acts like this. On January 12th 1998 during a demonstration by a group of Indians demanding justice, an Indian woman and her child were both shot dead.'

It had been 24 days since the main appalling incident, an incident that tears at the heart of any right-minded person. I moved on with sad thoughts. I pitched my tent behind a small shop and settled for the night.

Gathering of Indians in Chiapas

CHAPTER 12

Into Mexico

The road continued downhill to the Mexican border and beyond, a hundred miles along a valley of beauty. The mountains jostled to show off their grandeur as they stood in untidy line, and the river tumbled from boulder to boulder racing to keep up with the speeding cycle. The easiest border crossing of all, at La Mesilla: a charge of 50p in Guatemala, nothing in Mexico.

I was now in Chiapas. I spoke to people at every opportunity. They were helpful but cautious, jumpy, concerned for my safety. I was constantly told not to ride over the Sierra Madre, told to put my bike on a bus, warned that evil men hide out in the Sierra. I carried on and when it grew dark I left the road and slept out of sight behind the rocks.

Reaching San Cristobal I tried in vain to find the three English girls and later I passed within ten miles of the scene of the massacre. The road dropped to Tuxtla Gutierrez and then on to Chiapas de Corzo. Here I had a great problem finding a camping spot in the town. People were concerned and wished me well, but they didn't want me camping near them, they thought I might provoke an attack.

I carried on into the country and finally dragged my bike onto some scrubland. From out of nowhere the landowner appeared. He became very agitated.

'Get away, it's too dangerous. If you are murdered on my land I'll feel responsible.'

I moved on to the next town, still no beds. I was told that reporters from around the world had been prevented from writing the story. I could easily have been taken for a reporter. Darkness was closing in, and help came in the form of two racing cyclists impressed with my travels.

'Follow us,' they said, and set off on their stripped down machines at breakneck pace with this old man who had just done over sixty miles pedalling like mad on his heavily laden transport to keep up. They took me to a lakeside resort complete with armed security patrols. No problem camping there next to the river with all amenities available, this was the Canyon del Sumidero. In the restaurant the Mexicans grinned broadly when I spoke about the killings, several stating how much they hated the Indians. At the border a few days ago a customs officer had declared, 'We are pure Mexicans, they are just Indians.' Chiapas and its neighbouring state Oaxaca have the biggest concentration of Indians in Mexico with over seventeen tribes. One-third of the three million people in Oaxaca are Indians.

A late start next day because I took a boat trip, so I had done only thirty miles when I stopped at a café and asked for sleeping space. The very friendly people showed me to a large room where dances and parties were held, and my tent took pride of place on the stage. I knew now how Laurence Olivier felt. Although the owner had said she wouldn't open early she had a soft heart and saw me off with a good breakfast, and again a caution.

Time to stop again later, but people refused to let me camp. A woman told me that hundreds had been killed in the past four weeks, but nobody else confirmed this. I wondered what to do, all this talk of murdering maniacs was more than unsettling. Close by was an empty stockade with an eight-foot high surrounding wall. Could I sneak inside? Then came an amazing sight. Twenty-six state of the art luxury coaches came to a stop and disgorged over a thousand people. Eleven Americans led this cavalcade, the rest were mixed nationalities.

'We are on a pilgrimage to Guadeloupe to pray for peace in Chiapas,' explained a fervent American.

'Why Guadeloupe?' I enquired.

'Because two hundred years ago a vision of the Virgin Mary appeared to a group of Indians, so it is a holy place,' was his reply. Baffling to me but still, their intentions were good. All attention focussed on this cavalcade, I wheeled my bike to the back of the crowd then slipped into the stockade. I stood behind a wall for a while. I had not been spotted and soon I was asleep.

Hygienic butcher - Mexico

It is a long lonely road - Mexico

Questioned by Police behind the sand dunes

CHAPTER 13

Cycling through Mexico

I was now riding in the Tehuantepec isthmus, the narrowest strip of land separating the Pacific Ocean and the Gulf of Mexico. This was where the Mexicans had hoped to build the canal that was later the Panama Canal.

At Matias Romero I checked into a hotel room for two nights. A long distance cyclist soon looks a scruff and I needed time to wash and dry clothes. I threw away socks, shirts and underpants ready to buy new. The bank said they didn't change money, try the chemist, the chemist said he no longer did, try the ironmonger, and he did.

After a day of idleness I was eager to hit the road again and was soon enjoying the friendliness of Veracruz. At a lunch stop four children brought an atlas so that I could show them where England was, and I spent half an hour teaching them a few English words.

Riding through dense jungle I followed a narrow track to a clearing where I erected my tent. Several people walked the track and I greeted them all. Some came back with oranges. With a half hour of daylight left I sat in the mouth of my tent and watched a group approach, a bare-chested man holding a machete in striking position, a woman walking cautiously at his side and three children clinging to her skirt. They stopped about thirty feet away looking rather uncertain. Without speaking the man raised his hand in the time-honoured signal of peace. I rose to my feet and walked towards them imitating his signal. With a big smile the woman spoke to the children and they ran to me offering coconuts and oranges. Okay, it was like a scene from a second rate movie, but it was genuine.

Like the majority of country folk in Central America, Macario and Amanda had never met a foreigner. They had seen some on coaches that didn't stop, they had heard of the United States and presumed all foreigners came from there, but they knew nothing of countries of the world, couldn't read or write and had no television.

'You must sleep near us. Many people use this path and some are bad,' said Amanda, so I moved my tent next to their collection of humble huts. All the children whooped with delight as they crawled in and out of my canvas abode. A crowd gathered, the adults as wide-eyed as the children, including an old lady with more lines on her face than my map and a mouthful of bad teeth like black and yellow wasps. I had a splendid time with these uneducated but marvellous and caring people and rode away with a lump in my throat and my bike creaking under the weight of their gifts of bananas, coconuts and oranges.

I rested again in the lovely town of Catemaco, and spent time checking my bike. In Antigua I had found the rim on the back wheel was cracked. With brakes constantly applied the blocks wear through the rims although the spokes and hubs can still be used. It didn't take long for a bike repairer to replace the rim and meanwhile I allowed myself to be talked into taking another boat trip on the lake that brings the tourists here.

Two islands in the lake are homes to monkeys who swim out and even climb on board for bananas, Coyame Island being the location for the Sean Connery film 'Medicine Man'. Various props were pointed out, such as the fibreglass trees that were imported, because the real trees didn't look real enough.

Back on the road, a pickup truck going in the opposite direction turned round and came back. The driver and his wife swamped me with friendship. I told them about my travels and that I was headed for the town of Veracruz 120 miles away.

'We will take you,' they insisted, 'you can't ride all that way.'

I had already told them that four thousand miles had passed under my wheels, and now I explained that to take a lift would rob me of the pleasure of ten hours' cycling. They drove away shaking their heads in disbelief.

The Gulf of Mexico reached; I pushed the bike through sand dunes towards a tumbledown shack that turned out to be sheltering a man and two women. The wind was very strong and I huddled in my tent, but was soon aroused by a voice telling me to come outside. There I found five Mexican police all pointing firearms at me. They seemed surprised to find an old man, having expected to find some hippy type with drugs, and after a lot of questions they left me in peace.

Veracruz city: here in 1519 the Spaniard Hernan Cortes landed with 508 soldiers, one hundred sailors, sixteen horses and fourteen cannon. He burnt his ships to emphasise that there would be no turning back and he swept across Mexico to achieve what is regarded as one of history's greatest victories.

CHAPTER 14

Cordoba and Beyond

Next was a two-day ride to Cordoba. The first day it was pouring with rain. The front wheel threw up a stick into the back wheel and it broke two spokes. It had to be the back wheel and it had to be raining. All gear removed, back wheel out, remove rear cog and replace spokes, I carry spare spokes, inner tubes, tyres, brake blocks and all manner of things.

A shack café meant food and hot coffee but no shelter, so the tent went up under some trees. A long-distance lorry driver approached me and shook my hand.

'Bravo!' he congratulated me. 'I saw you weeks ago in Costa Rica.'

And now Cordoba, the hotel had hot water so the tent, the bike and I took a shower.

Riding along again I passed the rotting carcases of horses and other animals including pacas. The paca, or gibnut, is a large rodent about the size of a cat but resembling a rat. It is considered a delicacy in Belize and when the Queen visited that country in the 1980s she was served paca and rice. The British headlines shouted, 'Queen Eats Rat!'

When I came across a deserted ranch a six-foot barbed wire fence did not keep out a determined cyclist, and I was soon enjoying half a roast chicken, bread, fruit and lemonade, indulging in my favourite pastime – listening to the silence.

On the road again with a fierce wind and worse to come as I head north, I am riding so close to the sea that I can almost drag my foot in the water.

Emilio Carranza provided a room for £2.50, but at Poza Rica a room cost me three times as much, the reason being that I was on a route used by Americans on their way to Mexican resorts. They usually travel in long convoys of motor homes keeping close together, amusing the Mexicans, who laugh, 'They are frightened. They need to hold hands.' In fact, three Americans who invited me to sit at their table were fascinated with my stories, but agreed with each other that they would be too scared to undertake a trip like mine. This is orange-growing country, with trees smothering the land as far as the eye can see. The roads are awash with oranges that have fallen off overloaded lorries. A crowd of youths ahead, made me a target and pelted me with rocks. I escaped with a few bruises and was more concerned about damage to the machine, luckily not much. An unfortunate incident, but if you take on a task like this you have to expect trouble at times. After lunch in Tampico, I carried on until I reached a bridge where a sign declared, 'No cyclists. No pedestrians.' I had encountered this before and could see no reasoning. It could be many miles to the next river crossing, maybe to meet with the same sign. A surly soldier stood at the entrance holding a rifle across his chest.

'Sod it,' I thought and rode hard towards his left, changing direction at the last second and going to his right. He nearly fell over but I was already past with him shouting after me. I was gone and that was that.

The ramshackle town of Manuel was home for the night. I entered a cantina, these bars are as rough as they get. The men drink themselves into a very bad state and it's easy to see how much they've drunk, because they leave the bottles on the table to be counted. The abuse started as soon as I set foot across the threshold, but having learned a survival lesson in Peto, I followed my usual procedure and went from table to table telling them, 'I am English.' They were surprised and amused and I had no trouble.

The girls in these places are very attractive, but you wouldn't take one home to meet Mother. Just a nod will bring one to your table. After a hundred miles on the bike I couldn't even have managed a nod. The bleached blonde barmaid, with a huge exposed bosom that a helicopter could have landed on, emerged from behind the bar to make some attempt to mop up the phlegm on the floor, at times adding her own contribution. The Mexicans spit constantly.

So now I look east across the Gulf of Mexico to Florida where my kid sister lives. (She's only sixty-one.) By road it's about two thousand miles. Should be no problem.

CHAPTER 15

Into America

The state of Tamaulipas, Mexico, is sparsely populated, only four small towns in three hundred miles and the country is uninteresting. Cactus, mesquite and yellow grass, cattle tended by vaqueros (mostly waving vaqueros).

I got well off the road and camped by a narrow stream. The wind tried to blow the tent away and the ground was too hard to drive in tent pegs. I laid the bike on the ground and tied it to the tent, the other side secured by rocks. Three cowboys rode towards me. They leaned forward, hands crossed on the saddle.

'Watch their eyes,' John Wayne would have said. I expected to hear, 'We ain't letting no homesteaders squat on our land,' but they wished me a safe journey and warned me there were bad men around.

Perhaps my last day in Mexico, I set off again. The last few days had been fast runs, a hundred miles a day with comparative ease, much of it in wilderness. At a lunchtime stop three soldiers, one a sergeant, invited me to their table. They were impressed with my fitness and my fearless approach to my travels, and I kept them amused as I poked fun at Mexican food, women, customs and so on. They left before me and returned to their duties. I didn't realise that they intended to have the last laugh.

Soon I rode on my way and came across a military checkpoint. The previously met sergeant stepped outside, barked a command, and a dozen soldiers scrambled from sandbagged positions with rifles levelled at me.

'You are an enemy of Mexico,' shouted the sergeant. 'What have you got in your bags?'

'Heroin from Guatemala and guns from Nicaragua, but I love black beans and tortillas and your women are the most beautiful in the world,' I replied.

It was a hilarious encounter, made funnier because most of the rank and file weren't in on the joke and they thought they were going to get a chance of some shooting practice. The three I had met earlier grinned from ear to ear, and I carried on with fingers crushed from handshakes and back bruised from slaps.

Against a powerful wind that made it impossible to ride straight, I reached the Rio Bravo and crossed into Texas. From the word go it was good. The customs officers at Brownsville had a pleasant attitude, plus in less than a mile I passed three McDonalds, Pizza Hut and Burger King. I settled on Popeye's chicken and the young manager not only discounted my meal, but also sent me on my way afterwards with a bag of food.

I paid sixteen dollars to rent a six-feet square of grass for the night at a caravan park, but I was invited to join a party of people in an assembly hall and eat as much as I liked. I had entered the US on Groundhog Day, it was 2-2-98 and the sun shone warmly. Evidently the creature had not cast a shadow as it left its burrow, thus heralding the start of Spring.

I chose Richard's Restaurant for breakfast. I was warmly received, a couple of winter Texans were impressed with my story and without my knowing they paid for my meal as they left. I couldn't even say thank you. The waitress came over: 'The lady owner was going to pay for your breakfast, but they beat her to it. Will you accept this ten dollar bill?' I was overwhelmed. 'Thank you for choosing our restaurant,' called the owner.

The back roads are best to ride, but they lack facilities and more food and water must be carried. The ranches are out of sight and Texans are always on the lookout for illegal Mexicans, so I thought it would not be wise to climb a fence. A dilapidated shed looked good enough and I lifted my equipment over the gate and set up inside. I hung my brightly coloured sleeping bag outside in full view. Before it got dark a pickup drove through the gateway, two cowboys stepped out, each with a rifle. 'What are you doing, fella? Who are you? Where are you from?'

'I am an Englishman on a cycling holiday,' I replied. 'If I'm a problem I'll move.'

'No problem but there's lots of rattlesnakes around here,' was their reply.

In Mexico I had two pumas prowling round my tent one night. A slap on the tent sides had made them bolt, but this night every sound was a rattle.

Dilapidated shed I slept in

Does this mean back to square one?

CHAPTER 16

Through Texas on a Pushbike

Very cold as I set off, but the sun soon asserted itself and another glorious day's cycling followed as I met more generous Americans. I went into a Texaco station in search of breakfast, where two lovely women, Nora and Dessie, listened to my tales. I was pleased months later to send them my newspaper reports. Now it was breakfast on the house and a bag of fruit to take away.

It was to be a long ride through the Southern states and I had already learned one of the reasons they call it the Bible Belt, if you ask, 'Where can I get a beer?' there's a good chance you'll be belted with a Bible. Just the previous day I had stopped in a small town and approached two men talking outside a shop.

'Yes, siree, this morning I found a dog mooching in my back yard. I done got my gun and I shot him dead,' I heard.

'Excuse me, sir, where can I buy a beer?' I ventured.

George acted as though he had been kicked between his legs. 'A beer? You will surely burn in hell if you drink beer!' He launched into a ten-minute lecture on the evils of drink, then produced a King James Bible and subjected me to another long list of thou-shalt-nots.

'God has sent you these thousands of miles to me so that I can show you the error of your ways,' he claimed, 'but if you must drink then buy a can from a gas station, have them put it in a paper bag and you drink it out of sight round the back.'

'If I have to drink like that I won't bother,' said this sinner as he rode away. It would seem the Great Creator didn't create dogs.

But that was yesterday and now I was at Marie's Restaurant enjoying my best meal in ten weeks, chicken and rice soup, T-bone steak, salad, ice cream and at least four bottles of beer. 'I've only charged you for three,' whispered the waitress. I strolled over the road to a supermarket and stocked up with food. The manager stood in front of a gun display next to the Rice Krispies, snap, crackle, pop, bang bang. He handed me an extra bag of biscuits. I pitched my tent outside a ranch gate. That way, if someone comes along I might be invited inside further away from the traffic. Freddy, the ranch foreman, turned up only slightly puzzled at my presence. 'You sleep at the ranch,' he invited. 'Besides, there's rattlers here.'

This was a ranch where hunters stay and there were many lodges. Soon I was dwelling in the lap of luxury courtesy of another wonderful Texan family. Freddy knocked on my door in the morning and after breakfast of sausage, hot cakes, eggs and coffee I was on my way.

A lovely day, but I was getting very bored with the unchanging scenery. Miles and miles of nothing, head and shoulders country, all you see of people is head and shoulders when a car passes. Nobody walks, no cyclists. In the two hundred miles between Raymondville and Tilden are only eight tiny hamlets. My plan was to ride to Tilden, have a substantial meal then carry on another thirteen miles to Choke Canyon Lake. At Mac's Café and Motel in Tilden I was immediately made welcome by the owners and the other customers being interested and impressed. After my meal I announced I was going to camp at the lake. 'You sleep here. It'll cost you nothing,' said the lady owner, and I was again set up for the night. It meant that during the evening I was able to spend some time in the bar and mix with the locals.

A young woman asked me if I had noticed that a lot of the men had missing fingers. 'Many are cowboys and they lose their fingers roping horses and cattle,' she explained. I remembered that on the white water rafting expedition in Costa Rica the guide warned, 'If you go overboard we'll get a rope to you. Don't wrap it round your fingers.'

On again heading for the Alamo. A brief stop at a gas station and I traced on a map with my finger the route I had taken. That guide couldn't have done that, he only had knuckles. In the afternoon I actually saw two people walking. I stopped to take their picture and told them why.

'Oh, we're not just walking. We're collecting beer cans,' said the man as we shook hands, he only had knuckles. Apparently, some people make their living collecting beer cans. Drivers drink as they go along and they throw the cans out of their car windows, because if caught with an open container of alcohol in a vehicle the driver and passengers are dealt with severely.

CHAPTER 17

The Alamo and the Billy the Kid Museum

Statue of Billy the Kid - Hico, Texas

Six miles north of Kansas City I was allowed to pitch up on the car park of Shorty's Restaurant. It was fiercely cold, I slept fully clothed. In the morning the tent was sheeted with ice and it took a while to pack up with frozen fingers.

On now to the Alamo, which played a big part in Texan history. I spent a couple of hours with the ghosts of Davy Crockett, Jim Bowie and many other brave men. I studied one of the long guns and read that the firing mechanism had been made by T. Ketland & Co, Birmingham, my hometown. An alcove holds the flags of nine countries, a flag for every nationality that defended the Alamo, and the flags of England, Scotland, Ireland and Wales stand as proud as any other.

The Alamo - Texas

One hundred and sixty-two men fought seven thousand for thirteen days. They blew up the munitions store knowing that those still left would die, but that it would prevent the ammunition from being captured. By the end they had killed two thousand of General Santana's men and given General Houston time to gather an army that crushed the Mexicans.

In prison, Santana set Wrigley's on the road to making a fortune, he told them how to make chewing gum, something that the Mexicans had made for years.

I struck up a conversation with two very big bicycle-mounted policemen who carried enough weaponry to defend the fort on their own. I told them of my travels through the jungle countries.

'We wouldn't do that with an army,' they exclaimed. 'Man, you've got balls.'

At Dave Wilson's Steakhouse I received a surly 'no' to my request to camp. Papa Gallo's Mexican Restaurant gave me a warm welcome instead. After a pleasant evening I took up a position at the rear, where I was roused from sleep by the voices of two men haggling over the price of a gun.

'I want to try before I buy it,' said one voice.

'Okay, but be careful, there's a guy asleep in that tent,' said the other.

I lay in the blackness while several shots were fired. The deal was struck. No bullet holes appeared in the tent.

I carried on northwards, no serious hills, but they went on forever. Lunch at Johnson City, home of the late Lyndon Johnson, one-time US President and then further north I set up a roadside picnic spot ignoring the sign that said 'No Camping'. If anyone objects, I move on. The countryside was a little more pleasing with lush grass for the cattle, but considerable road kill, skunks, deer and coyotes. On the live side, an armadillo, a couple of jack rabbits, buzzards, eagles and two hilarious road runners. The road still had steep rolls but 112 miles covered in seven hours! I felt in peak condition and considered another twenty, but decided to stop at Hico, it's such a pleasant little town. This is where William Bonney was born and died, better known as Billy the Kid.

I was eating a delicious Dairy Queen ice cream while outside two men eyed up my bike.

'Where you from?' drawled Larry Lennox. I told him.

'Thank God for that. We thought you were a goddam Yankee.' These southerners think they are still fighting the Civil War.

Tent set up in Larry Lennox's Junk Shop - Hico

Larry owned a junk shop and suggested I sleep there, so surrounded by all sorts of bric-a-brac that's what I did, across the road from where Billy took his fatal dose of lead. Along with the assortment of oddments were guns and ammunition.

'Of course you can buy a gun, no permit needed,' he told me. 'I'm all in favour of people owning guns, even my wife shoots. If the Russians invade we can call out the biggest army the world has ever seen.'

'I wonder how they'll get the people out of their cars?' I thought.

Hico is nice, nice town, nice people. Of course, there is a Billy the Kid museum, and the main street has an old Western look. I phoned Texan Terry and he was amazed that I was almost on his doorstep, 'Yes, you'll be welcome.' So now I made my way to Arlington, between Fort Worth and Dallas.

Terry is a deeply religious 38-year-old. He worked hard to make me welcome and he drove his pickup to show me sights I wouldn't have seen without him. I had my photo taken in front of the grassy knoll that President Kennedy's car was passing when he met his tragic death.

The Book Depository from which President Kennedy was shot

Bob stands in front of grassy knoll where Kennedy met his end

Outside of opening hours we visited Billy Bob's Honky-Tonk Saloon, the biggest nightclub in the world. Every entertainment is here, with forty-one bars. Inside the vast building all the floors slope towards one end, in the old days it was a huge cattle-holding pen and the floors sloped to allow the huge amount of urine to flow away.

We went to Fort Worth Post Office. 'There is history with this building,' Terry informed me. 'It was built in 1937.'

'I was built in 1935,' I said.

I stayed two great days with him, then the tall Texan dropped the bike and me on the outskirts of town and I set off for Louisiana.

CHAPTER 18

Into Louisiana

The scenery was much improved, woodland, water, flowering cherry trees and a scattering of daffodils. About fifteen miles short of Jacksonville I set up camp in David Cemetery. Like the others there I rested in peace all night, but I was the only one warm enough to move off in the morning.

I pushed the pedals hard and long till the light was fading, then I stopped at the little town of Chireno, where I asked in 'Ethel Lamars' the one and only café if I could camp.

'No objection,' said the woman.

Mr Miserable Texan came to the door. 'You'd better move that,' he shouted. 'I'm calling the police. That's public land!'

'If it's public land then I'm staying and I'll be happy to talk to the police,' I replied. I took my meal in the hostile atmosphere of the packed café, apart from the waitress not a single person spoke to me.

Fully clothed I lay in my tent and waited. 'Hey! You in the tent, can I speak to you?' called Bill Boyle, the town constable. We shook hands and I explained that I was riding the American continent. He was very interested, a slow-speaking, patient and sensible man. After checking my passport he turned to Mr Miserable Texan, who had kept a certain distance away and said, 'This guy seems to me a right kind of guy and I see no problem.'

Then, turning to the ever-increasing lynch mob, Mr Miserable drawled, 'Ah've done tole him ter git outa town afore sunup.' The café's slogan is 'Where Friends Meet to Eat'. They should add, 'But Strangers Not Welcome.'

Crossing the state line I entered Louisiana, Gone 'With the Wind' country. I bedded down at Jefferson House, in the beautiful town of Natchitoches. The house was the last word in plush elegance and Gaye and L J its owners at that time were so pleasant to be with, real gentry. A rib eye steak and several beers in Papa's Pub before a great night's sleep and a belt busting breakfast.

I set off in light rain that quickly turned into a downpour, worsening every minute, it would be impossible to camp and there was nowhere to shelter. I reached the Red River and decided to take cover under the bridge. The river was boiling in torment. I leaned the bike against the bridge and surveyed the steep earth bank, it would be awkward but I reckoned with a few agile steps I could grab a lintel and swing myself into a dry area.

I sprang onto the bank. My feet went from under me. The rain soaked earth became a ski slope. I skidded down on my back, immediately aware how serious the situation was, with water rushing towards me. My hands scrabbled in all directions. Even as I fell I cursed myself for being an old fool. My heels carved out a groove in the mud and one hand grasped the flimsiest of newly exposed roots. I hung on for a few seconds then swung my feet towards the sanctuary I had sought. With a rapid movement I half rolled, half scrambled under the bridge.

Feeling very silly and covered in mud I made it back up the helter-skelter and headed back to Natchitoches. I checked into Louisiana Motel, unaware that I would be pinned down for six days, while Hurricane El Nino caused catastrophes across the Southern states. I still rode out every day, it didn't matter if I got wet as I had heating in my room.

The town is lovely so it was no hardship being stuck there. It has been the background to several films; the latest when I was there had been 'Steel Magnolias' starring Dolly Parton and Shirley-Ann Field. I signed the hotel visitors' book in their names.

CHAPTER 19

Mississippi, Alabama, on to Florida

At last on the road again and a night at Jena, Louisiana, where kind Aman said, 'You can put your tent on my front lawn and I'll try to be quiet when I return.'

On to Natchez, Mississippi, at the Tourist Office, the receptionist photocopied the article that had been published in the 'Natchitoches Times' about me and pinned it to the wall. In several places people had taken my photograph and even asked me for my autograph.

I rode an old wilderness trail called Natchez Trace, a scenic route, commercial vehicles not allowed. I slept in the forest, but with my sleep disturbed by deer and a violent lightning storm, come morning I packed up my sodden belongings, rode miserably fifteen miles to Port Gibson and checked into a motel.

Port Gibson's slogan is 'Too Beautiful to Burn' because during the American Civil War when General Ulysses S Grant's men wanted to burn the place he stopped them, 'It's too beautiful to burn,' he objected, and so it is.

But now I found no eating places open, nowhere to sit and relax with a drink in a glass. It seems in all these states you have to join a huddle of men skulking behind a gas station clutching a can of beer served in a paper bag. Does that really fool the police?

I made instant friends with the New Orleans Crescent City Cyclists and they invited me to the Mardi Gras celebrations. Parades filled the streets and I enjoyed the excitement of the crowds, particularly the girls who lifted their tops as the floats passed! On the famous Bourbon Street I sat at a bar where girls wearing nothing but high-heeled shoes walked along the counter stepping over the drinks.

It was goodbye to the cyclists next morning. 'You are living out our dreams,' they said, and called me Organ Donor because I never wear a helmet.

I rode past the NASA site where rockets are assembled and shipped across the Gulf to the launching pads in Florida. With so much swampland and waterlogged forests many bridges are actually elevated highways up to 28 miles long.

Through violent storms I battled on to Gulf Shores, Alabama. A lovely couple with three daughters befriended me, fed and fussed over me, and snug as a bug in their house I heard about some of the hazards of living on such low-lying land. They told me that during floods they occupied themselves shooting rats that climbed the poles the house sat on, and after floods it was not unusual to find alligators in the garden.

At the many holiday resorts in this area, all with gambling casinos and nightclubs, signs declare that a fortune can be made and each establishment offers 'the loveliest girls'. One neon sign even boasted 'Girls. Girls. Girls. We have the biggest sluts in America working here.'

Reaching Pensacola Beach, Florida, I ignored the no camping sign and bedded down after pushing a stick into the sand so that during the night I could check if the tide was coming in.

In this Florida Panhandle area I also spent two nights next to masts, a TV mast at Clarkesville and a telephone mast on Highway 98. The masts are set well back in the forest, out of bounds of course, with iron railings and barbed wire to scale. But I only stay one night, I light no fires, I leave no rubbish. The world belongs to us all.

CHAPTER 20

The Crazy American Lifestyle

My first breakfast in Florida was at Early Bird Café, Destin.

'Could I have some sandwiches and hot cross buns to take away?'

'Sure, and the boss says they're on the house and so is your breakfast,' replied a very cute blonde.

In a country as big as this there must be some glorious scenery, but the hundreds of miles I've ridden in Florida have been mostly boring, with no scenic beauty. I thought of Chiriqui Grande, the mountains and valleys of Guatemala, the rain forests and lake in Costa Rica, Picos de Europa in Spain, La Sierra de la Estrella in Portugal, and of course the stunning English countryside.

After a night in Hudson I moved on to Sarasota, passing through Tarpon Springs and Dunedin, among the most beautiful towns I saw in the States. It was seven weeks since I had talked with Sean in Guatemala and now I followed up on his invitation to stay with his girl, Mia.

Sean's girlfriend Mia. Sarasota, Florida

Goodbye from Bob to another worthwhile friend

She welcomed me with, 'If Sean says it's okay, then it's okay with me.' I received red carpet treatment and after a short getting-to-know-you talk, I was taken to a plush beachside bungalow where I would be left to my own devices while Mia and her mother slept elsewhere. Before settling down we took a walk on the white sand and watched a flaming sun drown in the sea.

They took me to an English pub, the Tudor Rose, and while we were sitting there enjoying a meal a man left a crowd and came across.

'Yer've left yer lights on, ar kid,' he said in the unmistakeable Brummie accent. He was a member of a Birmingham pop group touring America.

Mia came to see me off and was able to update me on Sean. While I had slept in luxury he had been sleeping on the floor of a bike shop and now he was calling off his tour to return home to his beloved dog who had cancer. Mia was anxious to see him, and I was surprised when she revealed that she had only known him for two days before he went away!

So with 7,500 miles behind me I reached my sister's house. I ate more food in a couple of weeks than I had eaten in three and a half months. Having such a good base, the plan had been to ride out every day and take in the landscapes. However, having already ridden deep into the state I knew there was precious little admirable countryside. The cycling became boring, no excitement, and I wanted the thrill of potential danger. I decided to fly back to Central America for two weeks and then return home for a short spell to see my grandsons.

The crazy American lifestyle was too much for me. Pedestrians are banned, cars used even for journeys of less than a hundred yards. Walking across bridges is banned, most roads have no sidewalks. I got talking to a lady about rambling clubs in England.

'We have walking groups here,' she told me. 'We walk around the air-conditioned shopping malls where there are always armed security guards on duty.'

'What about the thousands of miles of countryside?' I enquired.

'Too dangerous,' she said. So many Americans see danger everywhere. This skinny old man with map in hand approaches huge people to ask for directions, only for them to raise their arms and shout, 'Get away from me, buddy. I'll call the police.'

Then the compulsory tipping where staff demand at least 15%. As I left a café a waiter, with two others as back up, gripped my shoulder.

'You've only left 10%,' he grumbled. I went back to the table and put the money in my pocket again.

'We'll phone the police, you're stealing the tips,' he threatened. I climbed on my bike.

Drive-thru businesses are another curse. Everything possible is done while sitting in a car, drive-thru marriages, blood donation, restaurants, liquor stores, laundry, banks, pet shops, insurance, chapels of rest, the list is endless.

In Port Gibson, Mississippi, I stood at the counter in Sonic Hot Dog Drive-In. The assistant became flustered, she had never seen anyone standing up before. 'You sit in your car and we bring food to you,' she explained.

'I haven't got a car.' Now she was completely flummoxed. She had never met anyone without a car. I had to go outside and give my order through a speaker system. Due to the pouring rain I re-entered the shop.

'Customers are not allowed in the shop,' she snapped.

The bike rolled towards Miami where a plane would take me across the Gulf to Mexico. I reached the Everglades and pitched my tent opposite the entrance to Shark Valley Park, chaining my bike to a sign saying 'Don't feed the alligators.'

I drank coffee in the general store and met Byron, a 54-year-old Sioux Indian. Some years before, he had completed a remarkable 1,200-mile bike ride. Remarkable because while he was serving in Vietnam his helicopter was shot down, he was dragged to safety, spent six years in a veterans' hospital having numerous operations including hip and knee replacements, learned to walk again and then learned to ride a bike.

Morning dawned and I had time to ride the seventeen miles of Shark Valley to see an abundance of undisturbed wildlife. Here, at least, motor vehicles are banned. Alligators lying on the road made me jump when they woke and leapt into the water as I passed them. I saw raccoons, chestnut coloured rabbits, turtles, and green back herons.

A park ranger warned me that the crows would steal anything and could even unzip bike bags. His warning came too late, because after climbing an observation tower I returned to my bike to find my belongings scattered over the road and a cheeky crow perched on the saddle. It could have caused me huge problems, among the items was a pouch containing airline tickets, my passport and Visa card. If the feathered thief had carried his booty a few feet more it would have been lost in the swamp.

Over the top doorway - America

Irresistible character

CHAPTER 21

In Central America once more

Arriving back in Cancun I realised that I had now circled the Gulf of Mexico plus the 2,800-mile spur to Panama. The adrenaline flowed again. I rode in the dark and asked a Mexican where I could find a cheap hotel. My request brought only a shrug and a sullen expression.

'I'm not American,' I said. 'I'm from England.'

'Follow me,' he smiled and soon I secured my bed. I feel bad having to declare that I'm English to get what I want, after all, with only a few exceptions the American people were tremendous.

I arrived at Playa del Carmen where the startling brilliance of the blue Caribbean hurt my eyes after the nicotine coloured water off the Florida coast, caused by the mangrove trees. Among the thriving shops and hotels is a small campsite La Ruina, right on the edge of the silky sand beach. Many travellers spend time here, an 80-year old Canadian had been spending his winters here for nineteen years, at only four dollars a night.

The glorious beach at Playa del Carmen, Mexico

I left after only one night and took the road to Belize. Now there were people around as opposed to none in America, at every stop I was swamped by children. (Where were the children in America? Perhaps they are not born until they are driving age.)

The jungle appeared solid on both sides, but I knew people would be around because here and there a narrow track had been cut and to recognise the track to their abode people had tied objects to the trees, a coloured rag, a plastic bottle, a bicycle tire.

Medardo and his wife came to my assistance and together we followed a track to a village. Pleased, excited children surrounded me. I shared out large bottles of Coca-Cola and a big bag of sweets.

Darkness fell in this collection of huts without electricity and I recalled to myself a meeting earlier in the day, when I met two English cyclists at the Mayan temples in Tulum. They had been on the road for eighteen months starting in Alaska, and they spoke of the hospitality of the American people, they had collected over a hundred addresses of people who had helped them. Like me, they found they did not forget these great people.

The conversation turned to sadness when Stanni and Richard told me that the troubles in Chiapas had continued. When they had ridden through this bloodstained state four weeks ago an Indian had agreed to meet reporters to tell of the ordeal that the people were suffering. Returning home he was shot dead. Government-supported bandits were blamed.

Off again with children running behind and shouting, 'Come back, Beto!' Beto is Bob in Spanish.

At the beautiful Bacalar lagoon I rented a cabin. The landlady insisted on holding on to my passport. After a shower and a change of clothes I spent time in yet another grotty cantina. The scruffy drunk who came and sat at my table turned out to be the owner, who was constantly adding his own contribution to the spit on the floor. Thinking enough was enough I put down six pesos for the beer.

'It's twelve pesos,' he said.

'I checked the price when I came in and that's all you're getting,' I replied and took my custom to the next bar. Within five minutes he came in too, went behind the bar and with a big grin on his face he checked the takings in the till.

I returned to my lodgings, passing the main building where a voice called from an upstairs window, 'Robert! Robert!' My landlady in a flimsy nightdress was waving my passport, so I climbed the stairs to collect it.

CHAPTER 22

Belize to Birmingham

With the beauty of the lagoon behind me I soon entered Belize. On the way I looked into a church, where nine people were praying in identical positions. Each knelt in front of a low bench, lay across and over the bench with the top of their head touching the floor and their eyes directed at their knees. Does God respond better to people in this pose?

At Orange Rock River (I made up the name) I met my old friends and accepted Crocodile Jack's invitation to camp on his land. What an idyllic spot with the sight of the river to lull me to sleep. After breakfast and in intense heat I stopped at a roadside shack. This was the home of a black Belizian, Morgan. He spoke eloquently and with pride at being a British citizen, thanking the British for building schools and teaching people to read and write. 'It makes it possible for us to find work.'

The one that got away

Further on I called into Coz's Cool Spot to see Canadian Giselle, whom I had met previously, she was the person who had hitchhiked six thousand miles to make a new life in Belize. When I reached Cheers Restaurant and set up on my previous site the family was amazed at the mileage I'd done and the countries I'd visited. I spent the evening chatting with two burly soldiers who were aghast at my solo ride and doubted my sanity.

The bike had stood up well, but had needed attention at times, for example gear cable snapped, four punctures, saddle springs snapped, brake blocks replaced several times, clips on panniers broken, rear wheel rebuilt and new chainset, chain and block fitted.

I stayed at a school run by Mennonites. The women wore long plain dresses and a white cloth on their head. At breakfast they sat opposite the men, nobody speaking. The leader read out several verses from the Sermon on the Mount and invited me to say grace. I told them I am not religious, but I will take this opportunity to thank you good people and I include all the people who have looked after me in eight countries.

I reached the sea resort of Dangriga. A gang of fearsome looking dreadlocked men shouted insults. When I rode up to them and faced them they carried on insulting me, but I gradually got a laugh and a dawning admiration.

'You are making history, man,' and I drove away with some more friends.

I had to turn back at Dangriga, so again I rode the Hummingbird Highway. Another newspaper had interviewed me and I now had several clippings plus congratulations from a Florida senator.

"It's nice to read good news about you..."

Senator Burt L. Saunders

I used the same camping spots on my way back to Cancun, including my favourite at Jack's. To bathe I sat naked in his canoe and bailed river water over my dusty body while all around nature prepared for the night, 'Jesus Christ' birds took a last-minute stroll on the lily pads, a kingbird skimmed the water and a great egret stood silent in the shadows.

I now rode two hundred kilometres to the children at Tres Reyes, loaded up with cakes, sweets, Coca-Cola, oranges and sixty balloons. What a time they had! I cast off the years in response to their cries of 'Carrera, carrera!' (Race, race!) and joined them in a mad chase round the village. They clustered round me when I left. ' When will you come back, Beto?'

A canal runs alongside Highway 41, the road I took from Miami. I crossed the canal and slept behind an abandoned car, untroubled by Miami Vice. Next day with the wind behind me I rode 150 miles to my sister's in 9½ hours.

A flight from Orlando dropped me at Gatwick and I had two days of riding through English countryside to reach Birmingham. So many sights to delight my eyes, more in five miles than in five southern states of America. Lovely villages, fields of lush green grass, trees weighted with blossom, bluebells, daffodils, old houses with character, quaint cottages, and pubs serving drinkable beer where the staff don't put your arm up your back and demand a 15% tip.

At the Upcross Hotel, Reading, the pleasant receptionist said £67 for a room. 'I wouldn't pay half that,' I told her and we settled on £27. On through Cotswold country, dancing lambs and drystone walling instead of the miles of barbed wire in the States.

I sat at my kitchen table. Nine thousand miles had passed under my wheels. I thought of distant lands and the loveliness of people, the concern for my safety expressed by so many. I recalled the words of a young Mexican when I was only four days into my journey, 'Don't you think you are too old for this?'

I pulled a map of the world towards me and my finger led my eyes across India, Nepal, Burma…

'No! Not yet.'

CHAPTER 23

India

Delhi, a squalid city, a heaving mass of traffic and people. I spent only one night there and got on the road at last, though it took me hours to escape from teeming Delhi.

Heading south for Agra I found a fairly quiet back road, but I drew an ever-increasing throng of followers eager to be friends and curious to find a white man in their midst travelling by bike.

At every village more joined the procession, motor scooters, rickshaws and buffalo carts. The noise was worse than a main road. I rejoined the main road and they all turned back. The land was very flat. I took another back road and a small low hill gave me a camping opportunity, if I set up behind the hill I would be out if sight.

To my surprise a tent was already pitched. I set up Thrifty (the name I had given my accommodation, because it had saved me hundreds of pounds already). It was two hours before two armed men returned to the other tent. They stood speechless for a while then broke into laughter. They had spent several hours patrolling this private land looking for illegal campers and here was one on their doorstep. They were good-natured and let me stay but I got no sleep. They were guarding hang-gliding equipment and needed to stay awake all night, they did so by chanting.

Morning dawned and progress was held up by hundreds of cattle driven by loin-clothed herdsmen. The herd was enormous and it took me a long time to shove beasts out of my way to get to the open road. Within half a mile my back tyre punctured. I have never replaced a tube so quickly, I could feel cattle breath on the back of my neck as I pushed away.

Haryana Tourist Complex tempted me and soon I was throwing buckets of water over myself. Everything is so primitive, the showers have never worked, there are constant power cuts, electric cables run unprotected along the ground, and the grass is kept short by teams of sari-clad women who squat and cut it with small sickles.

Assorted animals were shown for tourist amusement, an elephant, a camel, some sorry looking horses and a muzzled black bear with a ring through its nose. The bear had been trained to dance, by having its feet burned with a hot poker, each time it is burned the keeper rings a bell, so the bear associates the burn with the bell and when it is brought before the public it dances to the sound of the bell.

Agra: I made my way through the streets, another seething mass of people, animals and machines. The whole area is an ever-increasing rubbish tip. The stench stings the nostrils and causes sneezing fits. The roads are dirt that has been worn, washed or blown away. With no sidewalks the road often turns into a lake of filthy black liquid from one side to the other. I push the bike through the filth and it reaches the hubs, engulfs the panniers and reaches my knees.

Only three miles from the Taj Mahal I had had enough of the filth, enough of the droves of people who swarmed around me, enough of the constant horn blowing. (The vehicles display a sign on the back telling traffic behind to hoot if they want to pass.) Only three miles from one of the wonders of the world and I had to escape. I turned away and after another five miles I put Thrifty behind a rice stack.

CHAPTER 24

The Taj Mahal and Holy Cows

Bike at the entrance to the Taj Mhal

I crawled out of the tent at 6am. A hundred people had gathered to see me. They stood silently, so curious, no threat yet nobody smiled. I shook numerous hands. They watched every move. I went behind a tree to perform a necessary function and they followed me. I had got used to seeing Indian people squatting at the side of the road, sometimes in a long line. The first time I saw this I thought they were praying.

Things looked better this morning and now I thought I couldn't be so close to the Taj Mahal and not see it. So I stood outside this truly beautiful cream marble structure, built 350 years ago by an emperor in memory of his beloved wife who died in childbirth. The area around the building and even its approach roads are fairly tidy, as this is a tourist section with smart hotels and restaurants.

I caught up with a large group of Americans being guarded by many armed men. 'What's this about?' I asked one powdered and bejewelled lady.

'We are seeing the world by Concorde,' was the haughty reply.

'You're not seeing the world at all,' I informed her.

A shopkeeper invited me in for coffee and started to spin me a yarn about his intention to see the world by motorbike, a concocted story. After a pleasant half hour while he gathered details of my circumstances and found out that I was not a rich man, he finally got down to the nitty-gritty.

'Will you take a package back to England for me? I'll give you £600. You see, I export jewellery and I've used up my quota.'

'How does that work?' I asked, completely disinterestedly.

'I will take your address and all your passport details, then when you arrive home my contacts will collect the package and give you £600.'

I rode away as he called, 'Is that not enough money?'

Question: How many people can you get on an Indian ferry?
Answer: One more. At Yamuna River I boarded a ferry that was massively overloaded and memories of past disasters filled my mind. On the verge of darkness a man invited me to be his guest. His young wife prepared food and their three children were fascinated with their unexpected guest.

Despite the amount of meat walking about most of the food is vegetables. Besides goats, sheep, pigs, buffalo and chickens there are thousands of well-washed sacred cows, some of them painted with fancy patterns. In this area of teetotal vegetarians, when people are not shoving vegetable mash down their throats they are fetching it back through their nose. They constantly grip their nose and eject all shades of green stuff. By forty-five, people here are considered very old or else they are dead. Serves them right for eating caterpillar food!

As the journey continued I had no time to myself no matter what I stopped for, to look at a map, put air in the tyres, take a snack, lie down and rest or take a leak. The road was never empty for more than a hundred yards. Always men and boys mobbed me. There seemed to be fewer women than men, the women live a life of terrible drudgery. A man told me that many mothers kill baby daughters at birth so they don't have to experience this dreadful life.

Now the country was flat, but pleasant, and wildlife had become more abundant. Cranes, egrets, flocks of blue birds and parrots flew above, monkeys dropped out of trees and a mongoose sprinted for cover.

A night's stop at Mainpuri. The hovel masquerading as a hotel had a choice of three filthy rooms: 30p, 75p and £1.25. I took £1.25 and placed Thrifty on the dirty mattress. My tent is clean and has a mosquito net.

Rolling along again, mixing it with the traffic. The dogs are regarded as speed bumps, but the holy cows are given every courtesy. At times when you are taking a meal in a restaurant a cow will stroll in and put its head over your shoulder. Buffaloes are tethered to a stake for long periods so that their droppings can be gathered, dried and shaped by hand into plate sized chunks that become cooking fuel. Road repairs are primitive, road gangs living in flimsy shelters by the road and moving along as repairs progress. The women, often clutching babies, crouch a few feet away, handing water or cigarettes to the men as they wield picks and shovels.

With great delight I came across eighteen children having an outdoor lesson. Some time back I spent a few hours learning how to make balloon animals, because balloons are small and light enough to carry as treats for children. So each of these children received a giraffe, a reindeer or a dog and with laughter and goodbyes ringing in my ears I rolled away.

Regular Indian scene

This woman is 35

CHAPTER 25

Nepal and a Chicken Dinner

Spending a night in a decent hotel gave me a chance to wash my clothes and have a proper shower at last. For breakfast I ordered two fried eggs. They had been boiled, the shells removed, eggs sliced down the middle and then fried. They remained uneaten.

A man on a bike led me through the squalor and the open sewers of Farrukhabad. He took me to see his doctor brother. As I entered the surgery a crowd gathered.

'You are busy today,' I said, and 'They have come to see you,' was the reply.

Never free from people I rolled slowly along. When I stopped to make balloon animals for children the adults snatched them instead and burst them in the snatching. At Kannauj I walked along a row of shops. One was more of an office than a shop, and a political meeting was taking place. A dozen well-dressed men sat round a large table. The main man sent one of his minions to bring me inside and soon I was sitting next to the important looking guy.

He explained that his spoken English was poor but that he was better at reading and writing it, so I wrote, 'Who are you?'

'I am A. K. Pandey, District Commissioner of Kannauj, State of Uttar Pradesh.' He indicated that I was to be his guest, provided a beer, and wrote, 'I am Brahmin, a very high caste. The people waiting outside to see me are low caste. Do not be friendly with those people.'

I spent a pleasant evening with A. K. Pandey plus various dignitaries and newspaper reporters. I handed out a few balloons, and the Commissioner's bodyguard spoke to his employer.

'He wants a balloon,' the Commissioner told me.

At 2.30am I looked out of Thrifty and saw the bodyguard. He sat on a rug with his back against the door. In one hand he held a Royal Enfield 303 rifle and in the other he held a balloon giraffe. In a flimsy shack nearby another 65-year-old employee of the Commissioner's slept with a balloon poodle at his feet.

Another two nights camping, riding until it got dark, because erecting the tent in daylight attracted hordes of people, and I was nearing Nepal at last. For ten days I had lived on biscuits and fruit, only rarely daring to eat the food in cafes.

Each village or town was as bad as the last. I feared disease as I manoeuvred through years of rubbish, rotting dog carcasses, open sewers and piles of cow manure. Men urinated wherever they were standing. At times I saw men little more than skeletons shuffling along the road completely naked.

Two surly immigration officers asked me irrelevant questions for half an hour, like 'Where is your wife? Have you children?' They only softened up when they read my date of birth, then they were impressed with an old man who rides a bike.

One official manned the small Nepalese border crossing. He was pleasant at first, but he turned awkward when I could not produce a photograph to attach to my visa and could not pay in dollars. A poster on the wall proclaimed '1998 is Visit Nepal Year.'

'I will go back to India,' I said, 'and I will write to your Government to say that you are keeping the tourists out.'

'That will cause me trouble,' said the young official. He issued the visa and accepted rupees.

At a hotel in Nepalganj I washed down a buffalo steak at last with a liquid that wasn't tea, and followed the meal with a stroll round town. The streets were clean, the little shops looked inviting, and men working on sewing machines were making all manner of clothes. I could move freely without crowds hemming me in. The children called, 'What's your name?' and the women showed their faces, waved and smiled. A smiling girl makes a man feel good.

I rode with uplifted spirits at the foot of the Himalayas, and an encounter with a New Zealand cyclist pointed me in the direction of Tiger Tops Jungle Camp. For one hour I was the only guest, until German Marcus cycled in, also directed to this isolated paradise by the New Zealander.

Marcus was quite content to eat vegetable mush, but a man sent off to get me some chickens returned with two live birds hanging from his handlebars. He tied tomorrow's bird to a stake, put today's meal between his knees and with a prayer of apology sliced off its head in full view of the staked bird.

In the morning Marcus and I sat in the sun not noticing at first that the tethered chicken had pecked through the string and escaped. All the cabin doors were open but it definitely knew which was mine, it flew into my room, crapped all over the bed and with a triumphant 'Cock-a-doodle-doo' flew over the fence and away.

Nepalese children

School bus

CHAPTER 26

Isn't it?

Marcus wasn't really a cyclist. He had met a girl in Kathmandu and when she left for Northern India she took his heart with her, so he bought a bike and he was following her.

With two guides we set off on a six-hour trek. We waded through three rivers. It was an interesting day with wild elephants, deer and monkeys to see, except that our bare arms and legs were covered in leeches, no sensation but the blood ran freely.

Riding in lovely countryside through Khalispur on to Butwal, I met Ranjit and bedded down in his brother's guesthouse. Ranjit spoke good English, but ended every sentence with 'Isn't it?' He phoned a newspaper and soon I was being interviewed. I jokingly said that I was looking for a Nepalese wife.

'We go to a restaurant and I pay, isn't it?' invited Ranjit. 'They have a television. Isn't it? You rode a long way today. Isn't it?'

I wasn't very comfortable with how close he was sitting to me. When we returned to the lodgings he was clearly disappointed when I declined his offer to see his bedroom.

'Goodnight. Isn't it?' I said.

Next day I had serious puncture problems. The spare tubes I had brought with me were defective and I soon used up my patches. I took refuge in a roadside tea-house and slept on a wooden platform. In the morning a lorry driver transported me forty miles to the nearest bike shop. The lorry had nine people in the cab, two dozen on the roof and at least another twelve clinging to the sides. The bike shop couldn't supply me with tubes or tyres, but they spent a long time repairing my much-punctured tubes and only accepted ten pence in payment.

The newspaper article with my picture was pinned to the wall in the bike shop, as it was everywhere I stopped in Nepal. It led to many men asking me to marry their daughter. 'It was just a joke,' I tried to explain, but, 'No! No! It is in the paper!' they insisted.

At Chitwan National Park I was recognised immediately again, and I spent three lazy days. I made firm friends with Mishwal and accepted his invitation to visit his home village, eighty miles away. We travelled on dirt tracks by motorbike to the most peaceful spot imaginable, no traffic, no electricity, nothing. Mishwal asked me if I wanted to marry his 25-year old sister. I declined.

While I was chatting with the guides at Chitwan a German woman holding hands with a local boy of about eighteen stopped and spoke for a while before moving on.

'She comes here every year,' the guides informed me. 'In fact several come here and pay for attention.'

'How many of you have been paid?' I enquired. Every hand went up. Oh well, what's sauce for the goose is sauce for the gander.

A two-day ride led further into the mountains. After food in Mugling I settled twenty miles further on, at a perfect campsite by a river. A group of young women left their work in the fields and surrounded me, laughing and chattering. I couldn't understand a word, but it was obvious what they were talking about. I slept with the towering Himalayas above me.

Pokhara was quite a shock, a large city swamped with tourists, crammed with cheap guesthouses, but I am happy to reach a tourist resort now and then, it means western food and the chance to speak English. The sight of the white-capped peaks is unforgettable and I realised that I couldn't leave without trekking in the mountains, so I booked a five-day trek with Sherpa Dilip as my guide.

The trek involved constant climbing on dangerous surfaces for six hours, very tough, but the illusion I had of walking lonely trails was soon shattered. Thousands of tourists were walking these paths, a non-stop parade of people. We climbed nose to bum and descended head to crotch.

The lodges had a novel way of keeping guests warm after 5pm when it got cold. A large blanket hung pelmet style from the table and reached the floor. We sat round the table with big pots of burning charcoal under it and pulled the blanket over our knees. We spent great nights and told great stories while our legs toasted.

To wake up every morning, step outside and gaze at the freshly iced, snow dusted Annapurna and Machhapuhhre was a breathtaking experience.

Dilip had passed the word about my advanced years and my bike travels. The guides were impressed by my fitness, they treated me with respect and brought me small presents. Dilip and I covered the ground at speed, although he admitted that he had groaned when he was told he had to shepherd a 63-year old man. The advantages of having a porter were numerous. Dilip waited on my every need, carrying all the equipment, insisting on walking behind, waiting on me hand and foot along the way, securing the lodge room and somehow managing to bring me my food before anyone else got theirs. He told everyone that he was honoured to serve such a famous man.

The rope bridge

Beggars

Sherpa Dilip

Himalayan village

Paradise spot - Ban Phone Noi

My dog friend

CHAPTER 27

The End of the Trek, and Over to Thailand

Everything, yes everything has to be carried to the lodges by a man, a woman or a donkey. A woman who complained about being charged 30p for an apple felt small when she was told that it took a man six days to carry it there.

On the third night we reached Ghorepani, the turn-round point only 500 yards below our destination Poon Hill. Apart from langur monkeys swinging in the trees, black faces surrounded by white hair, no wildlife was to be seen, not even birds. All the animals had retreated into the forest because of the mass movement of people. The Swedish girl occupying the next bedroom coughed all night, with only a thin sheet of plywood separating us. I knocked her door next morning and gave her a handful of cough sweets.

As Poon Hill is the highest point on the trek the object is to watch the sun rise. It takes forty-five minutes to reach the top and we began to climb at 5am. It was a tough climb made tougher by the darkness. Many lights bobbed as other torch-carrying sunrise worshippers struggled up. Dilip said that there were sometimes as many as five hundred people assembled on the highest point. Coffee and sandwich stalls were set up. To me sunrises are a non-event, sunsets are more striking, yet to see the floured peaks of Annapurna and Fishtail mountain begin to glow as they were softly kissed awake by the first rays of a new day's sun stirred the emotions in my heart.

I met some Swedish people on Poon Hill who lived in Indonesia. Fearing for their safety because of trouble there they had left. They heard on the BBC that riots were continuing, eleven people including some British had been decapitated and their bodies dragged round town tied to motorbikes. I had intended riding through Indonesia, I figured it should be all quiet on the eastern front by the time I got there.

Now it was downhill all the way, easier on the lungs, but harder on the ankles, knees and back. The Nepalese pointed at me and called me 'dai' (older brother). Being addressed as one of the family is a compliment. Friends come and go but relations are for life. Dilip and I descended the mountain, two men who had spent 24 hours a day together for five days and called themselves the fastest men on the mountain.

At the end of the trek we saw something ridiculous. A party of ninety French people with as many guides were just beginning the ascent, the women dressed as if they were attending a Paris fashion show, looking elegant, but also provocative, even though many signs tell tourists to dress modestly. They must have had no idea of the terrain they would be attempting, although they would of course appreciate the French style hole in the ground toilets.

A last look round Pokhara and with a stock of food it was great to be back on the road. My food was visible in a net tied to my carrier. Children ran alongside shouting, 'Apple! Apple!' I couldn't give out one apple when there were so many asking, but halfway to Kathmandu I left the main road and set up in a shack village. The people were delighted and I sorted out my food with an audience of 27 children and six adults. That's when I found the net pocket unzipped and an apple and a packet of biscuits missing. No problem, I had plenty of food.

In the morning tea was brought to me, no more than a mouthful, nobody had more. With two stale rolls in my hand I looked for somewhere to throw them. Hands outstretched and eyes pleading, the children begged for the old bread, so I broke the rolls into four pieces and gave them to the smallest kids. A riot broke out as thirty small bodies fought for a few stale crumbs. As I rode away I hoped that at least one child had enjoyed an apple and some biscuits.

A miserable day, the first rain so far and a steep climb into Kathmandu. On this road I witnessed the hard labour that people endured to earn a few pence, as they collected large round stones from the riverbed, pounding them with a hammer to make chippings for concrete. I stood and watched as four women crossed the river by means of a wire cable. One hundred and fifty feet below them the river ran wild and from the cable hung a flimsy platform. Three women crammed onto it and a fourth ran as hard as she could, pushing the death-defying cradle and leaping onto it at the last second. At first the contraption ran on the sag of the rope, but when it stopped it took a feat of strength to complete the remaining distance.

Twenty miles from my destination a Land Rover with GB plates and a banner reading 'England to Kathmandu Expedition' pulled up after passing me. The three British lads had seen my Union Jack fluttering from the handlebars and were gobsmacked to see an Englishman on a bike, even more so when I produced my cuttings to prove I had ridden thousands of miles. Three demoralised young men rejoined their girlfriends in the motorised pram.

Now it was getting dark and I was pushing my machine because the climb was so steep. At the top of a hill a policeman gave me the good news, 'Eight miles to go and it's all downhill.'

Kathmandu was blacked out with a power cut that lasted eight hours. It is another ant-hill of a place similar to Delhi but without the rubbish, a lively town with all manner of services, not least an Everest Steakhouse. In there I deliberated what to do. To reach Burma meant entering India again, which I was loath to do. I considered Tibet, but the Tibetan winter was setting in and it would be very cold. It wasn't possible to cross Burma because their government didn't allow freelance tourists. So I bought a ticket to Thailand.

Airport security staff at Kathmandu insisted on trying to push my bike through the screening cabinet when obviously it wouldn't pass through a 25-inch aperture. After several attempts they gave up and stuck a clearance label on the crossbar. I walked through the detection arch and the bag of spanners in my hand luggage set off the alarm. Nobody took any notice and I boarded the plane.

CHAPTER 28

The Bridge Over the River Kwai

A taxi from Bangkok Airport gave me a reasonable price and took me to a hotel. On the 45-minute journey the driver suggested all manner of sexual practices that he could arrange, they fell on deaf ears. I took an evening stroll in this city of ten million. I could have been in London, with the skyscrapers, bustling streets, modern shops, teeming traffic and choking fumes. The multitude of food stalls lining the roads were immaculate stainless steel units, the incredible variety of fish, meat, vegetables and fruit a delight to my eyes.

I returned to my hotel and sat in the bar with a jug of lager. Cora joined me, twenty-eight years old, pretty as a picture, hair flicked over her ears, almond eyes, smooth skin. Her skirt amounted to three strands of wool below her knickers. I could see why the country is called Thighland.

Cora turned her conversation to business. 'Do you want me? I am very good. We can shower together. I can give you massage. I can…. I can…. I will spend all night with you for forty pounds.'

I had learned more about physical contact in ten minutes than I had learned before in my whole life. I did a little mental arithmetic. 'How about a pound for ten minutes?' I bid. I slept alone.

It took more than three hours to escape the sprawl of Bangkok. Communication was a big problem, I couldn't understand a word anyone said and I could read only the signs on the main roads. Menus written in strange scripts, no English spoken, it was impossible to order a meal. At one time I sat with a bottle of beer (same word) and pointed at the menu. The girl looked at me oddly and brought another beer. I had to resort to buying at markets where I could see the food and indicate what I wanted.

At the first chance I left the main road and spent two days absorbing the countryside, probably riding in circles. The maps were useless. At the small village of Wat Kai ('wat' is 'temple', the only word I knew) I found a narrow path leading through a wood to some swampy wasteland. Not good, but I set up and sat outside my tent nibbling a few biscuits and reading a book.

I became aware that men were watching me, but trying to conceal themselves behind trees. I waved but nobody would come forward. I resumed reading and occasionally waving. It was getting dark and the men stayed in the woods. Was there reason for me to be alarmed?

Two motorcycles burst into the open and drove up to my encampment. After a hopeless attempt at communication it turned out they were off-duty policemen and they conveyed to me that I would be eaten alive by mosquitoes if I stayed there. I followed them back to the wat. With Thrifty placed there on a wooden platform, I could wash and stroll into the village to mix with the folks. I spent a good evening and returning to my quarters at 8pm found many villagers and three monks waiting for me. They all smiled happily, but it was impossible to converse so I made some figure balloons for the children. One of the monks was blessed with a permanent grin and rocked with laughter at each finished model. At my questioning glance he nodded his head vigorously, his nod embraced his fellows and all three went off to prayer clutching a balloon.

Away early, but only a short distance covered before a stop at a barber's shop for a cut-throat razor shave. The shop must have doubled as a youth club judging by the number of lads there. They sprawled everywhere sharing a bottle of whisky, and from the amount of empty bottles on the floor it was common practice.

The Kwai Bridge is a lively tourist attraction with big restaurants close by, including a floating one, lit up at night, reflections in the water, soft music and romantic atmosphere. I pushed my bike between the railway tracks on the bridge built with blood, my Union Jack flying from the handlebars. Maybe some lost spirits gazed down and felt proud to see the British flag on their bridge. When I reached the other side a group of Thais were pleased that I was camping there and brought me food. I fell asleep to the strains of 'Colonel Bogey' played continually.

On a visit to the War Museum before I moved off, I viewed the many instruments of death and the harrowing pictures of allied prisoners. A glass tank contains the bones of 106 men who died here and the cemetery has hundreds of crosses.

I was getting hopelessly lost on the country lanes so I returned to the main road and headed south. Almost at Ratchaburi I presented myself to the monks at Wat Pai and had a choice of identical cells all devoid of any furnishing. These wats are always alive with stray dogs. The Thai people usually own several though not many care for them as they should. The dogs all roam free and breed. With puppies looking so cute the older dogs are chased off. They mostly find their way to a temple, but that doesn't mean they are safe.

Tourists and most Thais have the illusion that Buddhist monks wouldn't hurt a fly, but on my travels I slept in many temples and witnessed first-hand some distressing incidents. At Wat Kai I awoke several times to the sound of dogs being beaten and next day a little scrap of a dog with a badly bloodied head limped by. At this wat too a puppy had incurred the wrath of a monk. The creature crawled under a large pot and the monk with several others stabbed at it with long sticks time and time again. The whining and whimpering puppy was forced out from under the pot to whoops of laughter and dragged itself away with injured legs.

At a food establishment they offered live guinea pigs and live snakes. I managed to get across, 'Have you any chickens?' The man grinned, 'Yes, two.' He led me to the rear and there on the terrace of a small arena a crowd of shouting blood-crazed men urged on two cockerels tearing each other to pieces.

Bike on bridge over the River Kwai

War Museum at Kwai Bridge

CHAPTER 29

You famous man

After an hour's hard riding I was feeling the effects of the sun. A café bore the magic sign 'Cold Draught Lager' and a large jug of amber liquid came with a frosted glass. I picked up the road to the floating markets, the boat dwellers are really worth visiting.

Anoni called to me, 'Come and stay with my family, only £5', and when I produced my clippings, 'You famous man, only £3.'

We sped down the canal in a boat and I sampled the primitive lifestyle of the boat people, no electricity, no tap water. They drink the rainwater that runs off the thatched roof, full of bugs and rubbish, or when there's no rain for months they drink the filthy canal water. They use this water for every other purpose too, washing themselves, washing clothes, washing dishes, and dipping their toothbrushes in the canal to clean their teeth. The clothes I washed were cleaner before I washed them, than after.

I had my own water and I gave the food a miss. On this trip I had met many tourists who had suffered serious illness from contamination. Leela, a bubbly young girl from London, had been ill with diarrhoea in Pokhara for eleven days, eight of them in a hole they called a hospital. She had swum in the Ganges, eaten with the locals and taken part in a four-day white water rafting expedition, where the drinking water was drawn from the river. Although this water was boiled I still wouldn't have trusted it.

A boat trip through Damnernsaduak Floating Market where the floating shops sell everything you can think of. Then I rode in the amazing canal system with banana plantations and coconut palms in abundance. So far I had seen few bicycles and I was constantly made fun of as I pedalled along, but there were thousands of motorbikes with riders younger than ten or old grandmothers. Many times, five people squeezed onto one machine.

Before leaving the market area I said goodbye to Anoni and his wife Prance. Copies of my cuttings were placed in prime position on the wall of the Tourist Information Bureau. I pressed on southwards and in the late afternoon my map told me I was only a few miles from the east coast, so I left the main road and headed for the sea. My night's stop was Puk Tien, where a partly completed house a few feet from the beach provided my shelter and the Bay of Thailand provided the view.

At a beach café close by the locals were friendly though they understood nothing of my language. We laughed at each other's attempts to talk. When the time came to sleep the women slept in the open on wooden platforms and the men in the beached fishing boats.

Should I stay or should I go? I decided to go. I see so many lovely places, but if I linger I feel like a lost sheep. First I had a slow puncture to mend. I needed to put the tube in the water to locate the leak but I needed something saucerish. The last slow puncture was in India, where I used my spectacle case. This time I used the China Sea.

I met up with Burt the Bike. Today was the first day of his bike ride and he had already travelled 45 miles, 38 of them by train. We rode together for less than an hour. He was pretending to look at the map every ten minutes, when in fact he needed to rest. I left him behind. Well, he was forty years of age; perhaps it was too much for him.

In fierce heat I took a break in the seaside town of Hua Hin and telephoned Duncan, the ex-husband of a woman I met in Nepal. He lived in Hua Hin with his 37-year old pregnant girlfriend. Sixty-one year-old Duncan urged me to stay and live there, but the anything goes party lifestyle isn't for me. After breakfast with Duncan I spent the rest of the day rubbing shoulders with the tourists and most of the night saying no to the girls. Prices were shocking here, a real holiday town, and I moved off next day.

It was cooler and I made good mileage, but had great difficulty buying a meal because of my complete ignorance of the language. I found a derelict house well off the road and dreamed the night away.

Morning brought another meeting with Burt and again we rode together. At what looked like a suitable breakfast stop we took a little food, but when it was time to pay, a young lout appeared with what must have been a well-deserved black eye. He dismissed the woman who had served us and presented us with a ridiculous bill. When we objected he snapped his fingers and three burly men encircled the table. While they punched the flat of one hand with the fist of the other Mr Black Eye threatened, 'You pay, you pay!' We paid. A tourist spending time at a resort can report these things to the police, but when a person is out in the boonies nothing can be done.

A lovely coast road and I stepped up the pace. 'I need to look at the map,' said Burt. 'Goodbye, Burt,' I said.

Floating markets - Thailand

Coconut plantations

CHAPTER 30

Thai islands

A fisherman's shelter became a cyclist's shelter for the night with a black and tan dog keeping me company. A few biscuits and what could have been a lasting friendship was born. The dog lay next to the tent all night and when I set off he ran after me a long way before he gave up.

It was a bad day plagued with punctures and equipment failure, plus ferocious rain. I found a sala (a shelter on the side of the road) but it took me four hours to make do and mend before getting on the road again, only to find that the rain was so bad it was impossible to ride.

A group of lads good-humoured, but excited on drink and drugs invited me to join them and I gave them 100 baht to buy a beer. At this time there were 70 baht to £1. When they came back with three pint bottles I realised how many times I had been ripped off, because I had been charged 70 or 80 baht at every stop for one bottle. I declined their offer to sleep on the floor, heavy rock music was playing and I was only sixteen miles from big city Chumphon, a hotel and a good scrub.

When darkness beat me I slept at the rear of an abandoned factory, then in the morning found good washing and shaving facilities at a modern petrol station. I arrived shortly afterwards at the ferry port I had been aiming for and now I had a twelve-hour wait for the boat to take me to Koh Tao Island in the China Sea. It gave me a chance to lounge on Sairee Beach ten miles away, lying in the sun and soaking up the surroundings. On the way I had marvelled at the monkeys trained to pick coconuts. They climb to great heights and twist the coconuts until they break free. One monkey had already half filled a lorry. 'Reward him well,' I said to the proud owner.

Back at embarkation point I waited for the boat to be loaded. These boats don't inspire confidence; they are loaded beyond capacity and packed with passengers. Two months before, a ship out of Surat Thani had sunk with the loss of fifteen lives, badly loaded with bags of cement on one side and bricks on the other, the cargo shifted and then came disaster. They had just started loading tons of cement on my boat so I wasn't looking forward to the six-hour trip in pitch darkness.

I disembarked at Koh Tao and found there are only four miles of road on this stunningly beautiful unspoilt island. Mostly scuba divers come here, so I rode what road there was and boarded another boat for Koh Samui. Lamai Beach had been recommended and before long I was talking to Englishman Harry who of course had the obligatory girl on his arm.

'I can fix you up with her 19-year old friend,' Harry suggested.

'Too young,' I replied.

I rented a hut next to Harry. Pretty hopeless, the room was so small I couldn't even walk round the bed, but thought it would do for one night. A nice woman approaching forty ran a little café and I sat there awhile. 'I can take care of you while you are here,' Lara offered, so that's how I found much better accommodation.

Lazy days now, plenty of restaurants and bakeries, plenty of Western food. I rode the 35-mile circular road round the island several times. Having coffee in Papa's (it was the King's birthday and you weren't allowed to drink alcohol that day) I was invited to sign the special golden book that he reserved for VIP guests. My name joined those of some film stars and a man who was walking across Asia, but I was restless and it was time to move on. Tears clustered round Lara's eyes. 'Of course I'll be back,' I said.

Not flooded - they live in the river

Another ferry

CHAPTER 31

Pineapple Trouble

I took the boat back to the mainland in the dark and pouring rain I approached two girls in a hairdressing salon. They were amused by my lack of language, but found me a room above the shop. Next day it was good to be on the road again and back to genuine prices, a Coca-Cola was now 20 baht, where it had been 70 baht on Samui.

The road took me to Krabi, the resort of Ao Nang and a lucky encounter with a likeable 36-year old Canadian called Dave. We rented a bamboo hut and I spent several days with the group that Dave had assembled. These beaches are rated among the top ten in the world (but I've been on much better). I visited many islands by long boat. One is named James Bond Island because 'The Man with the Golden Gun' was filmed there, and just then on Phi Phi Leh Leonardo Di Caprio was making 'The Beach'.

Three young women sat dejectedly on the sand at Ao Nang, unable to find lodgings. 'You can have my room and I'll sleep in the hammock outside,' I offered. So there was soon an assortment of teddy bears and cuddly toys hanging on the walls. Shira and Hira, just released from Israeli military service, said the army wasn't too bad. 'Twenty men to every woman,' they laughed. I had passed Surat Thani airport on the way to Krabi and two days later in a violent storm a plane crashed, killing 101 people. Shira was supposed to be on that plane, but having suffered fifteen hours in the air flying from Israel she had decided to travel the last stage by bus and lived to love another day. English Hayley had been working as a waitress in a Japanese nightclub, making £150 a night from tips: 'In five months I saved £3000 and hit the road.'

With Dave and a smaller group I spent a few days on Phi Phi Don and enjoyed another paradise spot, all the huts were taken so we slept on the sand. From there I went to Phuket, one of the biggest Thai resorts, and was pleased to hear my name called by the Swedish couple who had shared the same lodge as me in Nepal.

On the move again, a good day but tough riding and I was grateful when Wisuthi invited me to camp in his garden. While I was dining with his family I learned that Britain and America had bombed Iraq, in the following weeks I experienced the anger of many Muslims. It dawned on Wisuthi that I might need the toilet in the night and he scanned his English dictionary for the words.

'If you wanting excrement in the night you can coming in the house, but you no can coming in the house at two a.m. My wife she excrement at two a.m.'

Wisuthi's unmarried sister-in-law never left my side. She massaged my shoulders and feet, poured water for me, handed me toothpicks and so on.

Fruit stalls lined the road as I rolled along at peace with the world. I decided to treat myself to a pineapple and leaned my bike up against a stall manned by two men and a woman. I conveyed that I wanted the fruit sliced. The woman pointed to a bench about twenty feet behind. I sat on one end, one of the men sat on the other and we had the pineapple between us. The woman had been sharpening the knife, she passed it to the man, I sat daydreaming for a while, but wondered why he was taking so long and glanced in his direction.

He had been slashing the air with the knife, but then he turned towards me and lunged at me. I threw myself off the bench and skipped and jumped this way and that as the guy tried to stab me. For a few seconds I backed away barely able to stay on my feet on the uneven ground, and then I stepped towards him and grabbed his wrist. I grated my instep as hard as I could down his left shin. He squealed and dropped the knife, and I punched him in the throat. The other man and woman came running over, the crazy man clawing at his throat bent to pick up the knife and I kicked him in the face. The couple, very alarmed, gripped his shoulders and I moved away. 'I don't want a pineapple. I'll get some grapes,' were my parting words. Perhaps the guy hated foreigners or wasn't right in the head, but at least I didn't have to cope with the puncture he could have caused.

Again next day I had the annoying experience of a child motorcyclist riding alongside me for miles making exaggerated panting noises every time I climbed a hill. In India and Nepal the children play with spokeless bike wheels (as I did myself when a child) or they pull a plastic bottle along on a string. Here they ride motorbikes. The majority of people act as though they have never seen a bike before and constantly shout whatever they shout.

A crowd of women and children sat under a sala. I made the sleep sign and with good humour they moved. Malaysia draws near.

CHAPTER 32

From Thailand into Malaysia

This countryside was sparsely populated; perhaps the best scenery so far in Thailand, with mountains cloaked in green and the road a narrow country lane. I stopped for a snack at a roadside café in an isolated location. Several men were getting drunk on white whisky that costs less than £1 a pint. A fat girl served me some rice and a drink. When I had finished I gave her a thousand-baht note, having nothing smaller. The meal had cost one hundred baht. The girl spoke to the men, they all laughed and she walked out through the back door. I waited half an hour listening to these guys talking and breaking into laughter. Of course, she wasn't coming back while I was there, one thousand baht equals about £17 and once again, no tourist police to complain to.

In a large town I witnessed a small boy knocked down by a motorbike, fortunately a glancing blow and he was only shaken. Suddenly music issued from loudspeakers, the traffic stopped, the people stood still and all the police and soldiers saluted. I sprang off my bike and stood too. The music stopped, normal life resumed, people nodded their approval and I was pleased with myself for showing respect for the King. The then 73-year old King of Thailand was much loved, had done great things for the people and was the longest reigning monarch in the world. Twice a day at eight a.m. and six p.m. the national anthem is played, but this was the only town I had seen where people stayed stationary for sixty seconds.

With forty miles to the border I settled on the coast and sat with three fellows who had already emptied a bottle of whisky. A monk joined us, Australian Peter Walker, and from then on he did all the talking. Aged 53 he had an amazing physique, he looked and talked tough, had fought in Vietnam and after his wife died had become a monk. He claimed he was a devout believer, but he hated almost everyone in the world, the Americans for causing the deaths of his army friends, the English and Scots weren't worth talking about, the French he hated for just being French, and women were the biggest problem of all.

A lady-boy served my meal. There are many of these sad creatures in Thailand. Peter sank another whisky and smoked another funny cigarette. Using non-stop filthy language he described the many sexual tricks that lady-boys will provide. He certainly knew a lot for a monk who had given up sex thirteen years ago.

The three Thai men insisted I visit their farm. 'It's only a short distance,' and this influenced me. My equipment loaded into their pickup, now came a nightmare drive of 25 miles through remote countryside with these guys pouring drink down their throats. They got drunker and drunker, the driver showed off his skills with a bottle in one hand and the steering wheel in the other. I only pretended to drink, realising I had got myself into a vulnerable position.

We left the road behind and bounced down a track of mud and water through pitch-black rubber tree forests. My wariness increased when we arrived at the ramshackle farm to find no wives waiting – these men were all single. We sat in the dark and the drinking continued. I tipped my drink away, I wanted to be sober if anything nasty developed. All the booze gone, it was bedtime. I pulled the scruffy mattress close to the door but my fears were groundless. Within minutes the three were all asleep and I soon joined them. Their friendship was genuine and they all expressed disappointment at my early departure in the morning.

And so into Malaysia, after being fined £12 because my visa had expired three days before. It should have been £8, but you can't argue with immigration officers. A hard climb in humid stifling heat followed and walking not riding for five miles. Then from the peak the view of Malaysia took my breath away. It was now a comfortable ride to Kangar.

Hotel secured I wandered around and made friends with Amin, a professional photographer with media connections. Next morning TV and newspaper reporters interviewed me. 'Do you like Malaysian food?' was one question. Speaking into the microphone I replied, 'Last night I dined at KFC.' On my second visit to this eating-house I was presented with a book of vouchers entitling me to free KFC anywhere in Malaysia.

Back at Hotel Ban Cheong I was informed that the Chief Minister of Perlis State had invited me to the breakfast ceremony at 7 pm. The Muslims were in the first week of Ramadan when they were not supposed to eat between 7 am and 7 pm. With my new staunch friend Amin I attended the ceremony and felt privileged to do so, but word went round the large congregation that an Englishman was present and things turned nasty. I found myself in the centre of a horde of angry men shouting, 'You and Tony Blair are killing innocent Muslims in Iraq.' They were getting more incensed by the minute and it was only the intervention of the Chief Minister telling the howling mob I was his guest that saved me.

Lovely road to ride

Great camp spot

Another group delighted to see me

Television interview

Good friend Amin

CHAPTER 33

Christmas on the Road

On the day before Christmas Eve I dined out with Amin and his lovely family, wife Dina and two teenage daughters who reflected their mother's beauty, Aimi and Ismah. At the restaurant they were amused by my attempt to use chopsticks.

'This is my treat,' said Amin, 'but if you want a beer you must buy it yourself. If the religious police see me buying beer I'll be in serious trouble.'

On Christmas Eve morning I said my goodbyes. Amin presented me with a camera and the family waved me off. As I rode many people shouted and waved, they had all seen me on television or in the newspaper. I bought a copy in Malay and another in English.

I rode to Kangkong, a village on the edge of the sea, just a collection of houses, and went in and out of the village several times getting the measure of things. The people recognised me and were pleased to have a cyclist come TV star in their midst. Gradually I had a larger and larger crowd of men and youths on motorbikes following me as I surveyed the surroundings looking for the best place to pitch my tent.

There was no beach so I chose a rough patch of grass. I had an audience of about eighty fans, who behaved well, but wouldn't leave me in peace.

'There are snakes on the ground,' said one.

'Have you ever seen any?' I asked.

'No.'

'Then I won't see any.'

Even after dark they returned every half-hour till midnight, buzzing the tent and revving their engines.

'Are you asleep, Bob?' they called into the small hours.

'Are you awake, Bob?' at 6 am. Great people.

Last Christmas Eve I had camped a few miles from Volcano Arenal in Costa Rica. Alone in the loveliest of surroundings I had nibbled half a packet of biscuits and drunk a can of pop. This Christmas Eve I lived it up with three cans of pop, a packet of dates and some fruit and biscuits.

With Ramadan having weeks to run I had no chance of breakfast and I was one hungry cyclist riding along. Chong Huch Boon, a Chinese Buddhist, rode alongside on his motorbike beside himself with excitement.

'I've just been reading about you and here you are. What a coincidence. I'm so privileged,' as he wobbled excitedly all over the road. I took breakfast as Chong's guest at a shack restaurant that he favoured so much that he rode thirty miles once a month just to eat there.

After breakfast it was only one hundred yards to the mouth of a river. I crossed by boat, Chong insisting on paying the five dollars fare, and I waved goodbye to another brief friend. Then it was on to Butterworth and yet another boat to Penang Island. A short ride took me to the upmarket resort of Batu Ferringhi.

Before bedding down I had a pleasant change wandering the resort. I settled down and watched a video film in a bar, but I thought that two nights would be enough here, it was a poor resort considering the wealth of its visitors, the beach, poor with gritty sand, lots of rubbish, and buildings daubed with obscenities.

I didn't even try to get a room at the swank hotels. I placed Thrifty on a wooden beach platform under some trees. It was a mistake, when the threatened storm broke the rain cascaded down the tent and formed a pool on the platform. I still managed to sleep, even in a pool of water.

The next night I needed a bed, as all my equipment and clothing was soaked. I had a leisurely day riding the perimeter of Penang, 52 miles in a mixture of blazing sun and pouring rain (still the monsoon season). In Georgetown a hotel in fascinating Chinatown offered a room for £3.50 and an English-style pub nearby offered a happy hour session, bringing the absolutely shocking price of beer down to just another shocking price.

A Canadian who had seen me on Phi Phi Island thought he was making a joke when he enquired with a grin, 'Have you ridden here?'

'All the way,' I replied.

'God, that's wicked. That's awesome.'

Cyclists are not allowed on the toll bridge connecting Penang to the mainland, so I crossed by ferry again. A man having his shoes polished called out, 'Are you the grandfather cycling round the world?' and I sat with him while he sketched for me the best route out of the city. The weather worsened but I rode 56 miles and dripping wet I found a room in Taiping.

A good breakfast of tea and pancakes set me up for the day. Weather threatening, but better, and I made a night-stop in Ipoh. Here a mock palace was being built for the remake of 'The King and I'. The story was really set in Siam (Thailand) but permission to film there was refused, just as it was refused for the first film. The Thais regard the film as an insult to their revered king.

Most of Malaysia is as modern as Thailand. Modern means motor vehicle dominated, modern means the old ways die out, modern means jeans and baseball caps, modern means a permanent haze of exhaust fumes. But the people continue to be pleasant and helpful and I got many toots on the horn and waves from media followers. With English widely spoken it's easier to travel here than in Thailand.

Cameron Highlands

Penang Ferry

CHAPTER 34

Happy New Year

I left Ipoh on a gloomy day but it was a day that provided superb riding. Villagers so pleased to see me called me many times to stop and they guided me to a narrow road that would lead to the Cameron Highlands, a resort developed by the British many years ago. The Highlands are an escape from the heat, not to visit them would mean missing some of the best scenery in Malaysia.

For several days I had been warned that I would not be able to ride the steep hills to the peak: 'You will have to leave your bike and go by bus.' I scoffed, but privately thought they were probably right.

Riding through the jungle was a delight, meeting local people, adults and children, combing the forest and capturing enormous butterflies, giant beetles, spiders and scorpions for the tourist trade. Fascinating to see two men with eight-foot blowpipes and poison darts bringing down monkeys, squirrels and birds.

I reached Tapah. It had been a great ride, but the challenge started here. I got some food inside me and some Carlsberg fuel and began the 30-mile climb to Ringlet. It took me over four hours and I rode through forest so green that I longed to see another colour. Water cascaded at every bend and it grew colder. At Ringlet I bedded down in a Chinese hotel hoping I wouldn't be kept awake slapping fleas, as I was in the previous two. I had stopped counting the lumps on my body.

A flea-less night and I continued the short uphill ride to Tanah Rata, the town that I couldn't quite reach yesterday. In Two Pines guesthouse Kamala sat with her husband reading a newspaper. 'There's a story here about a grandfather cycling round the world. I wonder if he'll come here.'

'No,' replied Kishman, 'he will know that the road is a dead end after fifty miles. He won't struggle up here and then ride down again.' As Kamala put the paper down I leaned my bike outside. To say the couple were amazed and delighted is putting it mildly.

Many backpackers were at this youth hostel type place and I dined with young Kate from London. Her friend Lorna had stayed in, she was not well. 'They will eat this foreign stuff,' I thought as I devoured my steak and chips.

It was a long, slow ride downhill; the road was smooth, wet and greasy with tortuous hairpin bends all the way. I was still being recognised, with people shouting 'Happy New Year!' and 'Good Luck!' A stallholder gave me a bag of fruit and I carried on in a deluge of rain. Twelve months to the day I had been riding in the rainforests of Costa Rica, and I had thought that was the heaviest rain I had ever seen, but this was its equal. It slowed me down, but didn't stop me, and I still rode in shirt and shorts as the rain was warm.

I rode back west, destination Pangkor Island. I rode strong and in good weather, I would have made it in a day, but I pulled in at Teluk Intan and secured a bed in a small hotel. In the restaurant two uniformed men invited me to join them at their table in front of a large window where they could observe a police van. A man gripped the bars and looked at us forlornly as we wined and dined.

'What's he done?' I inquired.

'He's been dealing in drugs and we're taking him to be executed,' was the chilling reply. I thought it would be bad form to wish the prisoner a Happy New Year.

New Year's Day: A boring main road ride but dry. On the ferry to the island a group of fourteen students clamoured for my photograph and invited me to join them at their hostel, but I declined the offer and pedalled away. I was immediately impressed with the island, only ten miles of road, and I found a secluded spot to make camp. Although a room was only £2.50 I didn't want to miss the chance to economise, plus the wonderful feeling of freedom in a tent.

Arm outstretched, Pang approached me: 'I saw you on TV.' He ran a business on the beach, canoes, jet skis and island trips. Behind him was a heap of charcoal and blackened timber.

'That was my house. A week ago it was set alight during the night. I was asleep with two employees. We had to kick our way out through the walls. I'm doing too well, my rivals don't like it,' he explained.

I took my evening meal at the Hornbill Restaurant, where Tunku Aziz thought I was a very important man. Yet another establishment hung my picture on the wall.

Hunting with poison darts

Frame accommodation in Pangkor

CHAPTER 35

You one are?

On my second night I joined a gathering of backpackers at Joe Fisherman's Village. I met up again with Kate and her friend Lorna, now in good health. Joe is the big noise on the island; he is listed in the backpackers' bible, the Lonely Planet Guide. I don't know how these kids think they will find the lonely planet when they follow the advice so religiously on where to sleep, where to eat, where to catch the bus, avoid that place as it's too dangerous. What do they do for adventure?

Time to move on and shortly Nipah Bay would be just a pleasant memory. I rode out to calls of 'Bob the Bike round the world.' A formation of pied hornbills flew low over the beach. I was sure they dipped their wings. South for thirty miles and then east onto a perfect secondary road. I entered wilderness Malaysia.

Nobody spoke English. They all still smiled, but understood not one word. Gradually houses disappeared and I rode with waterlogged jungle on both sides. There would be no dry ground to camp on, and any minute the rain could start. The deluge began thirty miles from the next town. Nowhere to shelter and the monkeys cackled as I rode by. I had no choice but to carry on even if it meant riding in the dark, but then with twenty miles to go, a choice. At the side of the road stood a deserted fruit stall with a corrugated iron roof.

I set up Thrifty on the dry concrete and spread my wet belongings on the various tables. I had plenty of food, cakes, dates, apples, tomatoes and pears and water, so I was quite comfortable sitting in the last minutes of daylight listening to the jungle sounds. Lights from passing vehicles occasionally spot-lit the tent and I wondered if any mischievous minds might decide to cash in. What a place this would be to dispose of a victim, and if that victim was me I would just disappear with no hue and cry because I had no phone, no computer, kept contact with nobody, even my own family didn't know what country I was in.

I dozed off with thousands of frogs croaking. Visitors arrived at midnight. Two motorbikes roared to a halt a few feet from my tent, the intruding headlights were doused and men stood outside. On my knees with torch in hand I unzipped the flaps. Two men grabbed my shoulders and dragged me out. I got to my feet to find four aggressive-looking men surrounding me. Being naked made me feel more vulnerable.

Their spokesman could manage a few mixed-up words: 'You one are?' he demanded.

'I am one,' I replied.

He grinned, told the others I was alone and they all laughed.

'What you do?'

'I rest. I sleep.'

The four swaggered round picking up my sorry belongings, bits and pieces essential to me, but not much use to them: a little stove, packets of fuel, well-worn shabby clothing, a spare pair of battered shoes, spare tubes and tyres, my tool kit with chain link remover, block remover, spare spokes and various spanners. They threw these odds and ends around; disappointed with my junk, though of course they knew I must have money. But how much did I have? About thirty dollars in my wallet, but on my bike in one of the water bottles I had a thousand dollars. They didn't even touch the bottles.

I sorted out my Malaysian newspaper clippings and by the light of my torch they read about my travels, my invitation from the Chief Minister of Perlis State, my TV interview. They decided perhaps I wasn't such an anonymous person.

'You sixty-three. You very strong,' said the spokesman.

Yes, I thought, strong enough for one, but not four. I took the newspaper from the last man, and trying to speak with authority (not easy when you're naked) I said, 'Now I sleep.' I crawled back in the tent and closed the flaps. I crouched in the dark while they argued among themselves. I had shamed them, showing them I was doing something they wouldn't have the guts to do themselves. They kicked the motorbikes into life and were gone. The infernal frogs fell silent and I slept.

Off to a very early start. How lovely it is here, brilliant blue birds perching close by, langur and rhesus monkeys crashing through the trees. Who is more startled, them or me? As they launch themselves from tree to tree a branch snaps with a sharp crack and leaves slap loudly. I almost leap out of the saddle.

Now that I was in climbing country it was getting tougher. I wouldn't have been able to do these additional twenty miles yesterday. I reached Tanjung Malim and sorted out a KFC, I still had vouchers left. The manager had seen me on TV and was overjoyed to see me in his restaurant, though apologetic that he couldn't replenish my vouchers.

CHAPTER 36

A Flat-Headed Tarmac Snake

Twenty miles of strenuous riding, twenty of comfortable riding and then the turn for Bukit Fraser (bukit meaning hill). Uphill all the way, glorious countryside and a reasonable gradient. This resort is similar to Cameron Highlands but the approach is more natural, the jungle runs wild in a cascade of green. As I drew nearer it became more orderly, beautifully clean and manicured. Every blade of grass was dusted every day, a rich people's resort, no cheap rooms here.

'I have a cheap room. Thirteen pounds a night.' I ignored the call.

Drenched from the push-you-to-the-floor rain that I had endured for four hours as I slogged up the never-ending hill I approached a lady in her garden.

'I speak no. I man fetch,' she said.

Husband Hullis, speaker of perfect English, came to my aid. 'There is an empty house. If you are not fussy you can sleep there and shower in my house.' I kicked all the rubbish to one side and slept there, I've slept in worse places.

Hullis's house was in a row of cottages for maintenance workers, guys who work on the smart hotels. In the bathroom Hullis gave up trying to make the shower work. 'Use a saucepan to douse yourself and also to flush the toilet, the cistern doesn't work.' A tap about a foot up the wall had a piece of rag tied to the spout, the rag hung to the floor. 'The tap was dripping and kept us awake. Now the water runs down the rag and we don't hear it,' explained Hullis.

'Are you one of the maintenance workers?' I asked.

'Yes, I'm a plumber,' he said with pride.

At breakfast I realised what a down-and-out I looked when I ordered food in a café and the woman insisted, 'First you pay! First you pay!'

The road to Fraser Hill is narrow and it corkscrews, traffic is only allowed in one direction at a time, alternating every hour. The gatekeeper lowered the barrier just as I arrived. It was a lovely morning, too lovely to stand around. When he turned his back I ducked under the pole and was away. Keeping tight into the cliff I coasted down with caution, but met no oncoming traffic.

As I sped downhill both wheels of my heavily laden bicycle ran over a snake's head. I didn't know what breed it was, but it looked like a Flat-Headed Tarmac Snake. I had a good ride to Jerantut, receiving great encouragement from Malaysian lorry drivers waving and shouting, 'Good! Good!' At Jerantut I found a hotel, showered and scraped the whiskers off my face. I still looked pretty desperate, time to buy new shirts.

One hundred miles from Jerantut to Telok Chempedak and I intended to take two days to get there. It was not to be, no hotels from start to finish and waterlogged land. I rode eight hours in heavy rain and completed the journey in daylight, very appreciative of the apartment I rented for £5 a day.

Telok was a good small resort, suggested to me by a Malaysian, very few people about because still monsoon season. I made Kebab Corner Beach Pub my headquarters for a two-day stay. Shan and his wife were hospitable and Mrs Shan cooked a delicious Indian curry. Until my travels I never realised actually how much rice is eaten, I blame it on this generation. Rice was originally grown just to throw at weddings, except with fewer people getting married we now have to eat the surplus rice instead.

I was worried about my tires, they had worn so thin I could read the writing on the inner tubes. I had made the mistake of having a bike with 27-inch wheels, my Dawes Super Galaxy. Having used all my spares I combed the cycle shops in Kuantan with no result. I had to buy some very narrow racing tyres, unsuitable but they fitted, and I was able to continue.

With confidence brought on by new tyres I followed the coast road alongside deserted beaches, the angry North China Sea making it a spectacular ride. I could see with my own eyes the aftermath of the severe flooding that this area had suffered. The water level was subsiding, but many homes were still marooned. For hundreds of yards the road disappeared under water. I rode slowly to see the centre white line, jumping off and paddling when the depth of the dirty water obliterated my guiding stripe. Water, water everywhere and I was in the middle of it. To step off the mostly concealed road could mean stepping into deep trouble. People stranded on the top floors of their houses leaned out of windows, mouths agape at the sight of a man going boldly on. Anyone with sense would have bedded down a few days in Kuantan.

Fortunately the sun shone and I arrived at Pekan, the first guest in the hotel for a week and the restaurant still out of service. Cows wandering willy-nilly on the roads, reminded me of India. I rode on in the downpours, I'd got used to it and it was so warm that in the brief dry spells the road steamed in minutes.

Kuala Rompin was a disappointment. I had expected a large town but it had only a small collection of shops. I made myself comfortable in Hotel Kencana. I had ridden only fifty miles, but with the bad weather and not knowing where the next shelter would be, this would do.

CHAPTER 37

A Gift and some Bees

I was lucky to find a Chinese restaurant, as most of the Muslim restaurants were closed, and I found myself again in a place where few foreigners are seen. The staff sat within a few feet of me and watched my every move. Perhaps they had never had any contact with a man from another country. They all wanted me to speak English.

A pretty thirteen-year old Chinese girl called Chin Fah Kian asked for my address. My pen ran dry as I finished writing. (For a year or two in the future Chin wrote to me telling me how well she was doing at school.) 'Will you be here for breakfast?' she asked in shaky English.

Arriving for breakfast I finally spotted Chin partly hiding behind a pillar, reluctant to approach me. As I straddled my bike she ran forward, put a beautifully wrapped gift in my hand and ran away too shy to speak. The gift was two pens; she had noticed last night that my pen had run dry.

With this lovely gesture I set off for Pulau Tioman, another paradise island, rated among the top ten in the world, this is where 'South Pacific' was filmed. On the way I learned that it is an island for divers, snorkelers and sunbathers, no roads and not much point my going. I met Kurt, a Swiss long-distance cyclist, and we stood for an hour dishing up travel stories.

'I've just spent six weeks in the Philippines,' he said. 'Great, but constantly swamped by women asking if I wanted a wife. I prefer my bike, it doesn't answer back.'

I spent the night at Mersing, the ferry port for Pulau Tioman. Off in sunshine at last with a feeling of well-being, yet I was to experience fear quite soon.

Riding strong, I was crossing a river bridge, when too late, I saw a black cloud at head height. My head carved a path through a swarm of black striped bees. They were not pleased and the attack began. In panic and riding shirtless I tried furiously to beat them off with my left arm while steering with my right. My body was alive with angry insects. I jumped with every sting. I stopped after half a mile thinking they were gone, but they had clustered like a giant pineapple on my panniers and they attacked again. Another panic-stricken furious half mile and at last I was free of them. I pulled fifteen stings from my right arm and seven from my body. I couldn't reach the stings in my back. Now smarting in many places I carried in my head the thought of killer bees. How many stings can one person take? Some die after one sting. My fingers swelled like sausages and my imagination ran riot, I thought I was losing all sensation. Not actually the case, for following, on a roller coaster ride I covered a hundred miles to Desaru in 7½ hours.

I had now ridden from north to south of Malaysia, and from side to side, with more to come.

CHAPTER 38

A Visit to Singapore

At Desaru I added another ten miles finding a campsite with a toilet block and assorted buildings so that I could shelter if a storm broke. A storm in Asia is a storm to remember, during the worst of the recent weather nine flood evacuation centres had been put to use.

Desaru is a hotel resort, each one self-contained. No other restaurants, so I had no choice but to eat in these expensive hotels. I was the only diner in the restaurants, the only customer in the 140-bedroom hotels, and the only sunbather on the lovely beach edged by the foam of the South China Sea.

I pondered which country to visit next: I wanted to go to Indonesia, but newspapers carried stories of riots and killings. My urge to visit was heightened by an article about an area where a new road was under construction and the people from two villages that had always been in conflict forgot their differences and trekked four days to get their first sight of machinery. They had never seen lorries, bulldozers, motorbikes or any other form of mechanised transport. Indonesia is made up of seven thousand islands, some hardly developed. Malaysia is a prosperous country, but still has many poor people; another news article described how the would-be purchasers of government apartments for lower paid workers qualified by proving that they earned less than £300 a year.

After two nights in Desaru I headed for a village I had been told about, an old forgotten corner where time stands still, close to a little-used ferry to Singapore. Riding beside a sea fringed with coconut palms in a very quiet area I entered Kampong Java. Just an hour or so made this my favourite village in Malaysia, a laid-back place if ever there was one, a collection of corrugated iron shacks where Chinese and Malaysian residents relax everywhere, their only concern being getting enough food for the day.

A short ride to Tanjung Pengelih. I sat with Tong, unhappy owner of a small boat.

'Fifteen people need. Boat no go,' he lamented. 'You one, boat no go, fifteen people need.'

We sat for two hours and nobody came.

'Where do you live?' I questioned.

'Singapore,' came Tong's reply.

'Where will you sleep tonight?'

'I sleep home, my house.'

'Then it looks like I'm going to Singapore,' I grinned.

We boarded the boat. Poor Tong, he only made £1.50 and spick and span Singapore became my host country. Super-modern spotless slick shops, boutiques, restaurants and hotels, an offence to litter, chewing gum banned. Anyone caught littering is shamed in the newspapers as well as fined. To change some money I entered the plush Hotel Meridian, the sort of place where people eat bananas with a knife and fork.

'We only change money for our guests. Are you checking in?' said the lovely young lady eyeing the bedraggled Bob.

'Be a good girl and help an old man out. I'm cycling around the world and sleeping in a tent.' She helped me out.

I intended circling the island close to the sea, but I was brought to a halt at an expressway that barred cyclists. Chinese Ben came to my rescue and guided me through well laid out parkland. It seemed the whole Singapore population was on a keep-fit binge, jogging, cycling, walking, running and roller-skating. I presumed that camping wasn't allowed. I couldn't find an out of the way corner. I threw caution to the winds and erected Thrifty in full view.

I had been warned how expensive it was here and at one of the many fashionable bars half a pint of beer cost £1.50, until Australian Dave and Indian Gerald, impressed with my journey, bought the drinks and snacks for the rest of the evening. Filipina Mary-Lou and Singaporean Delores provided the decoration.

There are two road accesses to Singapore from Malaysia, a causeway north and a bridge west. Ben had suggested the bridge, but as I approached I doubted that cyclists would be allowed. Deciding to go for it I rode wide of the police checking vehicles and when they shouted I kept going. A young policeman jumped on a bike and set off after me. He had no chance, my leg muscles had been developed over thousands of miles. I left him well behind, then stopped to see him panting at the side of the road. He would lose a lot of face if he reported back without me. I rode back and let him give the impression he'd been successful. There was no problem, but they told me I could only exit on the causeway.

Who could resist this picture

Mary Lou, Gerald, Dave and Dolores

CHAPTER 39

Mooching in Malacca

Back in Malaysia and a leisurely ride before sharing time with three Malay Indians, conversation as always turning to the availability of women round the world.

'Yes,' I told them, 'girls are offered everywhere, usually young girls. I'm not interested in young girls, maybe someone forty or fifty could get me interested.'

They grinned in disbelief.

'We have girls from eleven to thirty-five, but finding an old woman of forty or fifty would be difficult.'

'I don't need any help,' I finished the conversation.

A few good pushes on the pedals and I was back on the west coast, heading north for Malacca with an overnight stop in a grubby cheap hotel in Batu Puhat. On a sparsely populated road a motorcyclist approached me in the opposite direction and as he passed his wallet fell from his side pocket. He failed to hear my shouts and his wallet contained $40, his driving licence, ID, three ATM cards and other items. In ten miles there were only four houses and nobody recognised the guy. At a café I had better luck, his ID was recognised and a messenger was sent straight off to his family home. A very pleased relieved man soon rolled up to collect his goods.

The warmth of greetings continued all the way to Malacca, where I booked into Sunny's Guesthouse. I don't know how he got that nickname, I never saw him smile. I consumed a good steak in Rock and Roll Grill and had a chat with Muslim Moses, the Assistant Superintendent of Police, who drove fifty miles here to drink where he wouldn't be recognised. He paid for everything, so another good day.

Mooching in Malacca I rode up St Paul's Hill.

'How are your grandchildren?' called TV-watcher Francis K S Goh. This artist, then 55 years old, had lived on the hill for eighteen years, a great character, he fed all the local stray cats with chicken scraps he collected from the restaurants. He explained his crazy idea that he could have his entire body tattooed with brand names; he thought they would probably pay him to have Nivea on his face, Vicks Lozenges on his throat, McDonalds and KFC on his belly, Levi's on his legs and so on. Months after our meeting he sent me one of his watercolours.

Time to make up my mind and in spite of being warned not to visit Indonesia I bought a ticket to Sumatra.

'You famous man. I give you 50% discount,' offered the agent, and this welcome bonus brought the price down to £6. Another steak at Rock and Roll and a second night at Sunny's, sharing my bed with a multitude of nocturnal fleas. With a couple of days to kill before my ticket came into force Bob the Bumps headed north. Not too far as I was reluctant to leave Malaysia. Is this the friendliest country in the world?

Twenty-three year old Hazlina stepped from her car. 'Can I have your autograph? And will you come to my house?' Her three sisters and one brother all waved excitedly. Flattered, I followed, and even though they were still fasting for Ramadan Hazlina produced an array of snacks in minutes. Half an hour and five autographs later I rode on and soon found a motel close to the beach. After some light-hearted leg-pulling with the staff I was allowed to use the bathroom facilities even though I intended to sleep outside. They pointed out a space among the tables and I pitched my portable home. I watched the sun set on the Indian Ocean and when it grew dark I enjoyed a meal and gazed at the pyramids of lights on the fishing boats moving across the water like floating Christmas trees.

The staff at Motel Tanjung Kling treated me like royalty, checking to see if I was hungry, did I need more ice, more light to write by?

Caree came to speak to me. 'Why leave Malaysia?'

'I'm looking for an Indonesian girl,' was my joking reply.

Caree went away, but was back within fifteen minutes with a broad smile on his face: 'I've got you Indonesian girl.'

CHAPTER 40

Into Indonesia

Still with time to spare I wandered back into Malacca and had breakfast at the Looney Planet Café, a favourite backpackers' hangout where my picture was pinned to the wall with those of other assorted celebrities. Many people wanted to be photographed with me, so I made the most of the limelight because I was leaving next day for Sumatra and anonymity.

Sorting out where to lay my head, I stood outside an abandoned building site surrounded by a high fence. I prised a couple of boards apart and lifted my bike through. An empty builders' hut stood invitingly with door swinging open, my night's headquarters.

My ticket said 9.30am boat departure, but the usual chaos reigned and 11.30 came before it inched its way down the Malacca River into the Straits. Before boarding I had become a millionaire when I changed £150 into Indonesian money and received 1.75 million Rupiah. With several young backpackers I disembarked at Dumai, what a shambles of a town.

'Lonely Planet says it's dangerous here. We must all stick together to the bus station,' they insisted.

'And what then?' I asked.

'We're all heading for Bali, so we all get on the bus.'

'I'm cycling to Bali,' I told the group of pretend travellers, and like Bob Hope and Bing Crosby I took the road to Bali, only two thousand miles away. I needed a map. I had already combed the Malaysian bookshops with no result.

'This is Malaysia. Why would we have maps of Indonesia?' they reasoned.

No chance of buying a map in this poverty-stricken shantytown knee-deep in rubbish. Nobody spoke English apart from 'How are you?' which everybody shouted as I passed. My arm ached from responding to the welcoming waves. No map, but I found out the name of the nearest large town and set off on a main road in what was now the late afternoon. I made it to Duri just before dark and settled into the Hotel Chitra. When I left Duri behind my picture was on the wall but I still had no map. By lunchtime I had seen plenty of shack restaurants with little to offer, then some men unloading a truck directed me to a supermarket. I spoke to the aptly named manageress, Mona Lisa, a beauty.

'Is that a Birmingham accent?' she enquired.

And there I was talking to a woman who had studied at Birmingham University. She was so pleased she phoned her husband, he arrived and we all piled into his truck. They were very happy to help a Brummie, they drove me into Pekanbaru and helped secure my bed at Hotel Linda. Next came a fruitless search for the map.

In a large shopping mall I asked the bookshop owner why he had no maps.

'I've had this store nine years and you're the first to ask for one,' was his answer.

We dined in what was supposed to be the best restaurant, all the food cold and the only drink hot water. But it was a privilege to meet this lovely recently married couple and husband Paul paid the bill. Still early and I strolled the tatty town. It could have been India, no bars but small stores sold beer and a shopkeeper put a chair in the little space he had. I spent a pleasant hour with him though not a word was understood between us.

Morning brought another search for the elusive map. This time, success! With a late start I headed for Bukittinggi. Soon the hills gave me tough riding but improved scenery. I was still a long way from Tinggi Hill and found no hotels. Suddenly I was outside a huge restaurant.

'Have you food? Have you beer?'

'We have food. No have beer.'

'Can I sleep here?' I pointed at a sleeping platform. I dispatched a boy to fetch me a drink from a shop I had passed a quarter of a mile back. He was overjoyed when I let him use my bike.

I made the best of what food they had, cold scraps of chicken, cold bits of fish and warm rice. I avoided any hot water. It was a good night's stop, with communication difficult, but everybody interested in my travels. All who entered the restaurant shook my hand and those who spoke English implored me to approach the newspapers.

'Please tell the world that we Indonesians are good people. If a man can ride alone through our country on a bike and come to no harm then surely the story will encourage other people to come here.'

I promised to do my best. After all, I would be speaking the truth. I retired for the night with my eyes tired from the glare of so many smiles and brilliant white teeth. My arm aching from waving at my well-wishers, I felt a lot of sympathy for the Queen.

CHAPTER 41

A Chain Smoker and a Tattooed Lady

I left the restaurant at Pasar Bawah and began the hard riding that peaked at over 7,000 feet. In superb countryside a man with a rifle over his shoulder was carrying a beautiful red-throated yellow bird in a small cage. The bird dominated all sounds with its delightful singing, but it was being used as a decoy: any birds attracted were rendered dumb by the gun and finished up on a plate.

Many people were dressed in traditional costume, or was it their normal wear? Three elegantly dressed women approached, each with an unusual headdress and balancing a flat circular tray on her head with a present on it. They indicated that I should follow and I found myself at a wedding.

How pleased the people were to see me. The Sumatrans go out of their way to show friendliness, and I would find out as I approached Bali that the same good-natured manner did not exist everywhere in Indonesia. The shouts of 'How are you?' and the warmth of their laughter were genuine.

I passed a hotel on the way into Payakumbuh, then met French cyclist Henri coming the other way. After a getting to know you chat we rode back to the hotel and agreed to share a room to halve the cost. Henri had ridden much of the world, such as Mexico City to Rio de Janeiro 12,000 miles in nine months, he had been robbed in South Africa twice in an hour and had spent a month in Thailand without spending a single penny on accommodation, sleeping every night in a wat.

Hotel Manghuto was rather swanky, it needed to be, at £4 a night for a double room. Strangely it had no bar and no restaurant. I solved the bar problem and within minutes the bellboy was on an urgent mission. He returned with beer and ice for me, none for Henri as he was teetotal.

He was however the most addicted smoker I have ever seen. I was amazed at his cycling capabilities considering he devoured a cigarette only to replace it with another, it was pointless even to close the packet. When we ate in town every spoonful of rice took its turn with every drag. In the morning he swung his legs out of bed and put a fag in his mouth before his feet touched the floor. As an anti-smoker all my life I should have had my own room even at £4 a night.

Bukittinggi was marked on the map as being of special interest. It was a dump, and after riding round for an hour I took to the road again, destination Lake Maningjau. Through rice fields and pretty villages in drenching rain, tough climbing and a dangerous descent with paperclip bends. People who have experienced it speak throughout Indonesia about this descent. Each bend is numbered, up to forty-four. Motor vehicles grind slowly uphill.

Once reached, Lake Maningjau is very inviting, reputed to have the clearest water in the world. It was probably the best spot I stayed in Sumatra. I took a bungalow on the lake edge for 80p a day, the balcony extended over the water and I lounged there taking in fabulous scenery.

Morning arrived and the rain was still heavy. I rode about twenty miles immersed in the beauty of my surroundings. A meal in a café was a repeat of other meals. No need to order, a selection of food was placed on the table, chicken, fish, chillies, vegetables, fried eggs and boiled eggs, all cold. Only what was eaten was charged for, the untouched food returned to the display in the window. Some of the food may well have been on several tables. Taking my time I was joined by local girl Cherie. As well as being anti-smoking I am anti-tattoo. I confess I am frightened of tattooed people. If they are prepared to mutilate and disfigure their own bodies, what would they do to mine? Cherie was a believer in self-decoration. Her ears had no room left for more rings, her nose bore the same scrap metal. Her legs, arms and neck couldn't be admired because of the graffiti printed heavily on each inch.

'I live at home-stay 44,' (named after the hairpin bends) said this once-pretty girl who had made herself ugly. 'Perhaps you can come round this afternoon. We can be friends while you are here.'

She stood up and turned her back to me, at the same time pulling down the brief shorts she wore to reveal another tattoo.

'I can show you plenty more,' she promised. I didn't take her up on it.

I will weep if Carol Vorderman gets a tattoo.

CHAPTER 42

Several Deaths

I joined a group of assorted hippies for the evening. Some of them had squatted here a long time, mostly lazing about on hammocks smoking funny-smelling concoctions. Claire was very pleased to meet another English person and amazed that I had arrived on a bicycle. She insisted that I joined a get-together at her somewhat distant homestay the next evening.

'There'll be apple pie and custard,' and with those words she made it definite that I'd be there.

So on a night of inky blackness on a dreadfully surfaced road I pedalled three miles to Rizal Beach and knocked on Claire's door. She responded to the knock, standing in the doorway with a towel barely covering her naked body and a big Indonesian man behind her similarly clad.

'Oh, Bob!' she cried. 'I'm so tired. I called it off. I managed to tell the others.'

I rode back to base crashing into unseen potholes swearing to myself, unable to believe that anyone would choose sex over apple pie and custard.

Lake Maninjau was glorious, but it was time to move on. I abandoned my plans to go to Lake Toba in the north, the resort that most visitors headed for, and instead I headed for the west coast which would eventually lead me to Java.

I spent the night in the large town of Pariman. I carried hardly any food so a power cut lasting four hours proved awkward and I went to bed in a fleapit hotel after munching a few biscuits. In the morning as I was leaving I helped a woman dragging a gas stove out of a storeroom. A rat had nested in the grill compartment and it ran up my arm before dropping onto the floor. I stamped it to death in a corner.

Strolling the early morning market where traders were setting up their stalls, I saw a man who had already prepared his oranges for sale having a furious argument with two women traders because they were setting up the same stall. The argument grew more and more fierce, vendors around and about thought it amusing and indicated that it was a regular occurrence with this bunch.

But the man was in an uncontrollable rage. He stalked back to his stall and grabbed a gun, shot one of the women dead then levelled the gun at the second.

The crowd screamed, 'She's pregnant!'

He paused, took stock of what he'd done and ended his own life with a bullet to his head. The police arrived within minutes, but nobody (including me) had seen anything.

Now I was heading south in glorious scenery, splendid riding, elbow to the Indian Ocean, else climbing mountains with tumbling waterfalls or travelling alongside the multitude of rivers with waters leaping joyously over the rocks.

I rested a while at a shop and enjoyed an hour of good company with English-speaking Merri. She suggested I stay at Painan for the night. It was a long way, a bit too long, and two miles short the darkness brought me to a halt. In a large restaurant I was told to sleep anywhere I liked. I gathered some mats together to make a softer surface and with eight other men scattered around the floor I dreamed the night away. I woke to find the eight men standing round me in a semi-circle, they wanted the prayer mats I'd been lying on.

I took a room at Balaiselasa for 30p and spent an hour at a local shop. Wherever I settled the people gathered to stand and stare. I moved seats continually to avoid the choking cigarette smoke, but there was no escape; they were just so fascinated with a foreigner. They peered over my shoulder as I brought my notes up to date, they took the notebook from my hand and studied it before passing it round, even though they understood not one word. It became irritating to be the centre of attention.

Glorious weather again in glorious countryside, at times tough going. Food was a problem, too much rice, unless you like rice.

A group of boys leaping in and out of a river shouted at me, 'Mandi! Mandi!' (Bath). I stripped to the buff and joined the naked youngsters. My skin by now was as brown as any Asian's, but only on exposed parts, and when I shed my shorts in front of twenty boys a stunned silence was followed by shrieks of laughter at my white bum. These kids have probably grown up thinking all Westerners are piebald.

CHAPTER 43

A Moment With Cendra

On the 80-mile ride to Muko Muko I passed monkeys riding bicycles. They perched on the crossbar in front of their master and gripped the handlebars as if they were steering. These working monkeys gathered coconuts and just like the people they worked for peanuts.

At Muko Muko I learned that a cheap guesthouse is called a wisma or a losmen. How many must I have passed when I needed shelter? At a wisma two grown-up sisters asked if I liked Indonesian food.

'What is there?'

'Rice,' they chorused.

After a language struggle they produced some potatoes and eggs. I demonstrated how to make chips.

'I'll have egg and chips,' I announced.

What a fiasco! First came a dish of delicious looking golden brown chips. I tried in vain to tell the sisters' elderly mother that I wanted my fried egg at the same time as the chips. She returned shortly with a scrambled egg. She had thrown the chips away. I gave up and strolled to the nearest shop, where the empty seating area was filled in minutes with thirty men and boys jostling to sit or stand next to this strange man.

Every yard of cycling was uphill, bukit after bukit and the map told me tomorrow would be the same. It was impossible to be alone, people lived alongside the road, ramshackle dwellings lining both sides for hundreds of miles, every house with a roofed platform smack up to the kerb edge, with somebody lying on it. I was never free from glaring eyes and I had never seen so many children. The shouts of 'Hello, mister!' and 'What is your name?' started first thing in the morning and continued all day. Better than having rocks thrown at me (as I'd experienced in some countries), but impossible to respond to all greetings. Then there were the motorcycles keeping pace, sometimes a queue formed as each rider waited his turn to ask, 'What is your name? Where you go?' Another fleapit for the night and a visit to a café to sample the local delicacies, a choice of a large, medium or small dish of rice with some unidentifiable goo. Twenty-seven villagers crowded round the table to watch my every move.

I have to admit that I developed a little joke of my own. I started to realise that they wanted to copy me, often repeating the last word I said, even though they didn't understand it. Let me explain their handshakes, as in Malaysia the custom is after shaking hands to place your hand on your heart, which I interpret as meaning 'My display of friendship comes from the heart.' If I'm correct then that is actually very meaningful, but for a little joke with the folks around the table I shook hands with each and placed my hand on my head. The first man slowly followed suit, the second man a little more quickly and after that they all adopted what they probably thought was a Western handshake.

After strenuous riding eighty miles standing up on the pedals in a deluge of water, while trees bent like boomerangs and branches snapped like matchsticks, I decided on a two-day stay in Bengkulu. I entered Hotel Vista dripping wet to find a tasty looking female checking in at reception. I wondered if I should tell her that three buttons had come undone on her blouse.

'Are you booking a room?' she smiled.

'That's the idea,' I replied.

'It would be silly to book two rooms,' she said, and we decided not to be silly.

Cendra and I spent time on Long Beach, a beach that the locals think is wonderful, but which is poor in comparison with others I have enjoyed. In Sumatra I saw miles of stunning coastline, but no good beaches and I found as I travelled further that I encountered no good beaches in Java or Bali either. Indonesian beaches carry permanent signs warning danger for swimmers. The sea is not only rough but has undercurrents that even the locals can underestimate. Eighteen local people watching the ferocity of a storm had been engulfed and drowned by a massive wave not long before my visit and a small child had lost her life while paddling.

On Long Beach I talked with 23-year old Safrial. He was married to Shasa, seventeen, and they couldn't afford the hospital treatment for their poorly one-year old baby. Safrial guided me to a shop where I could buy tubes for my bike, warning me to be careful because tourists had been robbed and killed in some parts of the country. I shrugged off his warnings, so far I had experienced no real danger in Indonesia, only occasional bullying and mickey-taking, insignificant compared with the warmth and loveliness of the many I had met, including Cendra.

I shopped in a large store and conveyed to the staff that I needed all sorts of things for a one-year old local baby. The shop girls were delighted and with an armful of this and that I returned to Safrial and Shasa. Safrail considered himself lucky if he made £1 a day selling fruit from a handcart, but the wheels were broken. I soon fixed him up with new wheels, to give him at least the chance to earn his £1 a day.

It proved difficult getting my bike ready for the off. Cendra wouldn't let go of my arm. Like all Indonesians she had to spit every few minutes.

'I like you,' spit. 'I want to travel with you,' spit. 'We can go to Bali together,' spit. 'We could get married. I am twenty-eight, but I don't care about the age difference,' spit.

I pulled myself away.

'Phone me when you get to Java and I will come to you. Don't forget me!'

'Course not,' was my goodbye.

I was invited to join the celebration

Cendra, 'Don't forget me,' she called

CHAPTER 44

A Stag Party and a Pelting

Staff at Wisma Omiko in a clean town called Manna were pleased to have a tourist as a guest, complaining, 'So few come here.'

'I'll tell you why,' I said. 'It's because there's no food and no beer.' I had just been served rice and a scrap of chicken. I watched many fishing boats unloading their catch, but where the fish went was a mystery.

A group of a hundred men attracted my attention as they squatted outside a mosque. They were in good humour and high spirits, it was a stag party. I accepted their invitation to join in and also accepted a drink from the choice offered. The choice was tea or coffee. At a so-called International Money Changer I tried to change some $20 bills, but, 'We only change $100 bills and we don't change English money at all,' was the response.

'You should take your sign down,' was my parting shot.

Two banks had the same conditions and Visa cards meant nothing to them. At my fourth attempt, but only after long deliberation, my passport scrutinised by every staff member and photocopied along with my ATM card, I was allowed to draw money: for £100 I received 1.4 million Rupiah.

With Omiko behind me, the best wisma yet and so it should be for £1.40 a night! The day was hot and the hills went on forever. Food remained a problem, although some men had written down the names of meals I could ask for. It was a waste of ink, because what you saw was what you got, never any bread or potatoes and all food served cold.

After forty-five miles riding I took refuge in a village shop with the villagers almost sitting on my knee. The shopkeeper's wife made me a dish of Pisang Goreng (banana fritters). They sure made a welcome change. The local doctor fixed it for me to have tea and scrambled eggs for breakfast next morning. They were served cold, cooked the night before.

The country became less populated, just jungle and screeching monkeys. When the road swung inward the surface was bad, the hills impossible to ride or even walk dragging the bike. But then the beaches grew better, the sand paler, and I risked a cautious swim. With twelve red flags displayed I kept close to the shore. Ten miles from last night's stop appeared a sheltered cove that kept the sea calm and a curving pale sand beach fringed with coconut palms. What a spot this would make for a resort.

Such strenuous riding seemed to take forever. Perhaps this was because of the milestones: at the start of the day a milestone declared 111km to Krui, but each stone added another kilometre rather than decreasing them. With a stone reading 118km someone must have nudged the road worker and he started again with 111km. I reached Krui at 103km. After a short lie-down I went for a stroll in the market. Two men with fists clenched and arms flailing like windmills rushed at me, shouting,

'Murderer! You bombed Muslims in Iraq!'

Other men came forward and cursed the two angry men, shook my hand and welcomed me. I continued my stroll.

Next morning, another confrontation in the market, a stall keeper started pelting me with vegetables. Ducking a hail of potatoes, turnips and whatever else he had to hand I walked up to him and offered my hand. He paused, rather surprised. Other stallholders came forward and patted me on the back. Shamefaced, the man turned his expression into a smile, shook my hand and touched his heart. In a few seconds I was helping him pick up assorted vegetables. I sat at his stall and ate the fruit he put in front of me. A crowd of delightful children gathered to follow me to a banana pancake stall where at 2p a pancake it didn't cost much to treat them all.

A few hours on the beach brought a meeting with Novi, a 24-year old mother of two who used to be a tourist guide. She was pleased to practise her rusty English. She showed me a building where women worked in appalling conditions, choking in dust and sorting out mounds of crystals used for making glass and colouring paint, earning 35p a day. An American boy had courted Novi and wanted to marry her, but she had turned him down on the grounds of different religions. She had married a local man instead, but he had beaten her constantly and the marriage was over. With two tiny children her tourist guide days were over. She had turned down the chance to live in undreamed-of luxury in America; now she spent her days in poverty.

I bought four potatoes and asked a man with a barbecue stall to cook them for me. With the meat I bought from him I had my best meal in Indonesia. But he had to go and spoil it, he went away for a while after asking if I slept alone, returning with his two daughters, one thirteen and the other fifteen.

'A man shouldn't sleep alone. Which one do you want?' The girls smiled sweetly.

Perhaps he thought I was Gary Glitter.

The town of Krui

35p a day to work in appalling conditions

216

Several countries butcher's shops

Who said you can't carry shopping on a bike?

CHAPTER 45

Trouble with Eggs Again

I bought a few things from the market before heading off. A throng of traders wished me well and I left with good memories of Krui.

It was a glorious day with superb scenery. I had to leave the coast now and turn east over the range of mountains that runs all the way down the west of Sumatra. I had crossed them east to west six hundred miles north of here and ridden alongside them to the south. Crossing west to east would bring me to the port for Java. I would start at sea level today but tonight would find me two thousand feet above sea level at Sumberejo.

A funny day people-wise, with some unpleasant incidents. At a stop I managed to shrug off a group of lads led by the town bully, whose behaviour was most disturbing, as yet nobody had laid a violent hand on me.

When asking for directions I have learned to ask several people out of sight of each other, just because some folk think it's hilarious to point in the wrong direction. Today I sought assistance from three different people out of sight of each other: perhaps it was a coincidence that they all pointed the same way, the wrong way. After five miles of hard climbing I had enough clues to know I was off course and a U-turn soon put it right.

In growing darkness in Sumberejo I met some troublesome guys who insisted there was no accommodation. I found a wisma, but I would have slept in a shop doorway regardless of dubious characters, I couldn't have gone on in the dark. The room cost me the tourist price of 86p. The Indonesians paid 70p and even at this price they crammed twenty-seven people into three rooms to share the cost, some lay on the floor. In the morning they lit fires inches from the doors and cooked breakfast. Nobody minded. These countries are so laid-back; as long as rice grows and they can spit they're happy!

I stepped out of my room to find a fan club had formed, all eager to make sure I had whatever I needed. Art teacher Henri, anxious to try his English, said, 'Come this way' and I sat with him, his two brothers and his wife. I was almost crushed by men and boys as I swallowed my rice and chicken. They loaded me up with oranges and bananas for the next day. The twenty-seven people from the wisma were here for a wedding. I was leaving, so I declined the invitation to attend, offered by a man who was very fluent in English.

'Thank you, but I must go now,' also adding jokingly 'besides, there's no beer.'

'We Muslims consider it a grave sin to drink alcohol or eat food during Ramadan.'

'Don't you wonder if you are the only one sticking to the rules?' I said. 'I have spent a lot of time now with Muslims and not many have refused to share my beer. I've been in many hotels where the doors are bolted and the windows shuttered, and Ramadan or not Muslims eat and drink, usually strong drink.'

'I don't believe you.'

I pressed home my unacceptable facts. 'Remember last night I was standing with you, when I was invited to join some people across the road?'

'Yes,' he agreed.

'Well, talk to them. I bought them all a beer.'

With the big climbs for the day behind me I rode fast to Kata Bumi for a lunchtime break. I managed to buy some cakes and found a stall selling beer and ice. To add weight to my previous argument four Muslims sat with me and partook of my drink.

At Bandar Jaya I entered a hotel to find four business girls hoping to make some wages. 'You like girls?' smirked the hotel keeper. My priority was to get cleaned up and as always to check over the bike because so often nuts and bolts start to work loose after the pounding they have coped with.

At breakfast for several minutes I tried to convey to a girl that I wanted scrambled eggs. Taking two eggs I held them over a bowl, pretended to break them and mix them. I pointed to a frying pan and sat down expectantly. Surely she understood? The girl broke the two eggs, mixed them thoroughly and placed the uncooked liquid in front of me, the opposite of the day before, when the eggs did reach the frying pan, but the woman didn't know when enough was enough and served me a black, crispy mess, with rice, of course.

CHAPTER 46

Over to Java

I noticed that almost every time I bought something, some street-wise man or youth followed me into the shop or sat near me in the café. He was telling the assistant to charge me double, I could see from the way they looked at me to check if I understood. Of course, they were making commission. I usually asked for the price to be written down and then I judged whether I would pay it. Even double it was still cheap, but these interfering entrepreneurs were annoying.

I was in the big city of Bandor Lampung and had already coped with hassle, shouldering off various unsavoury characters. With police around they hadn't tried anything. A likely lad followed me into a shop and when the girl filled a bag with cakes he told her how much to charge. Annoyed, I threw my purchases over the counter and snatched my money back from her hand. I delivered a few choice obscenities at the youth and left the shop while the girl shouted at him for losing her the sale.

This was going to be my last night in Sumatra. At the end of this tour I would decide that Sumatra was the best of the three Indonesian islands I visited: the people on Java weren't as friendly and Bali was one long traffic jam.

A sign pointed the way to a luxury resort and I pitched Thrifty on the beach for a charge of £1.75. It was more than I'd been paying for some hotel rooms, but I was in a lovely setting again in an empty resort. This place close to Kalianda was a great stop for my last night on the island, four circular bars, sweet music, spotlights on the sea and I was the only customer.

I boarded a ferry at Sumur and two hours later disembarked at Merak, Java, the crossing cost 16p. Anyer was close, but it turned out to be all expensive hotels. I had an amazing stroke of luck when out of all the bars I chose the Blue Moon and struck up an instant friendship with Ralph, its Australian owner. He was amazed at my mileage and my great age.

'My dad's the same age and all he does is watch TV.'

Several Englishmen among the locals said, 'Wait around a few days and you'll get plenty of marriage proposals.'

'I have had lots already,' I answered, but I put my foot in it by adding, 'I think it's silly for old men to marry young girls.'

An awkward silence before one of the three guys (all well over sixty) said, 'We've all got wives under twenty.'

Just then a young woman stomped into the bar and dumped a three-year old kid into the arms of one of the sixty-year old men. 'I'm fed up waiting for you. I'm off out with my friends. All you do is drink,' she snapped, and flounced out. The old guy ordered another beer.

I chatted with Ralph, a really nice fellow. 'You can stay in my beach house as long as you like. My housekeeper will cook and wash your clothes and my driver will take you anywhere. Take your pick of any of the hostesses. Everything on the house.' I was already having trouble taking my eyes off Leesha. We approached the house. Ralph asked if I was afraid of rats. I replied in the negative. As we stepped in, one of them was climbing the stairs. My new friend suggested that after opening the bathroom door I stepped aside to let them run out.

CHAPTER 47

The Rambo of the Village

Ann the housekeeper rustled up pancakes next morning and I was chauffeur-driven to Ralph's mountain home for a great English breakfast. I met Linda, his third wife, in their newly built magnificent wooden house, constructed by local tradesmen completely by hand.

A lunchtime drink at the Blue Moon brought a meeting with a brewery representative, keen to use me in an advertising campaign along the lines of 'This man rides the world and he finds Anker beer the best.' Photographs were taken and payment promised.

'I don't want any money,' I told him, 'just supply Ralph with a few free barrels of beer.'

Travellers whom I met later told me that they had seen a billboard featuring me, but I never saw one.

I hung around for a while, just because it was a nice place to hang around, but soon I felt I must move on. A violent cloudburst forced me to take shelter in a café.

'You sleep with my family,' invited the owner, and his family was pleased to have me. Neighbours from all over stepped into the house or put their heads through a window to look at this strange visitor. I slept on the floor with 23-year old well-educated Jophie. He knew that his country must change, get away from the unrest, violence and poverty. After dressing me in his own best shirt and trousers (mine were too scruffy) he took me to the city of Purwakarta because he insisted I should meet the Chief Officer of the region to express my opinions of Indonesia. It was a fruitless journey, however, as we had no appointment.

On the return journey to the village Jophie showed me his university and the squalid living accommodation that these future top men had to live in.

'What is your religion?' they enquired.

When I answered that I had no religion they asked, 'You don't believe in God? Why don't you believe in God?'

'Every day I see people living in appalling conditions, dying babies sucking on the breasts of dying mothers. Across the world I've seen people to whom death would be a luxury, who have never had a good meal in their lives, sick people born to live their short lives in filth and squalor. No God would have his subjects born into this.'

Silence reigned. Nobody spoke, but I knew that in a short while these people would all be back praying again.

So I took my leave from another fine family that took me to its heart. It had been great fun, the women giggling as they sorted out saucy phrases with the aid of a dictionary, the mildest being 'I want to kiss you.' I rode away with my eyes full of 'air mata,' tears.

It was hard to believe that I was riding a main road. The surface was broken up or missing for miles and I had to walk those surfaces. I had still not encountered 27-inch tyres and mine were paper-thin. Confused by road signs I sought assistance in a village. I pointed out my destination on my map to a young man who was rapidly joined by other men. He took my map from me and to hilarious laughter from the crowd he ripped the map into small pieces.

The Rambo of the village then flexed his muscles and to the delight of the onlookers demonstrated that he could break my puny frame in half. The nasty bunch dragged all my gear out of the packs and threw it on the road. Receiving many cheers Rambo rode away on the bike. I could do nothing but try and laugh as though telling them I knew it was only a joke, but I was anxiously worrying if he would come back.

He came back. I loaded up and hightailed out of there.

As light fell I found a builder's yard that strangely had no gates across the entrance. I wandered among the assorted building materials, stacks of timber, piles of bricks, bags of cement under shelter. I pitched behind a seven-foot stack of wood, keeping myself out of sight of the road, and settled down to sleep.

At 2.30am the sound of a lorry entering the site woke me. With my unlit torch in my hand and keeping as quiet as a spider's sneeze I left the tent and positioned myself behind a stack of bricks. The lorry was parked close to the timber that I had camped behind. It was very dark, but working without lights two men were rapidly throwing twenty-foot lengths of wood onto the truck.

Keeping myself in the dark behind my torch I switched on the beam. No doubt thinking that an armed security guard was behind the light the two men shouted in panic, jumped into the lorry and sped away. I had foiled a robbery and I resumed my sleep.

Half a mile on, in the village of Jasinga, the villagers poured on the friendship. Almost everybody shook my hand, what a difference from the previous village. I was amongst teeming traffic, absolute chaos, every inch of the road covered. I squeezed through gaps, the car and lorry drivers calling out, 'Selamat datung! Welcome! Good luck.'

Brickyard where I foiled a robbery

Official campsite in Malaysia. Tents sit on concrete ground - always wet

CHAPTER 48

Only Five Knives

Past Bogor the road was lined with hotels and eating places. I decided a clean bed and a shower would set me up. I settled down in Cipayung Bogor and in the restaurant Lesko the manager joined me. He was an experienced man who had worked in various countries. He apologised for his staff. 'They've had no education or training. They're pleasant and eager to please, but they don't understand what the rich tourists want. Some of those spoilt brats get annoyed at any incompetence.' Lesko explained his difficulties with advising his boss about running the restaurant. His boss would not supply knives, this was another country where people eat using their fingers or just a spoon and fork. A customer wanted to complain, because his party of six had all ordered steak, but the 400-seater restaurant only had five knives!

Lesko produced a wooden shield for me to sign, so now a plaque bearing my name hung on Sari Raya Restaurant's wall.

Ralph had warned me about the hills out of Bogor. I struggled for twenty-five crippling miles and after a brief respite the hills started again. I changed my route, but I still had two days' back-breaking riding before the roads turned reasonable. The change of route brought better countryside and people uninfluenced by the commercialism of the main road, but the road was cratered and inches deep in mud.

At Plered, motorcyclist Ade rode alongside.

'Where you go?' he asked.

'I go to Bali.'

'Not possible. We have no bus station.'

'I'm going by bike.'

'No! Not possible. Too far!' A discussion followed with the incredulous Ade, then he invited me to stay at his house. I followed him as he marched into a little courtyard and proudly declared that he had a tourist friend. His family and neighbours reacted as though he had won the lottery. Twenty-four year old Ade led the way for the evening meal and I had my first ride in a pedal rickshaw. After a terrible meal we returned to his home and I curled up on the usual mosquito-ant-beetle-flea infested mattress. I thought using my tent would be an insult.

Away again, still tough riding on bad roads with my tyres down to canvas. I had a good lunchtime stop, but impossible to relax, the room was dark from so many people crammed into the doorway or pressing their faces against the window. A young girl brought me coffee, hesitant at first, but with growing confidence.

'You American? You English? You have madam in England? You have girlfriend? You look for madam? You like Indonesian girls? You like me? You want to marry me?'

'I'm an old man. How old are you?'

'I'm nineteen. I don't mind.'

She tells me she earns £1 a week, gets her food provided and sleeps on the floor, so she sends the money to her family. Another girl desperate to escape poverty.

I was in tea plantation country, pleasant people called out, 'Hello, sir,' but not quite as many as the continuous hellos in Sumatra. No cheap rooms in Subang, so I forked out £1.30 for one of the best. Subang was a new town, clean with good shops and a proper market rather than the scruffy all over the road chaos in most towns. The people were all friendly and the police were a great bunch.

At last I had a road with a good flat surface, and I rode ninety-three miles in eight hours to arrive at the Hotel Asia in Cirebon, a large town right on the Java Sea with several shopping malls. I found a Pizza Hut, where I dined on chicken soup, salad, pizza and ice cream for £2.I drank one small bottle of beer in a café that sold it, but the owner mysteriously refused to sell me another. He even refused to sell one to me for Chinese Amin who was happily celebrating Chinese New Year in another corner of the café and who offered to buy me a drink. Amin was the first Chinese person I had seen, thousands had fled the country since the 1998 riots. Cars abandoned at Jakarta Airport by escaping Chinese could be picked up for nothing.

I walked back to the hotel, pausing to watch the rats scurrying from one pile of rubbish to another, sorting out the delicacies dumped by the food outlets. Wrecks of human beings competed with the rodents for the first pick of anything edible.

I had breakfast in Pizza Hut, opposite the immaculately clean KFC, the road in between a stinking mess of sewage overflow. People just paddled through it. A naked man shuffled along the street, then another one. I passed the city rubbish dump and watched the ragged clad men, women and children scratching among the discarded waste.

CHAPTER 49

Smelly Hotels and a Beautiful Temple

In blistering heat and with my tyres in a desperate state I headed for Pekalongan, stopping to swim in a pool after lunch. I still couldn't escape from people's attention, they meant well, but I wished for some time to myself. At the town I took a room and had a shower, then relaxed in a small shop, where twenty locals gazed at my every move.

I had an early start, rode for a few hours before I left the east coast and headed westwards. Still in blazing heat a very tired man looked for a room in Parikan. Although I can sleep anywhere and I am used to filthy rooms, even I drew the line at the first wisma I tried. Not only was it filthy, but the smell made my head reel. The two youths who showed me round just grinned when I held my nose. They were too busy watching the coconuts grow to be bothered with cleaning.

It was pitch black and raining heavily. English-speaking young Jantor offered, 'You sleep at my home,' but it was a special religious day and Grandma put her foot down, making it clear that she wouldn't allow a strange foreigner to sleep on the floor today of all days. Jantor took me to another wisma, as dirty as the first, but without the smell. Jantor was twenty-four, married with a four month old baby, so I treated him to a meal and slipped him a few dollars. Amy had been hovering outside the café, a good looking woman about forty, and she came in and sat close to me, pulling a face when I told her where I was sleeping.

'No need to sleep there. Sleep at my house.'

I had settled down with my things, plus I had paid 53p for the room.

'Too tired,' I told her.

I rode downhill forty-five miles to Yogyakarta, a favourite tourist spot, where the Superman homestay became my temporary abode, forewarned of my arrival by an email from Ralph. Backpackers arrive here by bus, but they were impressed to meet a real traveller and I was pleased to get some western food.

At the bird market in Yogyakarta some of the most beautiful birds I've ever seen were imprisoned in tiny cages, and as well as birds there were monkeys, lizards, bats, snakes and creatures I couldn't identify. Pigeon racing is a big pastime here, punters place bets on the outcome of short races. Owners attach a small plastic whistle to the pigeon's back at the base of its tail, so when the bird flies the whistle sounds, making the bird fly faster to try and get away from the sound.

At a well-equipped cycle shop I was finally able to purchase tyres, tubes and oil, have a new chain fitted and my handlebars re-taped. The young employee was told to drop everything to attend to me and the bill was just £7.50.

I spent the evening with Emma and Paul, a young English couple working in Singapore, who were paying $175 a night to stay in a swanky hotel geared up to provide for wealthy clients. All the staff wore traditional Javanese costume, but everyday habits prevailed, the commissionaire resplendent in authentic clothing still gripped his nose and ejected a stream of green snot onto the entrance steps. Emma and Paul went back to their posh hotel, glad to exit Superman homestay where rats ran freely in and out of the kitchen as we ate our meal. I retired to my 80p room annoyed that I hadn't taken one of the abundant 35p rooms available.

I rode to Borobudur temple, the most beautiful I had ever seen, spoilt only by the pedlars who refused to take no for an answer. As I was leaving a woman tapped me on the shoulder and asked if she could practise her English on me. We strolled like a couple in the well laid-out gardens. We talked about each other's circumstances, she was a widow of thirty-six.

'You are handsome, you must get many offers of marriage,' she said.

'I've had offers, but not because I'm handsome. It's because the women want to escape poverty.'

'Could I be your wife?'

We faced each other. I was lost for words. I could only say goodbye and walk away.

When I took refreshment in Café Citra the manager was impressed with my stories. He phoned the newspapers and soon photographs had been taken of me all around the temple. The Bernas newspaper and the Kedaulatan Rakyat printed my story and the café manager hung my picture on his wall.

Singapore Old Quarter

Traditional transport - Malaysia

CHAPTER 50

Bicycle Saddle – Horse Saddle

An election would be coming up in June and on this Sunday the opposing sides demonstrated their strength by riding in long noisy columns on motorbikes through the streets. They made a fearsome sight dressed in party colours and wearing masks, continually throttling their motorbikes in quick short bursts, with ear-splitting results.

Loaded with fruit and Dunkin' Donuts I set off for Bromo volcano, making full use of the map I'd bought in Bogor. The appalling traffic fumes bothered me more than the scorching heat. It's a worrying thought that all over the world people are unconcerned about the poison they introduce into our lovely world. I had a comfortable room in Sragen, only in need of a repaint, then on to Kertosono after an uneventful day. Next day in Lawang I refused to pay £4 for a room. Instead I rode down a narrow lane displaying a hotel sign, where I found a clean hotel for £2. Directed to a café I was amazed to find that the owner was an Englishman, Jim. He had lived in this backwater for sixteen years with his Indonesian wife. Jim was as surprised as I was. 'I saw you two months ago on TV, but I never expected you to turn up here.'

I have met expatriates in many countries and asked them, 'Do you think this is the best country you've been to?'

The answer is always the same. 'No, but this is the country where I found the best woman.'

Little did I know then that I would fall into the same honey-trap.

I chatted with Ula and Lisa. Ula was a teacher, married with two children, and Lisa her 32-year old divorced sister. Lisa made it plain that she wanted a western husband regardless of age, and Ula wanted to go to England. Ula earned £16 a month and lived with her mother while her husband worked a long way off for £24 a month. She had met him when a friend brought him to the house. They sat looking at each other, she thought he had a nice face and then, 'God whispered in my ear that he was the right man.'

'How would you feel if he took another three wives?'

'That is allowed in our religion. I would accept it.'

In reality most men can't even afford one wife.

Eleven miles outside Bromo it became impossible to ride, so I pushed the bike two miles to the losmen in Sukapura. Pleading for business in her little café the owner told me she could cook anything. Egg and chips would cost 50p and I paid first so that she could go and buy the eggs and potatoes, served beautifully with lettuce, tomato and cucumber. Morning dawned and I boarded a bus to cover the remaining tortuous miles to the volcano. Once there I mounted a different saddle, on the back of a horse. I was riding the black desert wasteland surrounding the volcano. Two hundred and forty steps led to the rim of the crater and choking on the acrid sulphur fumes I made it to the top. Another spectacular sight notched up and I boarded the bus back to Sukapura.

Off early I was pleased to be back in my own saddle, one that originally belonged to my hero the late Burt Griffiths. In his own very late years Burt also rode the world and fascinated me with his tales. At the time I never thought I would emulate him. He would be pleased to know that his saddle still roams the world. Some fast riding brought me to the seaside resort of Pasir Putih. There appeared to be nothing here at all, the beach cinder black sand. After some hard bargaining I got a discount of 35p on the price of my room, bringing it down to a more sensible 50p.

The seventy miles to the ferry port produced the best scenery with lush woodlands on both sides. Since Yogyakarta masked men had stopped me many times demanding money to support Megawati, daughter of Sukarno the first president of Indonesia, in her bid to win the election. The men wore red headbands and red triangular cloths over their faces, looking menacing, but not demanding all my money, just a donation for their party. After this had happened twice I bought a red headband and a red triangular cloth and if I saw the roadblocks I just donned my purchases and rode among them. Amused, they sent me on my way.

CHAPTER 51

A Broken Bone in Bali

A wet welcome as I disembarked in Bali. On through worthwhile country with many Hindu temples. Home for a few days was Lovina, a small resort with another black beach, but pleasant enough with plenty of restaurants and video films to watch.

On my second day I got up early and joined a party of tourists on a boat trip well out on the sea to watch shoals of graceful dolphins, who also wake early. I walked around afterwards and watched the children playing with their assortment of homemade toys, a plastic bottle pulled along on a length of string, clumsy trucks with tin cans for wheels, a flexible stick inserted in a hole pierced in a coconut making it roll on the stick as the child ran alongside. A piece of wood shaped into a propellor on a stick spun like a windmill as the child ran along holding it up.

A comfortable clean bungalow at Mega Ayu Hotel was £1 a night including breakfast, but even so after three nights I hit the road again. I was feeling a little lonely, maybe I would fly home in a week or so to visit my much-missed grandchildren. Chatting with an Australian couple I was surprised to hear them say, 'We saw you on TV3 in Australia.'

In a one-night stay at Amed I made the acquaintance of Ketut. At twenty-four he was young to own his own restaurant, but he explained how he worked every day before school at fishing, saved all his money and studied English and French. He had persuaded his father not to sell his land like so many others who although poor had at least been able to grow food. Now they had spent the money on cars, washing machines and fridges and they couldn't even grow food, while rich foreigners had built hotels and eating-places on the land.

The name Ketut means 'fourth child'. The Bali Hindus use four names for their children regardless of whether they are boys or girls. The first-born is Wayan, then come Made, Nyoman and Ketut. If more children are born the sequence starts again, with a second name to ease the confusion. The island was choked with traffic. I couldn't imagine what made couples choose Bali to get married. What could be better than an English church?

After a night at Candidasa I moved on, stopping for a while to watch young boys and girls working on road gangs. The boys wielded picks bigger than themselves and the girls carried rocks on their heads. It was a common sight to see naked men and almost naked women washing themselves and emptying their bowels in the river, and a lot of older women wore nothing above the waist as they went about the daily routine.

Ubud is a favourite destination, famous for its woodcarvings. It was my next target, but I almost didn't make it. I was riding through Klungkung in dense traffic when two girls overtook me on a motorcycle, then didn't get far enough ahead before they cut in back to the kerb. Their motorbike struck my handlebars and I plunged heavily to the ground. I lay there with the breath knocked out of my body, knowing without being told that my collarbone was broken and my ribs damaged. (An x-ray in England later confirmed the broken collarbone. By age seventy-six both my collarbones had been broken twice, three times by motorcycles cutting across me and not allowing for the speed I was travelling and once by my own carelessness.)

I was lifted and carried to the pavement, seated in a chair and given a glass of water. I was in agony. The two girls stood some distance away holding each other. They waited until I was breathing better before plucking up courage to apologise to me. I shook their hands and they beat a hasty retreat. I mounted the bike and moved off painfully, making slow progress until I reached a Chinese restaurant and consumed three bottles of Carlsberg painkiller. At Ubud I took the first available accommodation, showered and lay on the bed nursing my injuries, although the grazes on my elbow and shoulder were only slight.

I took it easy next day, exploring Ubud in a lot of pain. I visited the sacred monkey sanctuary, where 150 clever monkeys snatch any item they can, necklaces, watches, handbags and so on, offering them back in return for food. In the afternoon I took a gentle short distance ride three miles to see a herons' roosting area. The white birds clustered in hundreds looking like fruit growing in the trees. It was a lovely ride and I tried hard not to stare at the young bare-breasted women standing in the streams and washing themselves as I passed. Sorry, telling lies, I didn't really try.

CHAPTER 52

From Bali to Birmingham

Waking with just a dull ache to a glorious morning I stupidly booked a white water adventure. By lunchtime the weather had turned nasty and the rain was lashing down, before long we could have put the rafts on the roads. Twelve of us stood reluctantly on the bank of a raging river. Four frightened Australian girls asked the guides with trepidation if we should be doing this in a storm. I made some cracks about coming to grief, dropped to my knees and pretended to pray. The girls cursed me for making things worse.

We split between two rafts and plunged into the angry water. Frenzied activity followed as we struggled to cope with the rapids, the girls screaming and shouting words I didn't know girls knew. Within seconds I regretted my hasty decision to take part. Trying to control the heaving raft I was aware of the damage I was doing to myself. After two hours of contortions and frantic use of the paddle the pain had returned and increased, even though we beached safely. I lay agonised in bed and decided to stay in Ubud a few days. I had been very silly and it was three months before I was pain free.

I lodged at Manikan House in a quiet part of town with a good crowd of Westerners. Twenty-four year old Karin, a Danish girl with film star looks, had the room next to mine. She had started a world tour at twenty-two, financed by the sale of a house that her grandmother left her, and now she was rooted in Ubud after falling for a local man.

'There are complications,' she said. 'He's married.'

Like most people she was worried about the threat of violence in the coming elections. The Danish Consulate had advised her to leave, just like the Danish travel agent in town and his staff who were packing all their belongings.

It was an extra-special religious day and the men attached a flower petal to their right ear to show they had just come from prayer. The pavements looked a mess because of the flowers trampled underfoot.

Many tourists hired bicycles to visit the volcano but no way would they ride thirty minutes uphill. Instead they had themselves and the bikes carried up by motor vehicle and sat on the saddle to freewheel back. I doubt if the pedals on these bikes ever turned. I took the same trip without assistance and found the gradient not too steep until the last couple of miles.

During my six-night stay at Ubud I visited Kuta, the main tourist spot in Bali. The never-ending traffic barely moved. Bali is a huge parking lot. The Indonesians apparently regard this island as heaven. They must be easily pleased. I only spent two hours in Kuta. It was a nightmare, crammed with tourists, mostly drunken Australians.

Perhaps my best ride in Bali on quiet roads and I arrived at Sanur Beach, the second most popular spot but superior to Kuta, with a white beach that was the best I had seen so far in Indonesia (but still wouldn't make it onto my list of the best beaches I have ever seen). Prices were high but I talked them down to £2 a night at At Pollock Homestay, expensive but clean and tidy with friendly staff.

In town for the evening it looked like a talk-to-myself night, but 57-year old Danish Jens sat at my table and I found a soulmate. He was still trying to cope with the death of his wife two years ago from stomach cancer, which also wiped out my wife. Now like me he roamed the world.

The Somawati Restaurant where we sat together was good, built as most are from bamboo poles. The peace was disturbed occasionally when the owner grabbed a small-calibre rifle from behind the counter to shoot one of the rats scurrying along the rafters. I presumed he would change my meal if a rodent dropped onto my plate.

I had decided to end this tour so I bought a ticket home. I would leave in three days' time. The staff at the agency had seen me on TV and in the newspapers so they considered me a celebrity. They phoned the airport to tell them what day to expect a VIP and they discounted my ticket by $25.

My last full day's ride took me to Padang Padang. Karin had described this as the loveliest spot in Bali and so it was. Quiet because tourists mostly come on a day trip and return to the fleshpots. White beach, impressive cliffs and rock formations with no visible signs of hotels. A dozen good-natured women were sweeping up leaves. Amidst much laughter one called, 'Do you have a woman? Do you like me? I will give you a kiss if you buy a T-shirt.' All good fun and after a few photos I set off back to Sanur.

I gave the bike a thorough clean and took the airport road passing the salubrious Bali Beach Hotel where the Presidential Suite cost $3,000 a night. And this is a country where many people struggle to make half a dollar a day.

No rush at Denpasar Airport. I had a late afternoon flight to Manchester via Hong Kong and Paris. It was the easiest check-in ever because airport staff had been informed I was a VIP, so they whisked me through and many shook my hand. I was surrounded by the opulence always encountered in airports – swank boutiques, expensive gift shops, duty free liquor outlets. I looked at a shirt and enquired the price. It was £45. I pointed to the shirt I was wearing, 'Eighty pence.'

Back in England's green and pleasant land I headed home the pretty way through Cheshire, one of my favourite counties with its beautiful scenery, lovely towns and villages and nice people who call me Luv. I made a night's stop at the historic clean town of Nantwich, welcomed by Ellen, landlady of the Wilbraham Arms. She was a pleasant woman with inner warmth who knew how to use a kitchen, so I ate a delicious evening meal and a cracking breakfast with no sign of rice.

The morning brought the chimes of a church clock, the clink of milk bottles and the slap of the letterbox as papers were delivered, English sounds. I picked my way through a glorious network of almost traffic free lanes and took a leisurely ride to Birmingham. I had pedalled seven thousand miles and it was good to be home, to see my family and boast to my friends about my adventures.

It wasn't the end of the story, though, just the end of another chapter.

A large number of people could sleep under this shelter in Padang Padang

Last balloon animals made

Best beach in Padang Padang

CHAPTER 53

In South America Again – Rio and Onward

It was November 11th 1999. After a change of planes in Madrid I stood in the airport at Rio de Janeiro, Brazil. I had a problem already, my bike was in Madrid. I badgered unhelpful officials for two hours before they promised to deliver my bike to my hotel the next day. I insisted they paid for my taxi.

'Let's face it,' I reasoned, 'if my bike was here I wouldn't need a taxi.'

My Brazilian friend Valeria back in England had booked my room at the Pousada Girasol. I was lucky to get a room in Rio for just ten dollars.

At nearly midnight I strolled the main road of Copacabana. In a bar I met lawyer Marcello who told me that he was treated so well when he studied in England that he would take care of my bill now. Nina, a sixty-four year old widow out with Marcello, declared after twenty minutes that she had fallen in love with me and we should get married. I had been in Brazil for only three hours and had turned away 19-year-old girls as pretty as a picture in Asia. I was hardly about to take on board a woman with one foot as deep in the grave as my own.

I made my way back to my hotel passing the pavement sleepers. The more fortunate at least had a piece of cardboard to lie on. Two eight-year-old boys fought for space in a shop doorway. Outside a café where leftovers had been scraped into a bin a haggard old lady scooped out the slops and filled a bag and her mouth at the same time. The bin contained all kinds of rubbish besides her evening meal. She stumbled off to her pavement patch with her revolting mess of rice, spaghetti, pizza, chicken bones, eggshells and cigarette ends. Above the city on the highest point stood the colossal statue of Jesus Christ with arms outstretched.

I spent an anxious second day waiting for my bike. It finally arrived after numerous phone calls and being told time and again, 'I don't speak English.' The bike was damaged and it took two hours to get the buckled wheels trued.

I didn't waste time, though. Instead I prowled Copacabana Beach. Every girl was a potential Miss World, all colours with stunning shapes, but many so poor they could only afford one piece of a bikini. In the streets and even supermarkets they swayed around in the briefest of clothes.

I ate at a vegetarian's nightmare restaurant where waiters carried joints of meat on skewers from table to table, carving slices until you cried out, 'Enough!' The table was loaded with dishes of chips, onion rings, garlic bread, salads and chopped vegetables and the meal cost £4.50. Bloated I stepped out and tried not to see the street dwellers. A woman sitting on the pavement held a doll's hands and danced with it. I pushed a few dollars into her hand and quickly turned away, not deserving her gratitude.

Marcello had promised to organise a party for the evening but of course it was a set-up and he didn't show up. Nina, fresh from the hairdresser, new outfit, painted nails and two inches of lipstick, was brimming with expectations. Nobody spoke English and they all smoked a cigarette a minute. I suffered an hour of trying to converse but then carved a way through the dense smoke with my head reeling and staggered out of the door.

Two men approached. They exchanged a few words then parted company as they drew nearer. They intended to accost me from both sides. We were almost face-to-face in an empty street. I swung my arm up and pointed across the road. The man nearer the road looked to see what I was pointing at. In a flash I was through the gap between them and running like hell. They didn't come after me.

Navigating out of Rio was difficult, all long tunnels and no other cyclists. When I reached the airport three workmen loaded the bike into their van and carried me to the ferry that crosses the bay to Niteroi. Feeling better after two anxious days I started my ride in high spirits.

Throughout my life whenever things have gone wrong or I've felt down a ride in the country has always picked me up. However, this wasn't a road to relax on. Death or serious accident skimmed my elbows as I was constantly forced off the road, at times plunging into ditches. I feared damage to the bike but had no choice.

Traffic gradually thinned out further from Rio and although I hadn't ridden far I looked for a camping spot at Marica. A beaming woman on a bicycle was determined I got a good impression of Brazil. I can't speak Portuguese but we conversed with a little Spanish and I followed her as she made several unsuccessful attempts to find me tent space. One time stepping over a drunk she did her best to convince me he was not Brazilian.

Dora, the manager of a country club, allowed me with no hesitation to park Thrifty Mark Two (my new tent) next to the club swimming pool in a complex of luxury country homes. Beaming Crueza declined to share it with me.

The weather turned bad and I decided to spend several days in my tent under a canopy to keep it dry. Dora and her husband Nilson devoted a lot of time to looking after me, and Crueza came every day. I continued suggesting how cosy my canvas home was but she declared, 'My husband would cut my throat.'

Dora and Nilson took me to a religious meeting of folk fanatical in their belief of reincarnation. An English speaking woman got rather angry when I asked how the world would maintain all the billions of people who have died if they all came back again.

The rain never let up and I was glad that I had found this spot with Crueza's help. I enjoyed the peace and I was making so many friends. On Nilson's birthday he cooked a barbecue, reporters turned up, plus more and more guests. I learned that I had been on television and they all felt responsible for me, especially Crueza who brought me fruit every day. She gave me a strange cherry sized fruit with a bitter taste, to give me energy, she said. What could she be thinking?

Managed to find each a present

CHAPTER 54

Fame in Brazil

Crueza's teacher friend Sheyla took me to visit a school where she thought I would be an inspiration. The children didn't understand a word of what I said, but they clamoured for my autograph. About a hundred kids climbed all over my bike and wrecked the gears. A visit to a bike shop put them back in working order, but they were not as efficient as before.

I had good weather so I made my goodbyes. Dora tied flowers on the bike, Sheyla wrote a message in her best English, Crueza embraced me and kissed me on the cheek. It was a late start with everybody insisting they must say goodbye before I left, so I only had time to reach Iguaba Grande. I sat on the bed and read Sheyla's words

'There is a lot of ways to God
Cross a bike round the world
Know people and nature with open heart
Sure that's one of them
We will be missing you.'

Iguaba Grande was a good stop and a bed made a change after my concrete mattress. However, all fifteen restaurants in the town sold only pizza. The Extra newspaper hit the streets and it meant more autographs and photos. I look forward to media attention where I can't speak the language because the publicity explains what I've done and what I'm doing. Producing my clippings round the world has brought me free food and drink, free rooms and stopped me from being robbed or worse.

During a brief stop at Cabo Frio for lunch the waiter told me he had phoned a TV programme and they would arrive at four o'clock. It was only twelve o'clock and I said I must get off to Buzios. This was a lovely town with perfect beaches, where I lay on the powder sand and dozed before having to go and eat. I needed light to put up Thrifty Two. Pepe at Bananaland Restaurant rushed to find the TV crew who had driven miles and spent hours looking for me. For an hour they filmed me riding round the town, erecting my tent and making balloon animals for children. In England the interest is zilch.

Pepe and his daughter Michelle worried about me camping on the beach, sure I would be murdered, but I had a good night with the South Atlantic Ocean slapping the shore with irregular surges. A woman spoke to me at length in Portuguese. I took her across the road to ask Pepe to translate. It turned out that she and her husband owned a cycle shop and also gave guided tours. They wanted me to help promote their business. So five of us set out on a worthwhile ride followed by reporters from Brazil's main newspaper O Globo and some cameramen. The ride included visits to stunningly beautiful coves and beaches that I would not otherwise have seen. With my unladen bike I was at the top of every hill before everybody else.

I'm afraid I couldn't keep my mouth shut at lunch when they started the God talk. 'Rubbish!' I exclaimed. 'An earthquake in Turkey killed forty thousand people. Where was your God?'

Shushed to sleep by the sea I had visitors in the blackness of the night, but I heard no sound. Tied to my bike I found presents from Robert and Monica, the bike shop owners, two useful road maps. I was happy that we were parting as friends after my outburst. It was hard to leave Buzios, but it was time to start some serious cycling.

CHAPTER 55

Locked in the Lavatory

After the TV screening of my interview I was recognised everywhere. Cars stopped and people ran back to embrace me and take photos, lorry drivers waved newspapers showing my picture, some even had the picture stuck to their windscreen. Without even asking I was invited to set up my tent on the forecourt of a 24-hour petrol station, noisy but it had food outlets and toilets.

I left behind the splendid coast road. It was replaced with lovely countryside, cascading waters and crashing rivers, but the road itself turned into corrugated cratered sand and then into mud. I walked miles ankle deep with steep hills making conditions worse. I managed only twenty miles in five hours. Thoroughly exhausted I was relieved to see the tarmac resume at a village.

Germans Eva and Uwe owned Emporio do Dengo and they invited me to stay a few days. They were involved in many projects such as making pottery, canoes and running a farm. Uwe pointed out the containers holding assorted animal food, each container with a picture of the animal the food was intended for. He explained that his workers could not read so these pictures stopped them from getting the food mixed up.

I had a day out with Eva in Nova Friburgo, the Switzerland of Brazil. In the early 1800s hundreds of Swiss people set out to start a new life. Many died on the voyage and the survivors trekked across hundreds of miles of untamed land. Their venture was not a success. Immigration was encouraged, but the huge parcels of land they were given made it impossible for people to help each other, they were too far apart. Many more died and others returned home discouraged. The Germans who came later in large numbers fared better.

I moved on via Nova Friburgo again, where I bought a pullover and a jacket because the weather was still cold. Of course this was a signal for the sun to shine. My bed in Teresopolis was welcome after gruelling riding. I was so tired that I fell asleep immediately, to wake at ten pm and sit in one of the great ice-cream parlours that you find in Brazil. I was an immediate celebrity, posing for photos with staff.

I set off in blistering heat and dragged the bike eight miles uphill. A lifesaving drink from a coconut set me right for the descent. This was truly magnificent country with jagged tooth mountains, replicas of Rio's sugar loaf and smooth rain-washed giants. At Tres Rios there was some different awe-inspiring scenery in the shape of my landlady Carla, almost wearing a black top. Good food was plentiful although heavily salted. After placing the food on the table the waiters invariably added even more salt to it. At self-service outlets the routine was to fill your plate and then queue to have it weighed. Even ice cream was sold by weight. A Japanese Brazilian insisted on paying for my food and drink. Brazilians range from white-skinned blondes through all shades of brown to ebony black. Some of the staff serving breakfast rushed home to get cameras. The majority of places I find myself visiting are not tourist attractions, but perhaps the guy wasn't joking who said to me, 'You are not the first Englishman to come here. Charles Darwin has already been.'

My bike creaked off again loaded with gifts of food. The heat was health threatening, folks told me that this was still Spring and the heat was nothing to what would follow. I only managed forty miles but that was enough and Thrifty Two had pride of place beneath a canopy at Taberna da Sierra, with a breathtaking view of the mountains. The boss Fabio was pleased to show me round even though conversing was a struggle. Thankfully a lot of Portuguese words are similar to Spanish so we got by. On seeing the bathroom I put it to good use straight away for a much needed scrub. When I pushed the door shut I didn't realise there was no doorknob on either side, just a spindle. Scrub down finished I was locked in the lavatory and it took a lot of shouting before a staff member turned up with a pair of pliers.

The first child who waved at me got the fourteen bananas that Fabio presented me with. Progress was slow and every mountain scaled had a big brother behind it. I spent two hours trying to sort out the gear mechanism mangled by those pesky Marica children. With little mileage done I took a room at No Name village and was invaded for the first time by insects. Creepy crawlies landed on my head to create a diversion while others ate my food faster than I could. Charles Darwin should see how turtles have evolved now, they've grown wings and they call themselves beetles.

CHAPTER 56

Close Encounters of the Dog Kind

Close to Sao Joao del Rei I ate in a restaurant before settling down snugly under a bridge, where the river dropped to different levels forming waterfalls and a pool to swim in. Under another arch a family had constructed a permanent home with even a small garden. The woman in a torn ragged dress asked me for 30p to go shopping.

After an early start I managed to stagger to Lavros with tough riding and intense heat. Within thirty minutes of taking a room I was shovelling ice cream down my throat. I had a huge lunch for £1.80 and a pint of Skol for £1. I wondered about settling in the area as it seemed so cheap. On again with many miles passing under my wheels I reached Boa Esperanca by 2.30pm and decided to cover the extra twenty miles to Campo do Meio. The only living things I saw were lizards and birds, although the unseen monkeys were vocal.

The road turned to sand and I had drunk all my water. Mile after mile with no dwellings and I was desperate for a drink. A man on horseback told me there was water in half a mile and I found a farm with three vicious dogs on guard. Their barking brought no response from the house. No sticks to defend myself, but I urgently needed water so I opened the gate slowly and stepped inside. The dogs went frantic as I searched one step at a time for a tap. I found one and filled my mouth and my water bottles, expecting all the time to get torn to pieces. I wouldn't want to die like that. (In fact I don't want to die any other way either.)

'Life owes me nothing
Just one more morn
Is boon enough for being born
And be it ninety years or ten
I'll not question when
My life's been good, my life's my own
And I greet each day with gratitude.'

Considering the state of the access road, I was surprised to find what a lovely little town Campo was. I lodged in Bar Chapparal, not much of a place, the owner a large brutish type, but the word went round that the man who rides the world was in town. I got no peace as throngs arrived asking for autographs. A young woman put a card in my hand. The only English speaker in the town had written a message from her, 'If you wanting have time with me, it's okay.'

When I joined the dusty road again there was a lake to cross. I was the solitary passenger. After seven miles, another lake to cross. Neither captain charged me for the crossing. 'You have courage,' they said.

People say that, or 'How brave.' I don't see it like that, because there are actually only a few nasty people in the world. Sure, I've met some, but I remain undeterred.

The bike was taking terrible punishment. The road was so bad and the front wheel distorted every time I hit a rock. I jumped at the chance of a lift, four miles to tarmac. I sat and relaxed with a self-service meal. When my plate was clean a dog appeared, sitting in front of me with its head on one side. Although the counter had been cleared I asked the waiter for meat for the dog. He was astonished, but he brought me a dish of meat and the dog devoured the best meal he'd probably ever had or was likely to get again. Just as I was leaving a man told me that he had phoned the local TV station. Half an hour later they caught me up and filmed another interview, that I would never see on the screen.

I spent a night in a hotel at Alpinopolis, then another night in my tent after riding through Passos. The country was a birdwatcher's paradise, with toucans, cockatoos and all sorts of birds. I found it best to drink cold milk because the pre-made coffee on the counter was sickly sweet and the staff would never make me a cup without sugar. I reflected on the endurance test I was putting myself through, and the comments I had received on the craziness of it all. Indeed when coping with awkward incidents I ask myself, 'Why are you doing this?' But I know the answer. It is that I can speak with first-hand knowledge about all the wonderful people in the world. Making close contact using a bicycle is the most marvellous thing.

Studying the map I smiled at a town they must have named after me, Pratapolis.

CHAPTER 57

Superfit Athletes

I was travelling at speed along the fast road to Ribeirao Preto when thirty-seven year old champion cyclist Rosangela Mestrinel rode alongside. In 1999 she was fourth in the Hawaii Ironman Triathlon, swimming 2½ hours, cycling 112 miles and running 26 miles. She invited me to her family home where her press cuttings put me in the shade. Shelves groaned under the weight of more than sixty trophies from all over the world. A truly amazing woman she had ridden with top cyclists, carrying on racing until six months pregnant and only giving up when her belly got in the way. On two occasions she ran races until eight months pregnant and still finished with the leaders.

Rosy got on the phone and soon the TV crew arrived. The response I kept receiving was amazing. I recalled a friend in England contacting the BBC, no interest at all. When I am interviewed I am always asked what food I eat to keep fit. Interviewers suggest I should say I am vegetarian and teetotal to encourage people to maintain a healthy lifestyle. But I prefer the truth. 'I eat meat and drink beer and have never seen a doctor for my health.'

Rosy was very highly thought of in Preto. We rode through the streets with a police escort and spent time at the university that sponsored her. She carried out arduous training every day, running, cycling and swimming miles and then returning home to clean the house from top to bottom. She washed all my clothes and lent me her husband's shirt and trousers, and her three children gave up their bedroom for me and slept on the floor.

Sebastian from Panathlon wrote out a list of contacts that could be useful to me and invited Rosy and me to an awards ceremony. It was a posh affair, men in bow ties and dinner jackets, women looking elegant and me as scruffy as ever. Speeches unintelligible to me were made and awards presented, with achievements shown on screen. Finally Sebastian told this audience of two hundred superfit athletes that my achievements were considerable, that at sixty-four years of age I had already ridden more than 20,000 miles through eighteen countries alone. All these professionals shook my hand.

I stayed another night with this marvellous family and then it was time to move on. Rosy wanted to see me off, and Augustos who had been with her when we met also turned up. Her idea of seeing me off was thirty miles.

'What is your work?' I asked Augustos.

'I am a sailor,' he replied in his limited English.

'It's a long way from the sea. What do you sail?'

'I sail sweets,' was his puzzling reply and then it dawned on me that 'sail' was 'sell'.

At Jaboticabal it was goodbye, handshakes and hugs. After those days of such warmth and friendship I was overcome with emotion and my eyes brimmed with tears. Embarrassed I moved away, but they didn't understand my reaction and ran after me to hug me again before I rode away.

I had only been riding half an hour when Benedicto called me over. He said I must stay at his farm, but I couldn't possibly accept all the offers these generous Brazilians made, so I had a meal and moved on in 38-degree heat. I had been warned that it would get hotter the further west I travelled.

Docking at Itapolis after ninety miles I found a quiet bar that didn't stay quiet for long after I was recognised and the press invaded. I moved on in blistering heat and at the end of the day I was in a rather posh hotel that charged me £4.40 for the room and asked 60p extra for the bike.

The distances between food stops were getting longer. That's no problem for motor-assisted travellers, but at times it's a big problem for me. Without motorists of course there would be no food stops because the café is usually attached to the petrol station. Another lifesaver is the free cold showers. I was stepping fully clothed under them, my clothes dried in minutes. I was drinking Brahma beer. A few bottles of this in the heat and I'd be Brahma and Liszt.

CHAPTER 58

Snakes or Not

Seventy-five miles later in the smart town of Aracatuba I passed several bars before entering the one with the loveliest barmaid. There is nothing like a dame. The regulars were full of questions and once again a TV crew turned up and I was obliged to ride around the streets.

My bedroom was a field where cows and horses grazed around my tent. Three guys from the car repair business alongside, good-naturedly asked me some questions to check that I wasn't a potential burglar. My ride next day took place on good road surfaces and I saw armadillos where the sandy banks were full of burrows.

Gaucha Grill let me camp close by with a warning of many snakes. I was asleep by 8.30pm snakes or not. The next morning the staff had obligingly left the toilets open for me, saving me from squatting amongst snake-infested bushes. On the road again I saw that they were right about snakes, there were many, some crushed and others corkscrewing across.

At Tres Lagos there was a huge dam to cross. 'No cyclists,' the surly security guard told me, but three men in a truck came to my aid and we sped across. From Tres Lagos it was over two hundred miles to Campo Grande and my intention was to ride to this town in the west before turning south for the waterfalls of Iguazu. This movement would involve four hundred miles. I rested awhile in Tres Lagos then continued for an hour. From the top of a hill I could see the road stretching into the distance. Not a house, not a farm, nothing but shimmering heat. I turned back to Tres Lagos and decided that I would try another route instead, heading for the borders of Brazil, Argentina and Paraguay.

I took it easy for the day. Checking the map, I had ridden 1,200 miles. It turned out I was wise to return to this town for a violent storm broke, with raindrops so large they would have filled a tea cup. My flimsy tent would have been flattened and myself swept away. I rode forty-five miles on a deserted road towards Brazilandia in well under four hours. Stopping at a small town I attracted much attention. I had intended to carry on but I was told that the road turned to sand and there was nothing for another forty-five miles. I decided to tackle it tomorrow.

I sat outside the Sorbeteria (Ice Cream Shop) bringing my diary up to date, the crowd getting bigger and occasionally taking the book from my hand to stare at the unreadable words. They were highly satisfied when they recognised a word, usually the name of a Brazilian town. A man talking to me turned out to be a journalist and the crowd bunched together for photographs. I slipped into the local barber's for a much-needed haircut. I was charged an autograph.

Now I was on a nightmare ride to Bataguassa, twenty miles of sand, like riding a ploughed field and all the time worrying about damage to the bike. A solitary road, not a soul, nothing. Then at last, asphalt. I felt like imitating the Pope and falling to my knees to kiss the road, but better not as nobody was there to help me up again. So a fast run the rest of the way to Bataguassa and further on to Presidente Epitacio. The sun must have gone to my head when at Hotel Primavera I refused a second floor room and paid an extra pound for one on the ground floor, no lugging my bike and equipment upstairs. But in these temperatures a tent is like an oven overnight, whereas a hotel room offers air conditioning and a shower whenever I like. This night, about every five minutes.

It was eleven before the rain stopped and I got on the way to Presidente Prudente. For some reason I felt weak and it was a slow ride to this large city. With my hotel sorted out I took refreshment in a bar and watched the street beggars. One woman of about forty going on sixty came to me to beg. She stood in pathetic rags and I gave her a few dollars. She returned with a little group, so now there were three women, a boy, and a young girl already old clutching an 18-month old baby to her heavily pregnant body. They were all surly, but what had they got to smile about?

They spread on the counter the coins they had managed to beg. The bar owner counted them, less than a pound. A bargaining discussion began and he gave them some rice and vegetables. I ordered several plates of food and some sweets and placed them on their table. Nobody smiled or said thank you, but I wasn't looking for thanks. I just asked myself how they would eat tomorrow.

I had wandered into the seedy side of town where passers-by warned me of villains. The pub I entered seemed quiet enough, but word got out there was a tourist in town and the street girls turned up. Some of the ugliest women I had ever seen closed in, only they were not all women. They looked obscene in the weirdest of outfits or exposing bare buttocks in practically nothing at all. A heavily made-up man wearing a bra and hardly anything else squeezed into the little gap between my table and the counter in this narrow bar, with his naked backside cheeks separated by a thong inches from my face. In annoyance I snapped my fingers at the barkeeper and with a few sharp words he ordered the weirdoes out. They left scowling, laughing and making lewd gestures.

A poor breakfast started the day, and a night in a very basic wooden shack hotel at Santo Inacio finished it. No problem, I have passed nights in shop doorways, bus shelters, a junk shop in Texas a stone's throw from where Pat Garret gunned down Billy the Kid, beaches in many countries, floors of restaurants, churches, temples, derelict houses, empty factories, cemeteries and police stations.

As soon as I started off, drenching rain started too. With no cover I plodded on to Colorado where a lady café owner struck up an immediate friendship as the rain persisted. I could have drowned crossing the road so I stayed two hours in her café. I wheeled my bike into Room 66 at Hotel Bandeirante despite objections from staff. Colorado is a nice little town with a High Street similar to one in an English town. There are nice little towns all over Brazil, everywhere is spotless, a great country.

On my way to Maringa I called into a country restaurant. Three young staff members were excited to have what they considered a famous man in their midst. They showed me the shower. It had become my practice to step fully clothed under the cold water in my eagerness to cool down, but this time I stripped down to my underpants and revelled in a good soak. Ablutions finished I re-donned my dry shirt and shorts to join the two girls and a boy who were waiting with a thousand questions.

I sat opposite them chatting away while the water in my soaking wet underpants began to run down my legs and form a suspicious pool round my feet. The girls looked at each other and didn't say a word, just fetched a mop and dried the floor.

CHAPTER 59

Towards the Borders

I was riding the two-lane bike road out of Maringa. A large sign in English advised, 'Cyclists, take care of your life. Ride the cycle path'. A father and young son riding towards me stopped and dismounted. With their backs to me they stood holding their machines while the father pointed out something of interest. I was moving fast. The boy still with his back to me pushed his bike backwards into my lane. Brakes hard on I hit the obstruction. My back wheel lifted off the ground and I pitched over the handlebars. I got to my feet with skinned hands and elbow plus a twisted knee.

My first thought was to check the bike. Little damage, thank goodness. The father was concerned, muttering, 'He has no experience.' The boy pointed at me and said, 'Television.' I shook the man's hand and gave the boy a hug. I would have preferred to hug him round the neck with both hands. So much for 'Cyclists, take care of your life.'

Ten miles before Cianorte a car stopped. The two male occupants had seen my flag and were curious. They drove off but I guessed what was coming. Just short of the town the pre-alerted local newspaper staff waited for me, cameras at the ready, outside the police station. Interview over I accepted the police invitation to take a meal.

At my next temporary home once I had stopped cycling I became aware of the pain and stiffening in my leg, I hoped it would be gone by the next day. And indeed feeling in fine form I progressed next day through the lush cattle country on the continuation of my journey, English style country, but with ever-increasing heat. My pattern had become to start at 7.30am and say enough was enough about 1.30. Maybe only sixty miles, but any more became unpleasant. The men in reception at Hotel Iguarma slapped my back and poured on the praise. A dizzy blonde behind the desk looked bored to death. An adventure to her was a change of hairstyle and the longest distance she'd ever travelled was two hundred yards to the nail-bar.

It was nearly Christmas and every town displayed magnificent decorations. I'm not religious, so Christmas means little to me. My main concern is whether I will be able to get any food. I had spent the previous Christmas on the edge of the sea in Malaysia with a Coca-Cola, a packet of biscuits and some fruit. The Christmas before that I sat in my tent on the shore of Lake Arenal in Costa Rica listening to the periodic roar of Volcano Arenal, with the same feast minus the fruit.

I had maybe four days before I reached the borders and I was still undecided which country to enter next. Argentina was my favourite idea because I had been told that the northwest is great cycling country, and that Paraguay was ugly and mostly desert (which turned out to be true). With several stops to lie in the shade I found myself in Assis Chateaubriand with the cheapest yet B&B at £1.70. The town's excellent wide street supported the usual cavalcade of young women. Brazil is home to what must be the loveliest women in the world. Apparently females outnumber males six to one.

Off early from Hotel Central to reach the big city of Cascavel. On the outskirts the staff at the Restaurant Maxipeixe were not particularly friendly, but maybe it was because of the language problem. They still let me camp in the shade. When the café closed and was left empty in the evening I heard the seven-foot high gates being closed and fell asleep wondering how I would get my bike, my equipment and me over the gates in the morning. It wasn't a problem after all, the staff I thought were unfriendly had left the padlock unfastened.

Enjoying a meal outside at Medianeira I got ridiculed for riding a bicycle by a group of youths. They crowded round me making assorted wisecracks that I didn't understand, but drew a cheap laugh from the long-legged chicks they were trying to impress. Every ten minutes the chicks climbed into a car to be driven at crazy speed up the main road and back again. They all thought it was hilarious when I made myself a chip butty, perhaps I went down in history as the man who introduced chip butties to Brazil. I must be on par with Earl Sandwich.

The lads got out of hand when one of them snatched my glasses from my face and each in turn tried them on. It was time to show these car-cosseted high-spirited kids what a man can do. When I produced my newspaper stories their mickey-taking turned into respect. Shame-faced they climbed into their passion wagons and left me in peace.

It was Sunday morning and I was taking breakfast opposite and over the top church that looked like Sydney Opera House. Scores of swank worshippers' cars lined the street. I sat listening on the loudspeakers as the appointed man told the flock what is good and what is bad. The well fed, well dressed congregation emerged and returned in their luxury motors to their millionaire homes. Only a mile away I pedalled through shanty towns built from cardboard, polythene and strips of linoleum full of hopeless people and crying children.

At Foz do Iguacu I continued on to Iguassu Falls with the intention of staying several nights, but the hotels were all upmarket £100 a night, no backpacker accommodation. The falls rival Niagara, they are indescribably beautiful. Surprisingly there seemed little commercialism, the one and only restaurant closed at 6.30pm. With guards patrolling I had to wait until dark to pitch Thrifty Two. I strolled around watching the raccoons and black monkeys. When I returned to my bike a cheeky raccoon had gained entry to one of my bags and stolen a large fruitcake that a woman had given me.

The day trippers climbed aboard buses and disappeared. The guards slipped away as darkness fell. With the aid of my torch I placed my little house in what must be the finest camping spot in the world with the most stunning background possible. I was in residence on an observation platform that extended over the rushing water of the falls. The moon created silver rainbows and I slept with the constant roar surrounding me.

After two nights I was back in Foz at a cheap grubby hotel. The big city bustled with Christmas shoppers and the illuminations were works of art. I sorted out the best of the mouth-watering and cheap meat restaurants and kept busy visiting attractions. Itaipu Dam the largest power plant in the world is acknowledged as one of the seven wonders of the modern world, 32,000 people were employed in its construction and they used enough concrete to build fifteen Channel tunnels.

I rode to the zoo and found it closed, but the gatekeeper recognised me and let me in free. So there was only me and all the animals. I was glad that the Muslims in Foz kept their shops open at Christmas, though it was hard to eat with street dwellers begging for a mouthful. I changed my mind about Argentina, Argentinians kept telling me it was too expensive. At the border a sign read 'The Malvinas Belong To Argentina,' but that didn't deter me. What clinched it was the £30 B&B and the £2 pints of beer.

Iguassu Falls

Iguassu Falls facing Argentina

CHAPTER 60

In Paraguay

I checked my bike over in preparation for moving on. Most of the nuts needed tightening, unsurprising considering the rough treatment the bike had endured. It was December 27th and I had three miles to go to the Paraguayan border.

Amidst the usual border confusion the officer (another long distance cyclist) told me about a holiday in Italy where he and his wife boarded a train that separated without their knowing. They finished up in one place and their bikes in another.

'You are an inspiration,' he told me. 'Vaya con Dios.'

I needed to brush up my Spanish, but the first new friends I made were two Japanese farmers also far from fluent. We spoke in Japanese, English and Spanish while they nodded and grinned all the time. Their home-made ice cream was delicious. The gas stations were poor in comparison with Brazil, no food apart from crisps. I was looking forward to finding a campsite, but I saw no sign of anywhere to eat. It was looking bleaker and bleaker until at last I saw some dwellings in the distance and soon I had a room for £2 in Hotel Las Palmas. The Paraguayan currency was named after the first Indians who settled here, the Guarani, five thousand guaranis to the pound.

I got moving at 6am before it got hot and stopped for a snack in Caaguazu. Paraguay looked a poor country. The businesses along the road were just shacks and so were the towns, the food was inferior and no well turned out girls evident.

The temperature had reached 42° and I was struggling in the heat when from the opposite direction came Thomas and Charles, French cyclists who had been on the road for eight months and were planning to complete one full year. They had never cycled before and they told me Argentina and Paraguay were so boring that their enthusiasm was on the wane. My plan was to ride into Bolivia, but they advised that most of the roads were unrideable earth roads so they had entered Paraguay by bus. The two young lads had ridden six thousand miles in eight months.

'Keep it up till you're sixty and you might make a decent average,' was my joking response.

Head reeling in the furnace I was called upon to stop by two policemen demanding to see my passport. I knew what to expect, this had happened several times before.

'You have no permit to ride a bicycle. You must pay $10,' they informed me.

There is no such permit, of course, but in the past I had forked out the money in case officers turned awkward. This time I was well armed because Sebastian in Brazil had given me a letter of introduction to the President of Paraguay.

'We were at university together,' he had explained, 'and this letter will get you an audience.'

I produced the letter and my potential extorters had a rapid change of attitude. They both sprang to attention to salute me and I was on my way again. Hotel Maxi in Coronel Oviedo had the pleasure of my company. A shabby town and a meal not enjoyed among the choking clouds of dust that are a permanent feature of towns with unmade high streets. At last came a cool day and an hour of refreshing rain. I managed the 82 miles to Asuncion, meaning that I had covered two hundred miles in three days, so now I was in the capital among smart shops and McDonalds, Pizza Hut and so on. Yet at every road junction poverty stricken people sold packets of cocoa leaves to chew for deadening hunger pangs. The drug cocaine is produced from these leaves.

Several of the immaculate restaurants were called Sugar. I put my nose in the door and back out, too posh. I carried on wandering, paused outside another Sugar and this time the scruffy old man entered. The smartly dressed staff looked me up and down and muttered to each other. When I asked for a beer they pointed at the till, pay first. Looking down his nose the head waiter asked what had brought me here. I showed him my bike, produced my magic clippings and within minutes all the staff were shaking my hand and taking photographs.

The English-speaking manager was overjoyed. 'I have always hoped somebody doing such a big thing would come here. While you are here you drink free,' were his welcoming words. However, he forgot to tell the staff, and four beers later when I left they followed me outside and demanded payment. I convinced them that the manager had offered me free drinks and reluctantly they accepted, but one bright spark pointed out that I had already consumed one glass before the invitation, so I had to pay for my first drink.

I was warned, the Indians are dangerous, there are leopards and panthers, but the hazards I might meet don't deter me. Instead the lack of rideable roads decided me on flying to Bolivia and as I couldn't get a flight until 4th January I moved into a more comfortable hotel and settled down.

On a short ride into the country I found a memory embedded itself in my mind and it is still one of the strongest memories I have. A gathering of pathetic hollow-eyed men, women and children were digging holes in the mud. They dug a couple of feet down and waited a few minutes for a small quantity of brackish water to collect. Having scooped it up and shared it round they dug the hole deeper in the hope of a few more mouthfuls. I gave them my water bottle, perhaps this was the first time they had drunk clean water. It was the eve of the Millennium and all over the world millions of pounds were being wasted in fireworks. I imagined what use this money could have been put to.

All the restaurants were closed or fully booked, but a man with a small pizza shop invited me to join his family. I passed hundreds of street dwellers trying to beg enough to see another day. Millennium or not they would be as hungry next year as they were now. When life returned to normal 'You dine for nothing' said a restaurant boss who recognised me from Brazilian TV and he placed my picture on his wall of fame. I gave the price of the meal to some street kids. On my way to the airport I gave my remaining Paraguayan money to a small family of street people whom I had befriended in the last few days.

Now I would go to see what Bolivia would bring.

CHAPTER 61

A Bicycle in Bolivia

Santa Cruz is a big city only two miles from the airport. At a Chinese café the good-natured folks told me a room was £30. When I threw up my arms in a negative response the smiling lady led me further along the street to a £3 room.

Here again was appalling poverty, so many people with nothing. I almost stepped on a bundle of rags, glimpsing a baby's face only at the last second. Two other tiny children held out a hand as they would probably have to all their lives. Their mother looked like death, but she was no more than a girl herself. She glanced at me hopefully as I handed over a little money. I wish those bible-punchers would ride a bike round the world and then still insist on a supreme being.

I was off early having forgotten I had entered another time zone. I moved along freely in good country with the scenery improving as I reached the mountains. It wasn't too steep yet, but the heat was unbearable and the mosquitoes worse. I joined the locals as they washed clothes in the river, lying on my back in the water still dressed including shoes in an attempt to cool down. Back on the road everything was dry in minutes and I was baking again.

In a scruffy room at Bermejo I dragged the mattress off the bed and perched my tent on top so that I had a mosquito screen. The towns and villages were small and shabby, the people miserable, though out on the road was hardly a soul to be seen and few vehicles. Everywhere was dirty, the kitchens filthy, surfaces smothered with flies, plate of food, knife and fork, table-top and floor all surfaced with flies.

Bolivian cemeteries must be the most colourful in the world, decked out with artificial flowers providing an amazing splash of colour. The gardens of many houses are the same, where families bury their own dead. After the last house in the village of Mariana the road turned to loose sand, gravel and rocks. It was a tortuous ride as the bike lurched on three-penny-bit wheels from one rock to another. I smiled when a Bolivian man asked me, 'Why are you doing this? Are you making a sacrifice to God?' What a question from a man born into conditions like his.

Even though majestic scenery surrounded me I mostly had to keep my eyes on the road to seek out the smoothest route. I was in isolated country, miles of nothing, not even petrol stations. In the tiny villages petrol was sold in pint bottles. I reached Comarapa despite the heat and the terrible road conditions. With its sixty houses and two hotels this was the capital of the province, and Hotel Paraiso was clean unlike previous stops. There was hot water, too. How things change, for a couple of months the greatest pleasure had been a cold shower, but now the nights were cold and I needed a blanket.

One hundred and fifty miles in three days and considering the conditions I was reasonably pleased. That was the good news, now the bad, the road got worse and for mile after mile it was too steep to ride. There was no chance of a lift, in nine hours only three vehicles passed me, all grossly overloaded. Greta Garbo wanted to be alone. This was the place, complete isolation with only a handful of people who hardly responded to a hello. Any tiny stores had just a few tins of sardines, rice, biscuits and a couple of bottles of pop.

After nine hours of mostly walking I staggered into Pojo with blistered feet. During my trek a column of Quechua Indians each with a bundle on his head rounded a bend and we faced each other with maybe a twenty-foot gap between us. They all stopped in fear and shock. At a shout from their leader they dropped their baggage and ran well away from the road. They took cover behind rocks and peeped over the edge. I stood perplexed and formed the peace sign, but nobody moved. Did they think I was General Custer?

I had been told that the road from Pojo was surfaced, but no such luck so I hired a lorry and for £30 got transported fifty miles. To get to Pojo I had descended 11,000 feet. The lorry took me back up higher, but the highest was yet to come. Of the three scruffy hotels in the shanty village I arrived at only one had a room. I had to excuse the dirt and filth in this place, after so little rain for three years they were desperate for water. No clothes could be washed, no people or utensils, the primitive toilets could not be flushed. Every WC was piled high with excrement and people performed the necessary task in the surrounding scrubland instead. Water could be used for drinking or cooking only.

The food looked so revolting I couldn't recognise it let alone eat it, some sort of soup with goodness knows what floating in it. I paid up and left. A child ran to grab the dish before I was out of the door.

One of the shack hotels called itself the Hilton. I would be able to boast that I had stayed there. They conjured up an egg and some stale bread for breakfast and before long I was riding out of the village seeing the women selling goods from wheelbarrows. My fears about the road were unjustified. I had a superb cycling day on a surfaced road, beginning with eighteen miles uphill, a glorious thirty miles downhill and thirty more of level riding. Now I was in a broad valley with more people about, the fields lush with potatoes, radishes, onions and carrots.

After a fast eighty miles I reached Cochabamba. Never had I been so glad to see a big city. Everything was here. The markets had an unlimited selection of food and I dined on baked fish, rice potatoes and salad for 80 pence. It was time for a good hotel. For me this meant one with glass in the windows and not too many floorboards missing, so Hotel Americas fitted the bill. The one night I booked extended to three, not at all influenced by the seductive receptionist. I liked Cochabamba, built in the Spanish style with prolific arches, wrought iron balconies and shady courtyards.

I must include how before getting to Cochabamba I was desperate for food, but there seemed no chance. I slogged on and out of nowhere a small girl appeared, holding a banana. I tried to ask her where she had got it but from the look on her face she thought I was going to snatch it.

Girl with bananas

A man arrived who pointed to a tumbledown shack I hadn't noticed. 'Tienda,' he said, shop. I stumbled across the rough ground with seven excited children running alongside. The adults dressed in rags looked cautious and I couldn't see anything in the shop.

'We have nothing,' they said.

'I've seen a girl with a banana.'

The man looked at his wife for agreement. She nodded. 'Invitado,' he said, gift, and produced a bunch of bananas. Those who had nothing were prepared to give me food they needed for themselves. I reasoned with myself that close by were likely other tiendas and that these people had no money. They confirmed there were others better stocked. The mother protested strongly, 'Invitado! Invitado!' I took the bananas and pressed ten dollars in her hand. What had I got for the children? I dug out my little stock of toys and found something for each of the seven.

CHAPTER 62

Through the Barricades

The more time I spent in Cochabamba the more I liked it. Roberto, the owner of the sports shop where I bought more clothing, summoned the media and I appeared on Bolivian TV and in Los Tiempos the leading newspaper.

Roberto encouraged me to visit the home of Simon I Patino, Bolivia's most famous man. It was more like a palace, glorious in construction and décor. Senor Patino born in 1862 started out as a silver miner but quickly realised that silver was being mined to exhaustion. He and his wife spent years prospecting for other resources and together discovered one of the greatest tin deposits ever known. He became the richest man in Bolivia. During both world wars he supported the allies, reserving the whole of his ore output for them, essential for the war effort. He never slept in the house, because after a heart attack doctors advised him to live at a lower level where the air is not so thin. They say that only General de Gaulle ever slept here and the bed had to be lengthened for him. Simon I Patino died in 1947 and was buried in a white mausoleum in Cochabamba.

The Bolivian women are short and they wear a bowler or a trilby. They often look old but have a baby strapped to their back. The men wear a close fitting knitted cap with earmuffs. The streets are full of pitiful beggars, as many babies holding out a hand as men and women. Every day I gave away as much as I spent on myself.

Traditional Bolivian dress

I headed for La Paz. The road rose for sixty miles until the last pass at almost 15,000 feet. I was warned that I would have trouble breathing at that altitude. A nationwide strike began that day in protest against the government's proposal to increase the price of water. A lot of people would not be affected as their water came from a puddle.

The protestors intended to bring the country to a standstill. For miles round the towns and cities crude low barriers had been erected across the roads so that nothing could move. Every hundred yards was another barrier and spread across the road on the way to the obstruction scrap cars, tree trunks, rocks, barbed wire and a sea of broken glass.

'Buena Suerte,' I called out as I drew nearer, Good luck.

'Igualmente,' they replied – Likewise – and I began the task of getting across the barricades. I scrambled over the last barricade twenty-five miles later. Many times I almost collapsed carrying my bike and equipment over carpets of broken glass.

At the Cora River I had to unload everything and wade across. My legs were ripped badly, but I had made it past the barricades. This was where the tailback of vehicles started. For five miles both lanes were packed like sardines. There was no chance of riding for every inch of road was taken up with transport and the thousands of passengers being carried. These people had to eat, so fires had been lit, stalls erected and goods were being sold. Some were the goods that had been part of consignments headed for the city. A carnival atmosphere prevailed. A few hitchhiking backpackers were worried, I assured them they weren't in any danger. To many shouts of encouragement I pushed my way through and began my climb to the Alto Plano.

With traffic everywhere at a standstill I saw one other person on foot in fifty miles. The tiniest of settlements appeared and my canvas home was my welcome nest.

CHAPTER 63

The High Plains

Many times I was told (but I didn't need telling) that I was riding the old road. I realised that the paved road would have all the commercial outlets and guesthouses and would be more populated, but I was pleased I'd taken the wilderness route, I travelled in spectacular grandeur and breathtaking scenery. A sign pointed to Butch Cassidy's ranch.

The weather changed within minutes from brilliant sunshine to bitter cold. Worst of all I was amongst the clouds. I walked slowly inches at a time. There were no barriers, one wrong step and I would plunge hundreds, maybe thousands of feet, I was very frightened. But I had touched the heart of Bolivia, the rawness and the reality.

The roads remained empty. At the blockade I had been told that all the big cities were under siege and the protest would continue. On and on forever, mostly dragging the bike. At 13,500 feet I was dismayed when the road plunged for miles, I knew that the pass I needed stood at 14,750 feet. I reached the bottom, brakes applied all the way, and then the climb began that brought me disappointment again, culminating at 14,150 feet. Finally I took a photograph of the bike against the altitude marker at La Cumbre – 14,750 feet.

It was 6pm and so cold. I found a tiny shack, but the family was reluctant to let me sleep on their floor, understandable as they had hardly room for themselves. Morning began with scraping snow off the tent. After porridge and a cup of tea packing up was a miserable job with my freezing fingers, but within an hour the sun was burning my face. All the way to La Paz would be flat. In spite of the tough journey and the curse of scrambling over blockades I had done 105 miles in two days with 142 miles remaining to the capital.

I joined the Alto Plane at Carahuasi. A superb ride, but what a day for weather, scraping the snow off my portable home, followed by brilliant sunshine, a hailstorm, more sunshine, then far across the pampas a black curtain racing towards me. A sandstorm. I pedalled like mad to reach the edge but it was too fast. I dropped the bike and threw myself into a shallow depression. Blanketed by sand I lay choking and coughing trying to keep my nose, mouth, ears and eyes clear. It seemed an eternity before it blew away. The bike and I were buried in sand and it took some time to get on the move again. The day finished with heavy rain.

But still it was glorious to ride the High Plains, tremendous to gaze across the land where flocks of llamas roamed, too high for trees, no shelter anywhere. The poverty haunted me, when what little traffic there was didn't stop for the women and children sitting alongside the isolated road trying to sell cheese. I gave some of them the price of the cheese, but left the cheese with them. Little boys and girls shepherded sheep and cattle (no school for them). Way across the land two small boys saw me coming and ran hell for leather to cut me off, falling many times on the rough ground. Breathlessly they asked for 'plata' (money). Such an effort must be rewarded, but every which way I looked were hungry people.

Cold and with rain falling I bedded down for fifty pence in Patacamaya. It only took me ten minutes to get used to the smell and at least I had water for a wash. Water had been so scarce for days and nobody washed. I even felt guilty when I asked for drinking water, because although I was never refused I was reducing their supply. The toilets here were an education, communal uni-sex open-plan, four holes to choose and squat. I thought if the French ever heard about the place they'd make it their number one tourist destination.

Next day more traffic on the road meant the strike must be over. I felt tired, perhaps because of the altitude, but no breathing problems since I had a slow approach to these heights. I reached the great sprawl of La Paz. I'd taken three and a half days from Cochabamba. Some other cyclists had said five days, but they were only 35-year old kids. The market square thronged with people as I made my way through the stalls. Without a word a dishevelled man standing alongside started kicking my wheels. My old sergeant major used to drum into us, 'The British army never retreats, we just retire to a better position.' I retired to a better position.

Having got to the outside of three cups of coffee and two toasted sandwiches I wondered where to stay. A Brazilian athlete interested in my bike came into the café to ask about my travels. We talked for an hour. He was delighted to hear about the warmth of his people and my tears of emotion when I left Rosie, whom of course he knew. He left me a card for the Happy Days Hotel and I booked in for two nights.

At last, now ride the Andes Acto Plano

Heart breaking sight - Bolivia

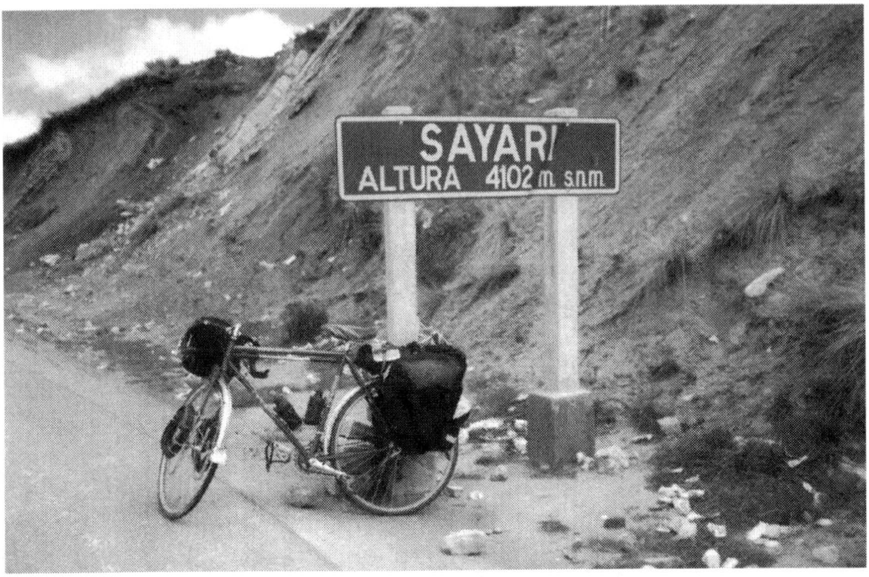
SAYARI
ALTURA 4102 m. s.n.m.

CHAPTER 64

An Abduction Attempt

'You must be absolutely crazy,' insisted Columbian Ferdinando when he learned how I got to Bolivia.

'So how did you get here?' I countered.

It turned out he had spent eight solid days on a ramshackle bus, and another two in front of him to get to Chile. Then ten days on a bus to get back to Columbia. I know who was crazier.

The old buildings in La Paz are historical treasures of atmospheric Spanish architecture, but most of the city is an untidy sprawl. On my first full day I mooched about in miserable weather, pouring rain and very cold. The locals were all wrapped in blankets. With Argentinian Marcus I took in a few sights. He had been three days in La Paz, two of them in bed suffering altitude sickness, splitting head, constant vomiting and heart pounding more than it did even when he had his first encounter of the female kind. We took a look inside San Francisco Cathedral. Marcus crossed himself and I dropped to one knee, my shoelace had come undone.

In the afternoon I was standing alone on the main road when an abduction attempt was made on me. A smartly dressed burly man engaged me in small talk, telling me he was a policeman. A small man (his accomplice) walked slowly past and Mr Burly put his hand on the man's shoulder and asked to see his identity papers. The man produced his ID.

'And yours,' said Mr Burly to me. I protested, but Mr Shorty all smiles said this was normal. I produced my passport.

'You must both come to the station to get these checked,' we were told. Again I protested and again Mr Shorty assured me there was nothing to worry about.

We walked slowly up the road in the opposite direction to the police station that I had passed ten minutes before, Mr Shorty encouraging me along the way. A car swung into the kerbside, the driver reached over his seat and opened the back door. The two men climbed in and told me to follow them, all so slick, so smooth.

'Hijos de perras,' I shouted (sons of bitches) and ran like mad.

Two days later I read in an English language paper that the body of a thirty-four year old French tourist had been found on a lonely road, killed by a blow to the head and with bruises and cord-marks round his neck. Only his passport was on his body, and witnesses said they saw him thrown from a car.

Leaving La Paz I tackled ten miles of steep autopista to get out of town, slow and gruelling with severe hailstorms and drenching rain, but with nowhere to shelter I carried on. My legs were smothered in angry red spots where hailstones struck my skin with the force of air-gun pellets. From the whistles I got I must have been the only man in Bolivia wearing shorts.

What a pleasure to see Lake Titicaca, the beauty spot of the country, a vast expanse with rounded mountains rising softly from smooth waters. The highest navigable lake in the world at over 12,000 feet. I arrived at San Pablo Tiquina having ridden eighty miles and was disappointed to find only a few rough buildings, not the resort I had been led to believe, and nowhere to sleep. Across the lake, San Pedro looked not much bigger, but more promising so I made the crossing by ferry, only to find nowhere to sleep. In the dark and bitter cold I persisted and was directed to a small grocery shop. The woman wasn't a pleasant sort at all, but she let me have a spare room for a pound.
'No toilet or bathroom,' she informed me, and produced a chamber pot. 'Only for piss', she stipulated and then the old misery returned to her counter.

I breakfasted with two naval officers. Commandant Captain Rodriguez told me about a classy house nearby owned by Dame Margaret Joan Anstee, an upper class English lady who worked forty years for the UN and became its first female Under-Secretary General. We visited this lovely house, it was a real privilege to be shown round by the housekeeper. Dame Margaret owns houses in various countries, including her main residence The Walled Garden near Presteigne. At a much later date Dame Margaret wrote to say she was surprised and pleased to receive the photographs I sent her.

Copacabana Bolivia (no comparison with Copacabana Brazil) is a small resort full of young backpackers. The youngsters I met were very good and seemed to think they should look out for the old man. But if we went on arduous treks it was the youngsters who struggled. I found some digs with hot water and settled down for a spell. I made friends with two young couples from Banbury and we all took a boat trip to Isla del Sol. The boat was crowded with twenty-year olds and I didn't much care for their language. One guy started joking about my generation's attitude to sex, to the assembly's amusement.

'Bob's age group didn't believe in sex before marriage,' he scoffed, supported by much laughter while his girlfriend hung onto his arm.

'And if you marry that girl, how many of your friends will have slept with her?' I answered as he went rather quiet.

Some hypocrisy was evident however, when on my third night at Copacabana a two am knock at the door disturbed my sleep. Carmen, who had come to Isla del Sol with me, stepped inside, threw her arms round my neck and declared, 'Bob, I love you.' But another new friend of mine sat up in bed and told her to go away, or words to that effect.

CHAPTER 65

Into Peru

Unable to get a map anywhere and with everybody saying the road to Peru was unrideable, I boarded the same bus to Peru as the kids, like them clutching the obligatory bottle of water and the Lonely Planet guide. At the border I was asked the address of my nearest police station at home in England, odd, but I suppose with computers officials can check anything.

At Puno I found a good homestay and strolled down to Lake Titicaca, shared between Bolivia and Peru. The ship on the lake was the Yavari, built in England in 1862, transported to South America in kit form, carried on the backs of mules across wilderness to Puno and there re-assembled. The whole operation took six years. The Yavari was featured in Michael Palin's bread and milk TV programme and a big sign had been erected on the shore: 'Michael Palin came here on his round the world trip.'

I wrote underneath, 'Not on a bike he didn't.'

After breakfast and still without a map I set off for Cuzco. Only one road so no getting lost, but with 250 miles to do a map would have shown me the distances between villages. Once over the steep rise from Puno was good riding on the High Plains again. Fantastic terrain, but how quickly the weather changes. At three pm a violent storm erupted in bitter cold. I had just reached Pukara, a scruffy little town, where I got an even scruffier little room for £1.

The day after started good, but as usual turned nasty, painful hail, drenching rain and then damn, a flat tyre. No shelter and unrelenting rain, luckily a lorry stopped and Bob and Bike climbed aboard to spend the remaining journey to Cuzco among sacks of onions.

I sat on the kerb in Cuzco at six am waiting for a café in this lovely city to open. Great Spanish architecture again, hidden courtyards, narrow streets and attractive balconies. I took the first room offered by one of the touts, but moved after one night to swap for a room with hot water. Cuzco was overrun with mostly Argentinian backpackers. Warning notices advised tourists not to enter a taxi alone as some cab drivers will place you in the hands of local hoodlums to meet an undetermined fate (shades of Bolivia).

On Sunday came a flag-raising ceremony, with soldiers on parade and orders called over a microphone, what would a British sergeant major think of a microphone? The packed square stood in silence as the flags were raised and then everybody joined the soldiers in singing the national anthem. The pride so many people have in their country, and yet I hear a rumour that God Save the Queen is no longer played at British cinemas.

On my third day in Peru I went to absorb some Inca history at Sacred Valley, first visiting Pisac, then Ollantaytambo, close by Machu Picchu. Splendid countryside surrounded me and the largest of the Inca cemeteries, but on me people always have most impact, here too they rushed forward at the sight of a tourist to do anything possible to earn a few pennies, little children offering to sing or pose for photos, others having bathroom scales, polishing shoes or as in Bolivia selling cocoa leaves.

I said goodbye to Cuzco and after twenty miles of tough riding I was in the midst of gasping scenery, verdant valleys rich in crops replacing pampas. Some of the valleys are at a depth where they never get too hot or too cold, so the farmers grow three crops a year. Shepherds waved to me, workers shouted greetings and children called out, 'Donde vas, gringo?' 'Where are you going, foreigner?'

After seventy miles I pitched my tent for the night. I heated up a pan of soup with a little audience of children and I made a few balloon animals. The two eldest boys, aged fifteen and twelve, returned after their regular twelve hours' work on the land, and although they had done more than one man's work each they too wanted a balloon animal. It had been a great day, no traffic, so peaceful.

In the morning the going got tough. Up, up, forever up. The tarmac gave way to earth, with landslides and rock falls. I reached the summit and for thirty miles the road was deep mud, a terrible descent into Abancay. I rolled into the town centre, my bike, my tackle and myself covered in mud. I hesitated to enter a café, but the owner waved me in, 'Have a wash. I'll watch your things,' he offered.

When I was fed and rested the staff brought a bucket of water and I started a clean-up job, but to my dismay I discovered the constant braking had worn through the rim of the back wheel and not only was it cracked but a piece of metal was breaking free. None of the bike shops could help me, so I bought a bus ticket to Lima, 560 miles away.

CHAPTER 66

Lima, a Desert Robbery and the End of the Journey

The bus for Lima was leaving at six pm. I clambered onto the roof (no ladder) and strapped my machine securely. The only other item on the roof was a live sheep tethered by the neck, oblivious of the ordeal to come.

The overloaded bus began its journey, with some passengers even lying inside the luggage compartment under the floor. The mountain scenery was spectacular, but the roads were shocking and the weather changed constantly. Sometimes rivers gushed across the road and sometimes passengers had to leave the bus and clear away boulders from rock slides. Across the gangway sat a young boy, baseball cap, cheeky face and a ready smile. I asked his age and why he was going to Lima, eleven years old and going to Lima to find work. He didn't know anybody in Lima and to buy the £6 bus ticket he had begged, run errands, cleaned shoes.

The driver deserved a medal for this trip, except that he probably did the same trip every other day. On through the night we went, pitch black with no road lights. When morning dawned the road was terrible, just a building site. We passed amongst dense cloud as we crossed the Andes so the unheated bus was intensely cold, and then at last a sight of the Pacific as the sun began to rise. With the moisture from the sea a fog developed in the desert and still we rolled on. After eighteen hours on the road the driver stopped for lunch.

Little Baseball-Cap wandered the café looking for scraps. I called him over and he told me he had only £1 to start his new life. I didn't let him go hungry and I decided that when he got off the bus he would have more money than he started with. On arrival in Lima the driver had been behind the wheel for twenty-one hours with only a half-hour break. He had driven on mud tracks, on roads that crumbled under his wheels, in total blackness, thick cloud, pouring rain, brilliant sunshine and dense fog. But the real hero had to be the sheep tied by its neck to the roof.

I scoured the bike shops and witnessed much headshaking. So many bikes, from sit up and beg sorts to clumsy mountain bikes with tractor tyres. On the point of despair I found a shop where somewhat reluctantly the Japanese owner agreed to rebuild my wheel. His heart wasn't in it and he cursed and grumbled all the time, but he knew his stuff and got me back on the road. Thousands of feet of altitude were now reduced to a few feet above sea level as I made my way through the huge desert. A roadside restaurant looked inviting, the pleasant owners let me camp in their well-maintained back garden, so after a good night I sped next day through the markers that indicated where the road was and the depth of the sand, where windblown sand had obliterated the road. The bike ran smooth as a watch.

A truck loaded with women and children stranded at the side of the road flagged me down. The men had no spanners to attend to a repair. I handed over my kit gladly and after an hour the lorry was running again, I had been keeping the kids amused with balloons.

I refused payment. 'Hermanos,' I said, 'Brothers'.

'Vales mucho,' they called after me, 'You are worth much,' and I was pleased with myself.

When it was nearly time to sleep I dragged my bike well clear of the road to the far side of some long sand dunes. There was nothing but sand as far as I could see and not a soul about. I set up for the night, all my equipment fitting into the one-man tent, but with no room for the bike. With nothing to chain the bike to I just put the chain through the wheel and went to sleep.

By the morning my bike had been stolen. I was devastated. Had somebody followed me at a distance knowing that I would have to rest for the night? I didn't know the answer to that, but I was gutted. I stood alone in the immensity of the desert and the faithful machine that had carried me over thirty thousand miles was gone.

Struggling back to the road with my packs I started trudging back to Lima, two hundred miles away. After an hour or so a vehicle picked me up and feeling very sorry for myself I arrived again in Lima. I had already established that there were no road-touring bikes and with the wind knocked out of my sails I was in no mood to continue. I bought a ticket to Florida and made up my mind to spend time with my sister before returning to England. I recalled the first time I went to crazy America, passing from Mexico to Brownsville Texas I had to sign a declaration stating that I would not join any criminal gangs, I would not deal in drugs and I would not join any groups trying to overthrow the government. I also had to swear that I would not try to assassinate the President. What would they have done if I had tried to assassinate the President? Slapped my wrist and said, 'Bad boy! You said you wouldn't'?

From Florida I contacted the Dawes cycle factory in my hometown of Birmingham and requested that they ship me a bicycle over. My unfinished trip had already involved 3,200 miles. I had been reconsidering and thought I might fly back to Peru and continue my travels into Ecuador, Columbia and Venezuela.

On the phone I spoke to some stroppy young miss who informed me, 'We don't deal with the public.'

'I'm not the usual public,' I explained. 'I've been promoting a Dawes bicycle through many countries on TV and in newspapers. I only want to buy another bicycle.'

'We don't deal with the public,' she snapped and put the phone down. Dawes went out of business not long afterwards.

When I returned home, in an interview with Birmingham's Sunday Mercury I told them about the Dawes reaction and they got in touch with the boss. His truthful response was that he hadn't received the message. He wrote to tell me I was just the type of cyclist they wanted to put on their website, but they'd had their chance and I'd already bought a Thorn Nomad.

I'd also bought maps of Vietnam.

CHAPTER 67

Man on a Saddle in Vietnam

Date: 23rd November 2000

Place: Ho Chi Minh City, Vietnam

My first impression is the welcome heat after the cold of England, but within minutes the heat becomes unbearable. Flying here to start my travels I have found that events in America have changed airport procedure forever: security checks are frustrating but necessary. I have a pouch hanging from my belt, the sort people carry mobile phones in. At my departure airport I empty my pockets, remove my shoes and so on.

Then, 'Hand me your phone.'

'I have no phone.'

'What's in the pouch?'

'My false teeth.'

In my small clean Thien Tung Hotel I have the foresight to put most of my money in the safe. Washed and changed I am as eager as ever to start exploring another country. Vietnam teems with motorbikes and there are no traffic rules. As I set off to find a restaurant I am accosted by dozens of rickshaw drivers all shouting that it's too dangerous to walk. Well, they would, wouldn't they?

I can't shake them off and then I realise they'll be able to show me a Western café (can't eat foreign stuff). On the three hundred yard ride I am flanked by dozens of girls on motorbikes offering me the time of my life. I'm looking for food.

No petrol problems

Local transport

The rickshaw driver calls back for me after an hour, but he takes a different route back. We get further away as he pedals down dark narrow streets. I jump out and start to run. The driver shouts and men burst out of alleyways. Five grip me, two of them press me against a wall, two rip my shirt open and each holds a hypodermic syringe against my stomach. The fifth man searches me thoroughly including places I wouldn't search, and they are all snarling 'Dollars.'

I have only ten dollars in my wallet. The five men argue whether they should beat me up. They give me a violent shove and run off with ten dollars. I should have chosen the time of my life instead of food.

After two nights in Ho Chi Minh City I am on the road with traffic thinning out and fewer girls pestering me. A motorbike girl rides alongside and keeps pace a couple of miles. She says nothing but she smiles occasionally. She speeds off, but appears again outside a shack and signals me to stop. We enter the shack and a toothless old crone appears who displays a wide grin and informs me, 'I love many GIs.'

I think, 'Well, you're not about to love a British Tommy.'

Motorbike girl pulls back a curtain to reveal three stunning women rolling around provocatively on a bed. 'Which one you want?'

It would have been like having to choose between Liz Hurley, Catherine Zeta Jones and Carol Vorderman. I accepted a Coca-Cola and ducked out, but I've kicked myself a few times since.

Fifty-five miles are far enough for my first day, and a hospitable family is happy for me to pitch my tent at their premises. I am off early to the resort of Vung Tau after a bit of unpleasantness from the village bully who plays to the crowd and pushes me around. I take charge by displaying humour and shaking many hands. Bully boy isn't getting the support he needs and skulks away.

Vung Tau is a pleasant resort although it's in sight of oil rigs. Few tourists are about and street traders all besiege me. Many Australians live here, they returned after the war and married almond-eyed girls twenty or thirty years younger than themselves. Allan, owner of Ettamogah Pub (named after the Aussie comic strip pub) makes friends. He's a retired prison governor and looks the part, big and tough. He tells me convict stories, including Chopper Reid the notoriously dangerous character who sliced off his own ears and nailed his feet to the floor to demonstrate to fellow inmates how tough he was. Actually I think I'm pretty tough, I've ridden a bike through Bangkok.

I talk to Jim who breeds greyhounds and has brought dog-racing to Vietnam. He tells me, 'I've always had the urge to do something unusual. I'm thinking of pushing a wheelbarrow round the coast of Australia'! He fixes me up with a secluded camping spot and informs me that his next greyhound's name will be Bob the Bike.

I'm lucky enough to find myself on Front Beach, which suits me because it's small, rather than Back Beach the main resort beach area. I make friends with a group of veterans and in one week spend only one night in a hotel, dingy but necessary for washing body and belongings. Taking advice I ride quiet roads to Phuoc Hai, only thirty miles, but I can't ride far in this heat.

At Phuoc Hai I lounge around most of the day waited on hand and foot by the delighted and delightful staff who are in stitches at my inability to speak a single word. It's a secure fenced and guarded complex and I find a cosy corner to snuggle down in. Everyone leaves, but a security guard tells me I must pay £1.50 to sleep in the compound.

'Okay, I'll sleep further down the beach,' I say.

'Too dangerous' is his opinion.

Faced with the unknown or spending £1.50, I decide to save £1.50.

CHAPTER 68

Swapping Stories

I sit up in my tent at daybreak and my throat hasn't been cut. I am once again on the road, where stalls sell delicious baguettes with cheese (some of my best bread ever) and there are so many food outlets. Much vegetation, rice fields and coconut trees in this countryside but the heat is intense and I have another short day before I enter a fairly large town not shown on my useless map. I spot a sign for draught beer at 22p. I have been paying 10p a pint up to now, so what, I saved £1.50 last night.

Eighteen-year old Khiem shows up. He works in the café for £9 a month and sleeps on the floor there. He can speak a little English. Together we ride to La Gi Beach, another stretch of silken sand. Then back to the café, where a grotty room is found for me and I am charged £1.50, so you see how important it is to save money - A good night with splendid townspeople. I lose count of the marriage proposals and the folks think my lack of Vietnamese language is hilarious. My ride proceeds and I join a main road with a hard shoulder to ride on. From the opposite direction approach my favourite people, other long-distance cyclists. Paul and Mandy are English and have covered many miles. We swap hair-raising stories, we could have talked for hours, but I think Paul's story tops mine.

Plodding to the top of a steep hill in Peru with Mandy twenty yards behind him, Pul gasped his way to the summit and paused to get his breath. A group of teenagers crowded round him and one pushed a gun under his chin. Not seeing the gun Mandy is shouting, 'Don't give them any money!' while Paul is saying, 'Take my money.'

Money in hand the lowlife want to see what else is worth stealing and rip open Paul and Mandy's bike bags. Meanwhile an unmarked police car gets to the top of the hill; a solitary policeman takes stock of the situation, reaches for his machine gun on the back seat and exits his vehicle, the lowlife run like rabbits. The policeman tells Paul and Mandy they are mad to ride bicycles through Peru.

At Cho Lau I stand on a river bridge and take stock of a camp spot. I am invited to pitch next to a flimsy café shack where the family treats me well. Their 29-year old teacher son turns up, making the evening a lot better because he can speak English with me.

An uncomfortable walk into town, with many shouts of 'Go back home!'

Morning comes and I settle for breakfast in a café packed with men. To begin with they ignore me, but with encouragement from the customers the surly café owner starts pushing his face up close and insulting me. To gales of mocking laughter I remove myself and cross the road to a food outlet where they are delighted that I am their customer.

In many countries I can only close my eyes to the cruelty shown to animals. At my last night's stop a squirrel ran constantly inside a two-foot square box. Here, a magnificent eagle has already spent two years in a cage not big enough to allow it to stretch its wings. This is duck country, ducks by the thousands. They are herded like sheep; it's common to see a column marching like soldiers, even stopping at the roadside until they hear the command to cross.

Today little bunches of Westerners on bicycles ride in the opposite direction, maybe fifty or so, and armed guards patrol them. Must be Americans.

At Nha Trang I encounter an Irish lad shopping for footwear because his shoes got stolen last night. He points me to the backpackers' area and the Sinh café where they hang out getting drunk and spending hours on the computer talking to Mummy and Daddy. They are transported from one resort to another completely unaware that through thousands of miles of the world nobody speaks English.

In Wu's café at lunchtime he tells me, 'Last month we had two hundred American cyclists here, riding in a big convoy with armed security and all their equipment in trucks.' Another bread-and-milk everybody-hold-hands bike tour.

CHAPTER 69

Rocks, Rain and Mr Pompous

On checking out I had to pay 25p for a towel I'd spoiled. Served me right, I shouldn't have cleaned my chain with it. Now I've spent a couple of traffic-free hours riding amongst curious villagers, occasionally stopping for a delicious sugar-cane drink squeezed using a device similar to an old-fashioned mangle.

Today people put on a friendly act but it's obviously false, because they're sometimes trying to charge me ten times the real price or else refusing to give me change. At one establishment I make a stand and demand my change. The crowd grows bigger; the insulting remarks increase and get more threatening, best to get out of here. I haven't moved six feet before the first rock hits my back wheel. With missiles dropping round me I ride a zigzag course until I'm out of throwing distance.

'Missed! You stupid yellow bastards!' I shout insultingly, and another incident has passed.

Joining the main road I meet a real cyclist, a young Belgian. He has visited more countries than you can shake a stick at, clocking up 16,000 miles in eighteen months and he's still going strong.

It must be National Rock-Throwing Day. A gang of young men whooping with laughter are stoning a chicken to death. On a pick-up at the side of the road a wooden crate is packed with dogs on their way to the cooking pot. They lie crammed on top of each other not making a sound. I can't look any one of them in the eyes. A beach with leaning palms, good food and a few jars of the acceptable drug all come with Ninh Hoa resort, Vietnamese beaches are among the best I've ever seen. I get the first Vietnam marriage proposal I've had. I thank her and shake my head, then make her a large heart-shaped balloon.

The first daytime rain. I enjoy the cooling down, but now comes a raging wind so strong I can't steer straight, it blows me off the road or into the path of vehicles, brings me to a complete standstill or forces me to the ground. Protective sheeting is being ripped from lorries, canvas and plastic sheets are scattered crazily across surrounding fields. A sheet envelops a truck and wraps around the windscreen, the now blind driver brings his vehicle to a halt with sad results. The map attached to my handlebar bag rips off and sails like a kite before landing in a crop of rice. It's essential to retrieve it although it may be useless now, so I empty my pockets and remove my money belt before wading waist deep through mud.

The wind stops but the downpour continues. Despite the conditions I manage sixty miles and smothered in mud pay the shocking price of £10 for a room in Tuy Hoa. With hot water available I spend an hour on a clean-up operation.

I'm stuck in the room for two days. The rain keeps falling and I wait and wait. I take a stroll to find cheaper digs in case I'm marooned for a long spell. However, by lunchtime I'm on the road. I head inland, the weather is still bad, but it's best to keep moving. It's going to be impossible to camp and there's no chance of a hotel. It appears there's more poverty in the countryside than on the main roads, but as yet not the level of poverty I've seen in other countries.

Nearing the time to lay down my head I try to indicate to an old lady that I want to sleep in her shop doorway. The lady is very nice, says no but guides me over the road to the family house where I am immediately welcomed and offered the family bed. To their amusement I erect Thrifty in the living room instead. I really enjoy my tent, inside it's my space and I can ignore any dangers that lurk outside. It gives me a feeling of security, even though sometimes it hasn't been secure at all.

I prepare myself for an invasion of people. Soon fifty are crammed into this small house and what a pity I can't talk to them, they're all lovely. Thank heaven for the balloons, such a simple thing, but they go down well. I sure had a brainwave when I first thought of them.

The village schoolteacher arrives, a pompous, arrogant know-all. His English isn't much better than my Vietnamese, but these poor, uneducated people are impressed by this busybody.

'Hotel! Hotel' he insists. I try to tell him it's pitch black and there's no way I can get to a hotel.

'Police! Police!' he says and climbs on his motorbike to ride away. The people are happy, especially the children, who think I'm a real novelty.

Mr Pompous returns with the police. Frightened villagers start slipping away. Using a table as a desk, Mr Pompous and the senior policeman sit one side, with me on the other and two policemen behind me. Mr Senior speaks harshly to my host family. I can tell they are apologising, now they don't think it's such a good idea to offer me shelter.

The interrogation begins. Mr Senior Policeman writes down a list of questions for Pompous to translate. (Only in the last few years have tourists been allowed to stay in a hotel of their own choice, before that they had to stay in government hotels.)

'What you do in Vietnam?'

'What you look for?'

'Why you no in hotel?'

'Why you no in tourist resort?'

'Why you no have motorbike?'

I'm not much bothered about this charade. If Mr Pompous had minded his own business the police would have been none the wiser of my existence. These jumped-up sorts can be found everywhere and Pompous is making the most of his ten minutes of fame. He copies every dot on my visa and passport.

'You sleep here one night. Tomorrow you report to police station and every day you in Vietnam you report to police station.'

'Yes,' I yawn.

'A policeman will watch you all night,' is his parting shot.

I was ready to sleep so I did. I woke up very early and the guard was fast asleep in a corner. Quieter than a mouse in carpet slippers I packed up and with a silent wave to my hosts I slipped away. I certainly won't be showing my face in any police stations.

CHAPTER 70

Da Lat

The deluge continues. The road is a nightmare of mud, rocks, holes and deep puddles. I am near to Cheo Reo when I fall off and the already mud-caked bike receives another coating. The panniers are well and truly dipped. In the town I appeal for a hosepipe and the bike is soon washed. I survey myself in the bathroom mirror of the own hotel. I am covered in so much mud I could easily get into Glastonbury pop festival for free.

Another day and at least the rain has stopped, except it's a day for punctures, because my tyres are holed from sharp stones. My spare tyres are somewhat distorted. The pressure of people is bad enough most times, but when the bike needs attention it can be intolerable. With all my equipment unloaded, tools, tyres and tubes on the ground, I'm hard pressed to keep my temper. People press ever nearer, tread on my gear, play with the pump, inspect my tools and interfere with the bike. It's almost impossible to attend to the repair and I'm worried about losing equipment as everybody wants a souvenir, but I must keep smiling.

The local comedian always turns up. Once he establishes I don't understand a word this one pokes fun at me, causing much amusement amongst my audience. I show annoyance and a monkey chant starts. Some of them push their faces within inches of mine, all chanting, 'U UH, U UH, U UH, U UH'. Not the best of experiences. Four times today I have to attend to punctures and I get similar treatment each time.

I get a room in Chu Chi and I'm checking my belongings and repairing inner tubes. After a light knock on the door a girl about nineteen enters. She doesn't speak; she just sits on the bed, then lies down. I stick a patch on a tube. 'I'm mending my bike, luv,' I say, and she exits the room. I bet she's never been passed over for an inner tube before.

I am riding well on the Ho Chi Minh trail. By the big town of Buon Ma Thuot I've completed 85 miles. The towns often have strange names and some don't sound very polite. Several times today I've asked, 'What's the way to Phuoc Long?'

Leaving my fleapit I dine at a swank hotel, where I know there will be Western food. The food is good when I can order what I want, but away from resorts or cities I have to eat what's brought, usually watery cabbage soup, a plate piled high with rice and maybe a little meat or cucumber.

I have left the big town pleased that I have been able to buy new tyres and this day is turning out to be the best so far. The hundred-mile road to Da Lat is hardly used and wanders past lakes, rivers, mountains and forests. It is sparsely inhabited, now and then there's just a shack that provides shelter for the poor souls scratching a living from the land.

The road gets worse and I have to walk a great deal mostly uphill as Da Lat stands at 4,900 feet. At 4 pm it's best to choose a spot before it gets dark. I stop at a shack shop, buy a drink (draught beer is 10p a pint) and play with some children. The balloons win the adults over, too, the folks are amazed and amused at me on my bike. The tent goes up and they bring me some food. But four heavily drugged men stagger up to my tent and start interfering with my goods, trying to ride the bike and pulling the tent about, occasionally grabbing me by the shoulders and shaking me. I re-pack my gear in ten minutes and it's goodbye to an anxious looking family of good people.

The search is on for another resting place and I settle a couple of miles further on, adopting my usual practice of first making friends. Now Thrifty is in position between two shacks and I sit down with a beer and a packet of newly purchased biscuits when my peace is spoiled again by another doped-up idiot. After some pushing and shoving he stumbles away and in the darkness, I crawl into my canvas house. It's the local lads turn now and the tent gets pelted with mud and stones, but they soon get tired and I get to sleep.

I rejoin the main road and the plus side is the abundance of food outlets, serving delicious hot baguettes filled with cheese and tuna, the minus side being the choking traffic fumes and the honking of horns. Da Lat is said to be one of the loveliest towns in Vietnam, dubbed Little Paris. As most towns are a shambles it hasn't got much competition, but it's pleasant enough and has shops that cater for everything.

The Peace Hotel is my headquarters for two nights. I try to sleep, but it's impossible because of a terrible domestic row in a shack below my window. Children are screaming and crying with fear as the man and wife rage at each other and finally I fill a large bottle with water and lob it as hard as I can onto the corrugated iron roof. A tremendous crash as it rattles down the metal sheets. Immediate silence falls and I have restored peace to the Peace Hotel.

CHAPTER 71

Vung Tau and Veterans

A lazy day wandering around the excellent market, visiting the bank with its corrugated iron doors and coincidentally meeting some New Zealanders, who not only live in the same city as my big brother, but actually play bowls with him. I haven't seen my brother for twenty years, yet here I am halfway round the world talking to some of his pals.

On the road again I easily cover the 70 miles to Bao Loc. A restaurant provides a menu in English and I settle on grilled leg of goat. Steamed goat's testicles are also on offer, but I figure two mouthfuls hardly a meal make. I've set off on the craziest route, which no four-wheeled vehicle could travel. It takes me through Da M'Bri and other villages to Xuan Loc, but there's no road at all. I cross rivers with no bridges and the path is only a few feet wide. This is the beauty of travelling alone, I've nobody else to consider and nobody to add fuel to the doubts in my mind as to how foolish I am.

The first obstacle is a policeman who is determined to turn me back to the main road. He conveys that my route is impossible and I must be mad to even try. Yes, I am, but if it comes right it will be worth it to find peace and quiet, enjoy the undisturbed countryside, experience the amazement of the people who live along the way. And of course, the feeling of achievement, tackling a track that Tarzan wouldn't try.

Three more policemen appear. Why are there so many about?

'You must go back. Show us your papers.' I insist I go on. They indicate to each other that I must be barmy and on I go.

Local people wade before me to show me where the river is shallowest and the bike receives terrible punishment. I make it to a surfaced road and a grubby bed in Xuan Loc. After a drink and an egg baguette with some puzzled locals I join the mosquitoes and snooze the night away.

In a few days I will enter Cambodia and with the thought in my mind that it may be a long time before I see the sea, I alter my route to head for Vung Tau and my Australian friends. A violent storm forces me to shelter at a petrol station where market traders are selling goods. The storm lasts over an hour and I receive a lot of attention.

A man speaks to me. 'We are all family here. Many young girls here. You can have boom-boom with any of them'.

He moves among the throng. As he places his hand on each girl's head she produces a smile of agreement.

'This one 50,000 dong. This one 70,000 dong.'

The younger they are the more expensive they are. The 70,000 dong girl can hardly be more than twelve years old. 50,000 dong is £2.50. I ride on.

At Vung Tau friendships are resumed and I set up camp on the beach. At least a dozen people insist I will be robbed and killed by drug addicts. On my travels I have become aware of how the majority of people seem to think a killer lurks behind every leaf or grain of sand. When my well-wishers pull down my tent for the third time I have to give in and take a cheap room. Next door is a nightclub and my boarding house turns out to be the place where the taxi girls bring their clients. The so-called bedrooms are the size of a broom cupboard and the walls are hardboard sheets about seven feet high. Standing on the bed it would be possible to take pictures of the next-door occupants.

Next day at the Ettamogah Pub Allan the proprietor invites me to camp in the back yard. I accept the offer, last night my neighbours were so noisy. I resume friendship with several of the Australian veterans. Many have returned after being divorced or widowed. It's easy to find a beautiful woman half your age seeking kindness, security and the chance to afford nice clothes. The hostesses at Ettamogah don't bother with me, I don't project the right image. I ride a bike and sleep in a tent, so that must mean I have no money.

There are some great characters here, Woofer, Sandy, Ace, Allan, Aitch and Greyhound Jim. The more I stay the more I like it. I've decided to stay three days and then cross the bay to Can Gio to give me a different route to Ho Chi Minh City and avoid 90 miles that I've already ridden.

Not far from Vung Tau is Long Tan, where the Australians notched up a substantial victory against the enemy in the early days of the Vietnam War. In 1966 108 soldiers repelled an attack by 2,500 Viet Cong and forced their retreat. Eighteen Aussies were killed and now veterans return to honour the dead and most likely to ponder over why there are wars in the first place. I am invited to be a member of a hotchpotch maintenance team for the memorial cross set up at Long Tan. I feel privileged to set off with six veterans in a minibus creaking under the weight of gardening equipment, cement, pots of paint, rollers and wire brushes. I bear the proud title of 'Painter of the Cross'.

Things turn awkward at Long Tan, where petty officials demand £5 a head, insist no maintenance can be carried out and limit our viewing to ten minutes. Uproar from the vets and the Battle of Long Tan almost resumes. Allan and his wife calm the situation, beer is passed round and a toast made to the fallen.

CHAPTER 72

Love En Route and a Robbery

With children shouting, 'Goodbye, Ong Noi,' (grandfather) I set off for Ben Da port to embark on the boat to Can Gio. The vessel is rusted rotten and crumbling and with no room at the jetty it is tied four boats out. These boats form the stepping stones and a board only twelve inches wide rises steeply to the first one. There's no way I can load the bike and equipment myself. A rather nasty looking brute takes charge of my vehicle and I lug my bags after him. We jump across a six foot gap to the packed transport. I give Mr Brute a five dollar tip, a day's wages.

'More tip,' he demands. I refuse.

He speaks to his fellow countrymen and they all laugh. In the middle of the bay Brute holds my bike over the side and with encouragement from the assembly threatens to drop it into the sea.

'More tip,' he again demands. I give him ten dollars. He puts the boat back on deck. The people groan with disappointment.

I disembark in an area of mangrove preservation where the mighty Mekong River enters the sea, acres of trees with spiders' legs. It is blistering hot, the traffic is nil, a very impoverished area, where I present a rare sight to the adults and children lining the road. A welcome shout from several teenagers means I will bed down here. There's no objection, they point out a hammock. Mother returns home, my heart skips a beat, she is sweetness itself. At forty-seven and mother of seven grown-up children, herself a widow for three years, Dung has a body that a childless twenty year old would envy. (It takes me a few hours to obtain this information.)

Nobody can speak English. Dung and I sit together and try so hard but it's hopeless. She is the right sort of woman, her loveliness shines from within. Steady, Bob, you're getting hooked.

In the village square a large screen has been set up for a film show. Two of Dung's friends, also widows, turn up and give her a few knowing nudges. She takes my arm and we stroll into the square to watch the film, but I don't understand a word and after half an hour she shows me round the ramshackle town instead. At the café we sit for several hours and only our eyes can understand our unspoken words.

It's dark now and I climb into the hammock. Maybe ten minutes pass and a hand touches my shoulder. I open my eyes and follow where she leads.

A few pleasant days. It's hopeless, we have no communication at all, but she's going to be hard to leave. I kiss the face framed in my hands, her forehead, her eyes, her nose. Be firm, Bob, the world is out there to see. A tear traces its way down my face and ends saltily in my mouth. I ride out of her life.

A major problem. Somewhere along the road today my tent has been stolen. It was in a bag strapped to my rear carrier, the straps have been cut through and now I'm tentless. I have ridden among the seething masses of Ho Chi Minh City motorcycles, they come from all directions. A rider has to swivel his eyes constantly, but I can't look behind. It would be easy for a pillion passenger to help himself; he probably didn't even know what he was stealing.

I swear long and loud, but remain collected, no point in getting rattled. I manage to purchase a waterproof sheet to make a rough shelter. I also buy a machete in order to cut a few branches as support. At the moment I am unaware that I will later use this tool to defend myself.

For now, with two more days left on my Vietnam visa I take a room in a smart hotel at Cu Chi.

Getting cosy with Dung

CHAPTER 73

In Cambodia

I sit and take in the scene from the pavement café of the Capital Hotel in Phnom Penh, Cambodia. My own hotel room is in the cheaper Hello Hotel along the street. Lonely Planet seekers from all over the world, I sit alone, listen and watch.

Americans over fifty and overweight dominate the café. They tie what little hair they have into a ponytail and most wear rings made from dollar notes on every finger. They make the rings by intricately folding the note so that the face of the ring shows its value, from one dollar upwards. The young waitresses give them a lot of attention and every now and then one of these overpaid and overfed Americans throws a ring across the restaurant. The girls squeal and fight to grab the prize, squealing more loudly depending on the value. It's a shocking display to poor people of these yobs' wealth.

So many beggars with missing limbs. I have been warned not to step off the road even to take a leak, because of unexploded mines. A seven-year old lad with half his leg blown away has latched onto me. He eats the bones from my plate, crunching and swallowing them like a dog while at the next table Mr America has just ordered his third meal. Another limbless lad asks for my apple core and I give both lads something to eat.

In a loud voice Fat Slob lets us all know his opinion. 'I never give them anything. They're lazy people who cut off their own limbs to make it easier to beg.'

I don't want to share space with people like this and I move on past beggars scrabbling along the pavement with flip-flops on their hands. Perhaps to emphasise that they have no feet.

It has taken me only one and a half days to reach Phnom Penh. The road was badly cratered at first, and motor vehicles travelled no faster than me. Chestnut brown naked children from stilted houses at Kampong Trabek gave me a great welcome. I answered their hello shouts in the hope of finding a sleeping space, but no luck. The family was good though and the son jumped on his bike to lead me to the school, where five different height desks pulled together made me a lumpy sleeping platform.

Next day is Christmas Eve and I share a table with Louise, a young Irish girl seeing some of the world before becoming an army officer, a good companion. Many Buddhist monks are about today collecting the expected food donation. I watch a woman placing food in the monk's container then raising her hands above her head in sufferance to a seventeen-year old boy wrapped in a blanket.

It's a good day on a good road leading to Siem Reap. Quiet, nothing like the attention received in Vietnam. At a meal stop I see the shelves behind the counter are stocked with jars containing assorted snakes. I settle for some rice.

Sim, who speaks a little English, befriends me at Kampong Thom. I am invited to sleep at her brother-in-law the schoolteacher's house. He brings his eight-year old daughter to see a white man for the first time. I show her my brown legs finish at white feet. Sim invites me to her house, apologising for 'no electric', and she and her husband show me their wedding album. Their four-month old baby is asleep in a hammock and her husband has no work. Eyes shining Sim tells me, 'I am no longer Hindu, I am Christian and God will find me a good job.' I think it best not to mention that there are millions of starving Christians around the world and God hasn't started his job creation scheme yet.

Boxing Day and I turn in at a guesthouse in Stoung. It's only three in the afternoon, but the journey has been difficult and my hands and wrists are sprained from constant jarring on the moon surface road, horrendous cratered sand with holes a car could fall into so its roof was flush with the surface. The food is very poor – soups, banana fritters, shredded cabbage, tiny scraps of meat. Still sixty-five miles to Siem Reap, it will take a full day if the road continues like this. A young man weeps at the side of the road, his shoulders heave as he sobs. He manages to tell me that his wife has sold their baby to people from Malaysia. I leave him with his grief, nothing else I can do.

Further on a crowd struggles to drag a water buffalo out of a hole it fell in during the night. The poor beast's heart has failed as it fought to free itself. I join twenty people pulling on ropes and levering with lengths of wood to free the carcase. A pause for breath when it finally lies on the road and then the body is butchered.

The road is bad but I have arrived at Siem Reap with one stop to swallow a meal of stuff that's better thrown at weddings. I book in at the Family Guesthouse for a three night stop to enable me to see a wonder of the world, Cambodia's main attraction that tourists visit in their thousands, the Angkor Wat. Reluctantly I pay £15 for a day ticket and marvel with the rest.

At resorts where tourists gather and Americans are forever flaunting their wealth, throwing dollar bills around, prices multiply as you speak. I am paying three dollars a night for a clean room while at the Grand Hotel down the road package tour Americans pay nearly two thousand for their suite. I leave Family Hotel with many handshakes, write a few lines and sign my name for Sinbad. 'I will keep this note all my life,' he says. 'Never did I think I would meet such an important person.'

There is much concern for my safety. 'You are an old man. You must stop cycling, your heart will fail.'

I am riding towards Thailand. Yes, one day my heart may fail, but better it fails on a bike than in front of the television.

Main road in Cambodia

CHAPTER 74

In Thailand

I take my place in the line of mostly Cambodians anxious to get into Thailand. As we shuffle forward I watch visa-seekers placing money on the desk. The surly official slides open his desk drawer, scoops the money in, stamps the passport and attends to the next.

Now I'm the next. If there's a charge I pay the charge, but I won't hand over extra money for a visa I'm entitled to. The official opens my document, finds it empty, snarls as he throws my passport to the other side of the room and tells me to get out of the way. I stand to one side while he deals with another three or four people, then he calls me back to the desk. He has to walk across the room to retrieve my passport and he stamps it with considerable force.

Stepping into Thailand is an experience in itself after spending time in countries like Vietnam and Cambodia. I am prepared for the experience as I've been here before. It's a much more modern country; there is poverty, but nothing as bad as I've seen elsewhere. I'm glad of the superb tarmac roads and the availability of everything I need. Within a short time I have a sought after piece of equipment, a tent, not a particularly good one, but it will suffice.

In the wet I look for a hotel, impossible to read the Thai alphabet signs. I can't determine which premises provide accommodation as the Thais relent only at resorts and erect a sign in English. Funny that in Cambodia there are English signs even out in the sticks.

I convey to a young woman that I need to sleep and she leads me to what turns out to be a love hotel, bring your own woman. I enter through a carport with a curtain across the entrance so that the car can be immediately concealed. Edge to edge mirrors cover the ceiling and the walls of the room, carpets, curtains, bedcovers and towels are patterned with hearts, packets of contraceptives in profusion and half a dozen pornographic videos. This must be the first time the room has been occupied by one person.

I have bought a poor map to replace the one that disappeared while I was mending a puncture in the last few hundred yards of Cambodia. I had found a deserted spot in a lorry park, but it wasn't deserted for long. Have these people never seen somebody repairing a bike? Everybody wants to pump the tyre up, inspect my tools, collect a souvenir. Result? Map missing.

Tomorrow is New Year's Day and I'm heading for the coast to pitch camp by the sea and be alone in my private space.

I meet up with Dutch cyclists Helga and Philippe who are nervous about entering Cambodia. I reassure them and they draw some money for me from the newfangled money machine that I gave up on fifteen minutes before. ATMs, computers, cell phones… I don't belong in today's world.

Riding on smooth roads the blazing heat sends me almost to sleep. I can't remember falling asleep on a bike before. At Soi Dao a police station offers tourist advice and a policeman considers he has a VIP to deal with. With a police escort I find myself at Khau Soi Dao Wildlife Sanctuary, joining Thai families who have escaped the cities for the weekend.

'Put your tent close to ours,' they advise, 'because a tiger prowled the camp this morning on the lookout for scraps.'

As the year ends I sit in the dark with these families, campfires, torches and candles casting shadows. No drinking, no need for noise, just enjoyment of nature.

CHAPTER 75

The Real Thailand

In my new tent I sleep well, I always sleep well for free. Dawn brings the jungle chorus greeting the day with shrieks, grunts and roars of assorted animals.

I head for the coast on this first day of the New Year, trying out the secondary roads. My map doesn't even show them and I ride in a circle that brings me back where I started. No matter, the scenery is good and I'm in no hurry. The countryside is much better than the flat, waterlogged ground I travelled on in the last two countries, although no doubt there was beauty I didn't see.

Standing on the river bridge in Chanthaburi I am captivated by the old teak houses in the Chinese quarter. I walk the narrow riverside street with ancient wooden houses and shops that have never changed. This is where I'll sleep tonight. I get a room right at the river's edge for £1.60 and pay the same for one beer (they will only sell me one). I walk to the city centre, but quickly turn back to escape the traffic noise. The shabby café opposite my hotel makes me welcome and charges me half the price of my room for a beer. The cook is a wizard with her different food offerings. She is twenty-nine with two children and no husband. 'She likes you, she wants to know if you are one,' says the boss.

The ferry service to Ko Chang (Elephant Island) has only been operating for a year, I'm told. It is a resort well served by holidaymakers, but prices are on par with England. I pitch my tent on White Sands Beach and bring a storm of protest from Thais all demanding money. At first I ignore them, but it will not be wise to leave my equipment when I go to eat. I know that on a campsite they charge £4 and I have just spoken to an Englishman paying £2 here. Okay, £2 is the price except 'No! You have supplied him with a tent and I have my own.'

Mr Rip-off: '£1.60.'

'I'll give you £1,' I respond. Deal done.

I make some good friends here and word goes round that the man who rides the world is in town. Ko Chang is a gem of an island, absolutely beautiful sands, warm sea, paradise. But the lovely place is spoilt by constant raising of prices and it will get worse because the government has declared it wants to turn Ko Chang into another Phuket. The place will finish up too pricey for backpackers. I thought I had made friends at the bakery where I breakfast every day and slip in often for coffee and ice cream. Breakfast of three doughnuts and a coffee is usually 80p but I'm leaving today and they can see from my loaded bike it's my last visit, they charge me £2.

Back on the road at Laem Ngop the ride is good until a fragment of glass pierces my tyre. I need shade to sort it out so I push the bike to a house come eating-place. Riding creates a breeze that makes the heat bearable, but to walk, stand still or crouch to work on something is impossible. I'd best buy something as I'm using their forecourt, so I purchase an unwanted beer.

The Thai woman who serves me greets me in a similar fashion to the way people reacted at the end of World War Two. Then she brings herself a glass for the beer I don't want and sits so close to me that we are nearly in the same pair of knickers. All I want to do is get back on the road, but she clings to me like a leech, waiting on me hand and foot, pumping up my tyre, wiping the sweat from my brow, occasionally putting her hand between my legs and applying a squeeze. All her family are present, but unconcerned. 'You stay here,' she invites. 'You one. Me one. We two.' She curses me as I ride away.

Back at Chantra Hotel in Chanthaburi on that little old road by the river, resuming old friendships with shopkeepers who charge the right price, it's better than ever. What an amazing way I have chosen to see the world, tough, sometimes boring, exciting, at times dangerous, mainly a rewarding way.

Today I am in the real Thailand. I have followed a road for seventy miles that has taken me away from the big highway, away from the seen-it-all-before people who live on the main roads. Pitching Thrifty Two on a concrete slab in a wat (temple) I join the orange clad brigade for coffee. Thailand is the easiest country to doss down in, not only in the wats, but the salas (roadside shelters) and the areas in villages where they burn bodies, which all have benches under cover and toilet facilities.

The monks scoff at my wearing shoes and demonstrate how they feel no pain by grinding their feet on sharp stones.

Sitting at a café outside the wat I am surprised when a man from the temple buys four bottles of white whisky, the most popular drink for Thais at less than £1 a bottle, roughly the same as a bottle of beer except they can't get drunk on one bottle of beer.

When I return to my quarters as darkness falls there's no chance of sleep because the monks and some locals talk louder and louder as the drink takes effect. Cockerels crow all night and numerous dogs bark and fight. The whisky drinkers unzip the tent and insist I drink with them. When I refuse they throw a few insults at me. I spend a restless night with gongs and chanting added to the rest of the noise.

Finally it's light enough to pack up and that's when I can't find my shoes. I placed them outside my tent and they're gone. Now let me make it clear that no tramp would wear those shoes, they've pushed pedals for probably 2,000 miles, paddled through rivers and been immersed in mud day after day. That's why they have to be left outside my sleeping area. One of last night's jokers probably stole them. I complain to the head monk and he talks to the amused brothers. A baby monk is sent off and returns with a pair of Adidas trainers, so I'm soon on the road again.

The girls came on strong before, but with my designer label shoes I'll be swamped.

CHAPTER 76

Smiles and a Punch

Riding again this delightful country road with the heat dictating when I need to stop I have taken a side road to Nadi and pitched tent outside a police station. I love the laid-back way of life in this country, no sooner have they given me the nod to camp than they show me the showers. I imagine the response from a police station in England, but when I think about it, why shouldn't a tax-paying citizen be allowed to use the police station facilities?

I am in the area where the badly damaged vehicles are kept. From the state of them I reckon many people must have met their deaths. A coach in particular with its front and side caved in makes me shudder.

Taking Highway 304 I rely on my stops to provide interest for the day and it works out well. After a pause to make porridge I respond to shouts from the highway police and they serve me coffee. Up to now the Thai police have been very helpful. I leave them and hit some serious uphill stuff. It's rideable and I am encouraged by the thumbs-up signs from the drivers of heavy downhill lorries that crawl with safety in mind. But near the top is the aftermath of a truck that has crashed through the barrier on a bend and plunged over with its load of tree trunks scattered far and wide, another death, vehicle for the police compound.

The useless map shows almost nothing, few roads and no heights. After mountainous terrain the road levels out and a long downward spin puts me on the flat again. I stop for ice cream and get a lot of attention from three female shopkeepers. (I knew these Adidas trainers would pull the birds.) Two of them are single and they make sure I know they want a husband, forty year-old Susie is the attractive one.

'Where you sleep?' she asks. I point at the shop floor.

'Yes, here you sleep can.'

Riding on I wonder why when I meet a nice woman I get cold feet. Six years ago when my wife died I was affected by the panic reaction that occurs with many when they lose a long-term partner. I attended singles clubs for two years, but modern Western women aren't my type. I'm the age group where women waited on men, that's long changed, but my opinion hasn't. I once passed through an airport where the baby-changing facilities were in the MEN'S toilets. What's the world coming to? Although I met some nice women in those lonely hearts clubs most were painted ladies in posh frocks. I didn't supply the right image, for a start they didn't like me turning up at their house on a bike, didn't look good to the neighbours. Then their idea of a date was dinner in a swanky restaurant and mine was riding out twenty-five miles into the countryside for a pub lunch and a ramble across fields for ten miles or so. They thought I was mad.

A sign at a crossroads in Nakhon Ratchasima points to a hotel. They want £11 a night so I ride back to the crossroads and occupy one of the empty shacks among the many food outlets. In the nearest café within minutes it's Mister Bob this and Mister Bob that.

'Can we put ice in your drink, Mister Bob? Will you have these candles for your tent, Mister Bob? Shall I get you some chicken, Mister Bob? Take your shoes off and wear my flip-flops, Mister Bob.'

Somebody takes away my shoes to wash; the laces are removed and washed as well. As I read my book a woman sits beside me and places her finger on the page I'm reading to stop the wind interfering and at my nod she turns the pages as required. A local man tells me he is sixty-eight years old. He was born in 2476 and now it's 2544 in Thailand. My word, it only seems five minutes since the Millennium. I didn't realise the difference in years, I've been thinking they must have an amazing way of keeping food fresh because I've been buying packs that say 'Best before 2544'.

A policeman with his teacher wife and baby turn up, her sister owns the café. They speak enough English to hold a conversation. The teacher is determined to make sure I'm looked after, which includes attempts for me to take her sister on board. It's turned into a great day, I'm the centre of attention (I'm getting very vain), food is constantly placed in front of me, and three women are smiling me to death.

Breakfast finished and I'm off. Leaving good folk behind emotion wells and I stem a tear. I join a nasty main road. The standard of driving here is shocking; few have any licence or insurance. Driving is on the left, but many please themselves what side they drive on and near collisions occur regularly as vehicles pull out of side roads without a pause. A motorcycle carrying two youths speeds out of a narrow lane and I don't know how I manage to avoid it. They stop a hundred yards on to speak to some others in their age group, so I stop and give them the lash of my tongue. They understand not a word, but it's obvious they are being told off. Their friends laugh at them and they've lost face. I proceed and half a mile further on the lads draw alongside me, the pillion passenger punches me hard in the back and with a twist on the throttle they're away. I crash to the ground with the breath knocked out of me and it's a few minutes before I get to my feet. I sit at the roadside gathering myself together. Injuries amount to a few cuts and abrasions, the bike's survived. The show must go on.

CHAPTER 77

Village Life

Most people have been great and I've had marvellous experiences, but I've been robbed and attacked, always by more than one man. I promise myself that if I get in a one to one situation the best method of defence will be attack. With this resolve I proceed happily on my way.

I've got used to being a figure of fun, amused people thinking I'm some cranky old foreigner riding three or four miles on his bike. When I prove with my newspaper clippings the distances I've ridden a shout goes through the village and respect is shown.

Back on cycling roads and collecting some laughs along the way, the day rolls on. However, I'm suffering discomfort in the crotch area from riding long distances in unbearable heat. The constant chafing takes its toll and my inner thighs are on fire. I need a few days rest but I'm a long way from a resort and the map doesn't show any lakes. A python killed by a vehicle lies on the road. Seven feet long and thick as my arm, it's a fearsome creature even in death and it gives me food for thought when I make camp.

Roadside stalls sell assorted clothing and I buy a shirt. Scorning the cheap shirts on offer (after all, a man with Adidas trainers has an image to keep up) I settle on a neat black number that sets me back £1.25. Inwardly I wince, but that's the sort of price you must pay to impress. A haircut costs me 40p, not being able to speak the language I can't ask for pensioner's rate. I approach what I hope is a town, Thep Thi, but it's just a collection of shacks with a dirt road that at last is being laid with cobblestones. No rooms anywhere so I set up quarters in the wat. The bathroom is primitive, but welcome and I take full advantage of the drum of water and the baling saucepan. Scooping pans of cold water over my body has become an addiction.

I stroll into the village in search of sustenance. The road workers have finished the day's toil and gone home. The villagers with all manner of carts are busy taking up the freshly laid cobblestones and wheeling them away for their own use. Tomorrow there'll be a vacancy for a night watchman. I sit down with five women more interested in whisky than cobblestones. They had shouted hello as I passed by, but they're so drunk I find a Mom and Pop place over the road. One of the drunks follows me and sits as close to me as my shirt.

'You buy me whisky,' she pleads. I buy her a half bottle for 68p. 'I live close. You sleep in my house.'

I pick up my bits and pieces and move to another table. When some men suggest phoning the TV station I decline because although I know the value of coverage I don't fancy sitting round waiting. I return to Mom and Pop's for breakfast, boil myself two eggs and make coffee to my liking in their kitchen area, never any hassle.

Another good cycling day: The road twists and turns, rises and descends as it searches for a route to avoid the highest points. I ride between wooded hillsides and look down on fertile valleys. This is my kind of cycling, the hills not too steep and the breeze downhill a bonus. I can stand up and pedal and downhill there's no leg movement. Non-cyclists think flat country is ideal, but the opposite is true. Flat country means you are always sitting on the saddle and your legs are constantly rubbing against it, plus flat country is boring and on windy days it's hard to ride with nothing to break the wind.

The heat today has been intense. I find a quiet lunchtime spot and friendship is soon established. The young lady here spends a long time writing the menu in indecipherable Thai. I borrow her chalk and add 'Roast lamb, new potatoes, baby carrots, Yorkshire pudding, mint sauce and gravy'. Some hopes.

I leave with a bunch of bananas that would feed King Kong for a year.

CHAPTER 78

Stop Me and Buy One

Doing some necessary laundry in my hotel bathroom at Wichian Buri I take a brave quick look in the mirror. Next time I must do this with my eyes shut.

I ride into town on my unloaded bike. I've made the right decision to stop early because the heat is incredible. I am attracting great amusement, an old foreign man on a bicycle. Crowds gather to laugh at me and I can only join in the laughter, but once I manage to convey what I have achieved the derision turns to handshakes and I'm no longer a silly old fool, except when I look in the mirror. I stop in the market to buy a takeaway chicken that I intend eating in a shop come café I have spotted. The lady is not at all concerned I have my own food, she takes it from me and comes back with it cut into bite size pieces on a plate of free salad.

I've taken my own food into restaurants many times in Thailand and had it cooked for a few baht. But I sat in a pub in England nibbling a few biscuits and the landlord told me in strong language, 'I sell food. You can't eat your own food here.'

'You sell cigarettes, but customers still bring their own,' I replied. Somewhat deflated he left this old man alone.

Beer Chang (Elephant beer) is the brew I've been drinking. Perhaps that's why we say a man is elephant's trunk when he's drunk. A large bottle is 35 baht (46p) and three are 100 baht, but at resorts one bottle costs 100 baht upwards. A meal I am served all the time is Khao Phat (pronounced cow pat) a dish of fried rice that tastes how I imagine a cow pat would. At Phetchabun having covered 72 miles I buy two charcoal grilled fish and sit in a café to eat them. As before, my food is put on a plate and I am supplied with cutlery and several sauces. I continue my journey on the main road to Lom Sak, then follow some back roads that are bewildering, but worthwhile as they travel through unspoilt villages. I find a beautifully laid out garden where the boss and a group of artists think I'm very important and take many photographs of me.

The uphill now becomes serious, mile after mile after mile too steep to ride, and I'm a pathetic figure dragging the bike in the blazing sun being ridiculed by villagers and road workers who shout out 'Farang' – the name they call all Westerners. A mirage approaches me, it's not a mirage, it's a Mr Whippy stop me and buy one. Somewhat refreshed I struggle on and a pickup truck gives me a much needed lift as the road spirals on and on. The driver is amply rewarded when we reach the destination I've been striving for, Phu Hin Rong Kla National Park. Here I encounter another example of the gold fever gripping Thailand, as Farangs are charged ten times the entrance fee of locals. This applies to all attractions.

The park is good and I soon make friends with Natalie and Adam from London and a couple from Holland, Janet and Martin. Food as usual is rubbish, rice, noodles and terrible chicken, little more than grilled bones. A Thai army major asks me to come to Bangkok, informing me that he trains the army cycling team and wants to introduce me, but Bangkok holds no attraction for me.

There must be some good trekking here, but I only take part in one that leads me to the old Communist headquarters built in 1975. The caves here were used as air raid shelters. The highest point is Flag Pole Cliff where the communists raised the hammer and sickle flag each time they scored a victory over government troops. I chat to a group of Thais under the leadership of an English doctor, who work for Norwegian Care for Landmine Victims.

I am cycling back to the National Park when the ferocious barking of three dogs makes me investigate what the commotion is. They have treed a cat, which is quite safe on a branch. A man with a long bamboo pole forces the cat off the branch and it lands in the middle of the dogs, where it is ripped to pieces in minutes. The guy thinks it's the funniest thing he's ever seen. How I wish I hadn't stopped.

My bike is chained to a tree and as I prepare to leave I find I've lost the key. Out comes my machete, the chain is chopped through and I'm on my way. This machete nestles on my rear carrier under the roll of my new tent, the handle protruding like a sword from a scabbard. It can be drawn out quickly though I can't see there will be any need for that.

Little did I know...

CHAPTER 79

The Drunk on the Floor

How pleased I am that the road runs downhill for twenty miles to Nakhon Thai and then continues mostly level. I am well received at Wat Thong Saen Khan and I seem to be getting on well with the couple at the café-shop across the road. They show me their wedding and baby pictures until it's time to pay, then they try to charge me double. I deduct 25% from the rip-off price.

With monk provided coffee inside me, I set off again next morning on superb surfaced roads with the mountains keeping a respectable distance. At a large restaurant near Uttaradit I point out what I want from the good selection of food on display, they still bring me Khoa Phat. Among the photographs of celebrities who have dined here, TV stars, singers, sportsmen, my photograph now adorns the wall. Another wat provides shelter where an all-purpose market with deafening music occupies the grounds. At early evening when the traders have all gone, a monk with a catapult chases off the dogs. He's a crack shot, peace reigns, no gongs, no chanting.

I set off at 7.30 in the morning without coffee or food, expecting some nearby food outlet. Thirty-eight miles and three hours later I'm starving. A café provides four cups of hot black coffee and a meal without rice and I'm ready for action again.

With my groin area feeling very sore I decide to stop a spell at Lampang. I pause outside a shabby café where a man calls out, 'I buy you beer.' I keep moving, my current priority is to buy a bike lock, for which two sweet girls give me a discount. The voice calls out again, ' I buy you beer. I have won the lottery.' I sit with the excited Sirhat who tells everybody passing he has won the lottery. Am I sitting with a millionaire? Still very pleased he reveals he has won £50.

Bedded down at Tip In Guest House for £2.50 a night I review the day. It's been a good one, ending with grilled snapper fish in the Riverside Restaurant. After two nights in Lampang it's sixty miles to Chiang Mai, Thailand's second biggest city. I'm surprised at how quickly I've got here, considering the roads are far from flat and the police have ordered me to stop twice. All traffic has to halt to allow a smooth journey for the King's sister.

Chiang Mai throbs with tourist bars. Streets and markets are an amazing concoction of goods and food. From hundreds of guesthouses I choose Daret, but I stay only one night because it's so noisy. A crowd of young Australians insist I tag along for the evening, but I manage just half an hour of wall-buckling music in a room like a coal cellar with the lights out, and I'm in bed by eight o'clock. That's eight hours before everybody else, no, not quite correct, with such an availability of women, people are actually in bed at all hours of the day.

I move into Ratchada Home Stay, leaning over a drunk spread-eagled on the floor against the reception desk while the beautiful manageress checks me in. I intend staying several days. Sitting quietly reading a book on my second day I listen to the young guys smooth-talking 43-year old Nong and when she brings my drink over I add my chat line, 'I bet all the men fall in love with you.'

Nong returns to the counter. I look up occasionally and see she is weighing me up. 'Bob, I am forty-three, you are sixty-three, that is just about right. I can take care of you. I am moving you to the room next to mine. I never lock the door'.

It turns out to be quite a cosy arrangement and I get fond of this lovely woman. We go out together several times, stepping over the ever present drunk on the floor. I decide to take things further. 'Are you sure about wanting to get married?'

'Yes, but first I must divorce my husband,' is the bombshell reply.

'Where is your husband?'

'He's the drunk on the floor.'

I check out. There are enough single women without fooling around with a married one. Murders are committed over that behaviour.

Nong with nephew

Chet

CHAPTER 80

Injuries and Idyllic Times Together

I had enjoyed a ride with Chiang Mai Sunday Cycling Club before leaving and I'd met up with fifty-three year old American Robert. He was on the last day of a four-week cycling tour.

'It's been my first ever cycling tour. It's been fantastic,' he declared. 'I can't recall a better time. And now meeting somebody twenty years my senior who looks capable of doing it again has encouraged me.'

I have spent two days of superb cycling with night stops at wats and I'm sitting in a shop bar with my shoulder almost touching the Burmese border. This crossing isn't for tourists and the people can't understand why I'm here.

There's conflict in Burma and border disputes with Thailand. A magazine I read called SS Army News contains stories of massacres, beatings and people being driven from their land. At first I'm not too alarmed when my sleep is disturbed by explosions, must be a firework display, but it continues all night and when I look out of my tent I see no bursts of coloured lights in the sky. I hear gunfire and the scream of shells, an outbreak of machine gun fire and moments later a defiant response. I lie there somewhat unsettled. The battle shifts. Sometimes the shots sound close, at other times some distance away. My new camouflage colour tent doesn't inspire confidence, so I crouch instead under the floor of a stilted building.

Battle sounds continue as daylight dawns. For the villagers it's business as usual, but they scurry about and return home afterwards instead of gathering and gossiping. I ride away through the forest and see units of heavily armed soldiers making their way cautiously through the trees. People tell me the road I'm taking is too dangerous, but like a fool I carry on and curse them for being right.

My useless map informs me it's nine miles to the main road. It turns out to be forty and for twenty of them I drag myself and the bike up practically the steepest gradients I've ever encountered, I'm whacked. When the drop comes it's brakes on full. A snapped cable would mean curtains.

After spending a little time at Nam Nao Caves to admire the stalagthingies I get a room in Fang. I don't realise at first, but it turns out I've done the right thing. At a good restaurant where you cook your own food at the table I join a middle-aged German couple with a young Thai woman.

'They are both my wives', says Karl.

'Yes, he has been with her four years now,' his unruffled German wife confirms.

The Thai girl has just obtained her driving licence. £20 has been handed over to an official for the necessary document, which has been stamped at the police station where a further £10 changed hands, so now she has a driving licence.

Karl breaks off mooning over the maiden for a moment to tell me, 'Tomorrow I am going to show her what the three pedals are for.'

On my way to bed I cross a dark stretch of road not knowing that what happens next will affect the rest of my life. Two paces from the kerb an unlit motorbike travelling fast hits me. It spins me over, I land on the top of my head and go briefly unconscious, lying in an untidy heap on the road. I come round and sit dazed, blood dripping from my head and forming a stream down my leg. The motorbike has gone.

Thais gather on the pavement saying 'Farang! Farang!' They always laugh at any accident or death, they're strange people. A man steps forward, grabs my ankles and pulls me onto the pavement. The motorbike handlebars have ripped a big piece out of my shorts, my underpants and my left buttock; my collarbone is broken again, my ribs must be cracked and my head is split open. With the greatest pain coming from my shoulder and ribs I limp and stagger away wondering if motorbike man got his licence the same way as Karl's Thai girl.

It's a terrible night. I can't move for the pain, my bed looks like a butcher's block, the pillow is a mess of dried blood and my underpants are stuck to my bum with the same liquid. The struggle to lift myself out of bed confirms what I already know, it'll be a while before I can leave. I dress awkwardly, but I can't fasten my shoelaces. I wash some of the matted blood out of my hair, but stop when my head begins to bleed again. I improvise a sling from luggage straps. A pathetic figure goes out to find breakfast on the streets of Fang. Fangs ain't what they used to be.

A lot of Thais enquire about my injuries and they all think it's hilarious. They've reacted the same along the way when I've told them about robberies. They're strange, their funerals are party events that go on for days, nobody the least upset that they've lost a close relation or a dear friend. They line up to have their photograph taken with the corpse in the open coffin.

And this is how Chiamchit comes into my story and eventually causes my life to change.

I limp into her restaurant and one of the girls seeing my appearance brings her to my table. Shocked she becomes my instant nurse. While I have breakfast she washes and dresses my head wound, removes my shirt to apply Tiger Balm to my bruises, and gently massages me. Chit speaks five languages and like all women she is thirty-seven (forty-seven).

I move out of the hotel and intensive nursing begins. All right, I'm not the first to fall in love with this nurse, but some wonderful days follow. Chit drives me out into the country, bringing along her pet python. I'm comfortably daydreaming in the passenger seat when the python slithers over my shoulder and down into the well of the car. I soon get used to it, although sharing a woman's bed with an eight-foot snake is rather odd. I suppose living in a town called Fang a snake is the obvious choice of pet.

Apart from the pain I'm in, I enjoy some idyllic days and nights. Our closeness becomes stronger, although it's hard to make friends with her resentful fifteen-year old son who cries when I put my arm round his mother. In a year or so he'll be putting his arm round a girl and his mother will take second place.

Chiamchit gives regular English lessons to a little class. I take a turn in front of the blackboard and suggest they all say a few words of English. Everybody co-operates except a nine-year old boy. When I insist, he sits up straight and asks, 'Why are you so old?'

Chit lays on a special evening meal of two roast chickens and red wine, and I can see the writing on the wall.

'My man walked out on me when I told him I was pregnant. There's been just the two of us ever since. My son is so precious I can't endanger the love between us,' she tells me tearfully.

I give her my address. 'Send for me if ever circumstance permits.' No harm in dreaming. Fully loaded I leave while Chit is out shopping. As I pass she runs out of a shop calling, 'Bob! Bob!' We stand at the kerbside a few minutes. 'I'm sorry. My son...'

I'm on the move. A broken heart hurts more than a broken collarbone.

I should have rested longer. I can hardly handle the bike. Every movement brings a sharp surge of pain in my ribs and shoulders. It's agony to change gear or pull the brake levers, although thankfully the buttock wound is above the sitting area. I have to walk even the gentle hills.

At Mae Chan I meet up with Jaap Spijkers, a Dutch film star who is also a cyclist. He takes a room in line with a film star's wages at £8.50 while I sleep on the concrete floor of the temple. My attempts to get to my feet in the morning are too pitiful to describe. We decide to ride a couple of days together, most likely Jaap realises the old man needs help. True enough, I can't even pump a tyre up. I slow Jaap down considerably, but he never complains and we enter Mae Sai, the most northerly point of Thailand. I am refused entry to Burma for the second time and even a phone call to the Burmese Embassy produces negative results.

'You couldn't ride across Burma anyway. It's too big,' declare the immigration officials.

I don't bother to tell them that the 25,000 miles I've clocked up would make Burma look like a duck pond.

Jaap and I head for Chiang Khong with a stopover in Chiang Saen, where I splash out and pay for a room. In Chiang Khong I share a room with a guy I met in Chiang Mai, Roy from Narberth in Pembrokeshire, Wales, and Jaap takes accommodation again more in keeping for a screen idol. He has a lot of email to catch up with, then he intends to take a boat on the Mekong River to sail into Laos, but I decline his invitation to join him, I feel too guilty about my slow progress.

Jaap, Dutch film star, crouching to make me look tall

Temple floor, good enough for me

Wat, Ankor

Chiam Chit

Love me, love my python

CHAPTER 81

A Stuck Pig

I make some good friends in Chiang Khong and find my favourite spots, the Chinese bakery, the bike shop and the coffee shop. Then I decide to set off for Hippy Paradise, a town called Pai. It's been well known for years as a hangout for the great unwashed. Some of the hippies have been here since the days of Flower Power. Old men with ponytails and I don't think those are cigarettes they're smoking.
On the way I sleep on the floor at Wat Phaeng, where one monk is in residence with an Australian who has been nursing a broken heart for four years.

If I say it's a hard ride here, then it's a hard ride here. A notice board at the edge of Pai invites those who have made it on a bike to go to the town office. I do so and am presented with a certificate for protecting the environment. My photograph goes on the wall.

Pai is a great spot, full of backpackers but lovely surroundings. I set up camp by the river with the intention of staying three days, and I make friends with Rex and Tip from Singapore, wonderful people and Tip bakes delicious bread. After an enjoyable rest at Pai I am ready to return to Chiang Mai to collect my visa for India. I'm past the collection date, but it will still be there. Spending the night again at Wat Phaeng I slip on a smooth wooden staircase and land heavily on my left side. My almost healed side is flooded with pain. Perhaps I should be in charge of a Zimmer frame not a bike. At the café in the village I admire a boarded-up detached house. The café owner tells me it's for sale at £3,000. A tempting proposition, perhaps I could come back here in the future.

Soon I'm back in the city and in possession of my visa. Tomorrow I begin the trek to Bangkok Airport to board a plane for Bangladesh. I'm disappointed to have been refused admission to Burma, but just today (February 11th 2001) fighting has flared again on the border with seven fatalities. I'm heading south, it's very hot and I finish up at Hot because that's the name of the town. I take refuge in a temple again and the monks look after me well, seeing me off and giving me thirty pence plus bananas.

Early afternoon and a 'hello' call encourages me to stop at a roadside café. The young girl aged fifteen who said hello is Lada, who informs me, 'My papa is English'. Even before she's gone off to fetch him the woman who runs the stall has established that I am single and the usual marriage suggestions are being made. Lada returns with her 36-year-old mother and her three-year-old stepbrother. The boy is named Johnson after the powder sprinkled on his bottom. How close was he to being called Pampers? I take up the offer to stay at their house and I meet 70-year-old Robert, who isn't pleased that his wife Tat is trying her hardest to get a 65-year-old man to marry his stepdaughter.

'Settle down here. I will give you a piece of land. You can build a house. I will give you my daughter,' suggests Tat. I stay two nights and the conversation is similar the whole time, but there's no way I'm taking on a fifteen-year old girl.

Tat admits she was a taxi girl. 'Robert keeps telling me to go out and earn some money to help with the bills,' she says. Robert nods in agreement. He has lived in Thailand fifteen years and speaks not a word of the language. He drinks to excess and spends his life in front of the TV with a wife who speaks a handful of English words. I am invited to see the pigs. In actual fact one is being slaughtered. Vegetarians, skip the next two paragraphs!

Five men grasp the luckless animal, holding feet and ears so it's well and truly hogtied. They lay it still struggling on the table. A man each side holds the pig in a vice-like grip, a flat piece of wood pushed against its belly with maximum strength. A young woman holds a large dish under its neck and a narrow bladed knife thrust low into its throat is twisted repeatedly to improve the blood flow. What else can it do but squeal like a stuck pig?

With almost the total quantity of its blood now in the bowl the pig is thrown on the floor. A club makes its appearance. Two heavy blows to the head and the pig enters pig heaven. The women bring forward the water they've been boiling and the men produce razor sharp machetes. With hot water poured over the pig they scrape away its hair and surface skin to leave a white body. The business of carving up the pig commences while the blood is put into plastic bags and given free to the assembled people for use in cooking.

Things are getting too serious with this family. I have had my photo taken with my arm round Lada. Tat places a coloured cloth bracelet round my wrist.

'That means you are married,' she says. 'Tonight you sleep with my daughter and after that you will not be allowed to leave the village.'

As if to back up her conversation a couple of guys turn up and she starts an earnest conversation with them, nodding many times in my direction. I recollect the stuck pig.

It's too late at night to move off. I enter my bedroom and lock the door. In the morning the two guys are still here. Tat speaks to them, obviously telling them I haven't slept with Lada.

They go away and so do I.

CHAPTER 82

My Machete Proves Useful

I have a room at Sarah's Guesthouse in Sukothai, a backpackers' gathering place with an assortment of young people and where my method of travel puts me in an elevated position. It's good to stay here, but one night is enough and I'm back on the road again. The mountains left behind, the riding is easier but I'm still suffering with my shoulder and ribs.

Another wat becomes my abode, where I am told to erect Thrifty Two in front of a row of golden Buddhas. The monks rouse me at 4.30 so prayers can be said; I don't know why they placed me here. It's too dark to move off, but it's warm. It takes an eternity to get light. I stop to make coffee and porridge at the first roadside shelter and think what a marvellous life a bicycle tramp leads. I love it, the rougher the better.

Close to Khrok Phra I share a room in a temple with two monks and a seven-year old boy, having run the gauntlet of women in Khrok Phra asking, 'Are you one?' You must understand that most of the women are good hardworking women trying to get out of poverty. I have no doubt they would look after a husband 100%. The bar girls on the other hand become streetwise and hardened. I don't condemn them. Their choice is between gruelling work in the rice fields for £2 a day or selling their bodies for ten times as much. They send most of this money home to support their families.

In the temple the two monks drape me in their orange clothing and take my picture. We prepare for sleep and the younger monk indicates that he wants me to sleep on the floor next to him inside a mosquito net. I take up this position with a six foot space between us. The seven-year old boy climbs into a double bed with the older monk. Perhaps he's a Catholic Buddhist.

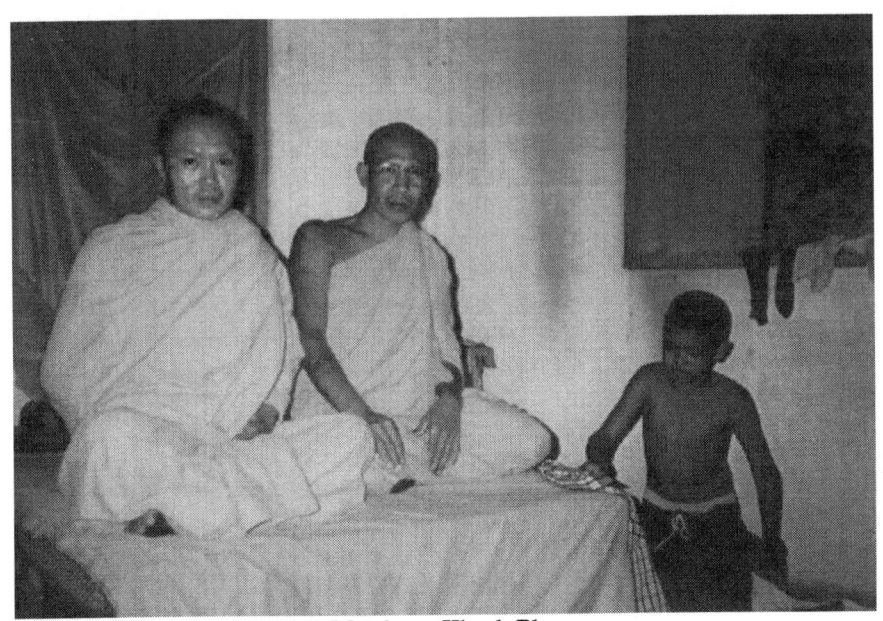

Monks at Khrok Pha

If you can't beat them, join them

Having a lazy breakfast in a café before I leave, I watch two cyclists wheel their machines past me. They see my bike, but after a short glance at me they walk on a short distance before leaning up their bikes and walking back, circling the café until they get back to the front again.

Disbelief in his voice one of them asks, 'Is this your bike?'

I nod to confirm.

'We didn't think…'

'You didn't think a man as old as me would be travelling like this,' I finish the sentence for them.

We are all riding in the same direction so we set off together. 'You young guys will be riding much faster. Go ahead. I don't want to hold you up,' I insist.

'We're having a job keeping up already,' they gasp. And gradually the gap widens and I leave them miles behind, young whippersnappers.

Another day brings a fearsome confrontation. I've ridden hard and long, I'm shattered, my body is crying, 'Enough.' The ever-present problem is the availability of substantial food. I simply can't eat the concoctions placed in front of me. I've seen better stuff squeezed out of dogs.

Eight more miles to Dan Chang, all uphill. I need to rest, but find no suitable camp. I need a wat and while I'm drinking a Fanta some people tell me there's a temple three miles on. They also chatter on trying to explain something to me that I can't understand. I carry on and worn out I reach the elaborate entrance I've been looking for, where I say hello to an ugly huge brute of a man swigging whisky from a large bottle as he leans on the gatepost. He has a dagger tattooed on his neck and a strand of barbed wire tattooed round his shaven head. I keep a healthy distance from him, but he lurches forward and starts kicking my panniers.

With a few pushes on the pedals I'm away. I find myself in a vast sugar cane field. Nobody's about, but a rough dirt track leads onwards. In about half a mile I understand what the people were trying to tell me. There's going to be a wat here, but it's not yet built. Like it or not, whacked or not, I must carry on to Dan Chang.

Pushing my bike I retrace the path. Coming towards me is dagger tattoo man with a male companion. Before they reach me they stop. Dagger man is encouraging the other man to rob me, or worse. The man will have none of it. He throws his arms in the air, violently shakes his head, turns on his heels and speedily departs. Tattoo man closes in. The bike is between us but he towers above me. With banana-sized fingers his right hand grips and digs into the muscles in my already damaged left arm. His left hand holds the neck of the now empty whisky bottle. In a flash I draw the machete from its makeshift scabbard and my arm describes an arc that finishes by chopping at his neck. The viciousness in his eyes turns into unbelievable shock, he lets go of my arm, throws his hand to his neck and seems transfixed. He knows he's hurt. I move away backwards, holding my weapon defensively or threateningly. He starts to run back to the main road. He needs to get the dagger tattoo stitched together.

Exhausted but unconcerned, I reach Dan Chong. It was him or me, it wasn't me.

Too worn out even to appreciate the swaying hips of the waitress I throw myself into a chair at an open-air café, until she utters those three little words that a man longs to hear.

'You want beer?'

CHAPTER 83

Back in Bangkok

Finding a good room is difficult because off the beaten track the hotel and guesthouse signs are rarely in English. Come the morning and after a breakfast of coffee and grapes I move on to a lunch stop at U Thong.

Sitting in the market I spot the stallholder using her cellphone, so it's easy to guess who she's phoning. Before I've even swallowed a few mouthfuls of rice Susie turns up. She's received the news that a Farang is in town. Unusually for a Thai woman she has a substantial upper structure; most of them have breasts like fried eggs. She looks nice, forty years old, and she doesn't beat about the bush. Within minutes she lets me know she wants to marry a Farang. She tells me her circumstances, which include looking after her aged mother and her brother who is brain-damaged from a motorbike accident.

Rice swallowed I roll away, halting near Kanchanaburi where a restaurant owner lets me set up on his car park. In the evening I enjoy a proper meal while sing-a-song girls displaying a lot of flesh entertain the diners. One of these girls brings me a note on which is written, 'I am an air traffic control officer at Bangkok Airport. Thank you for coming to Thailand.' I join him and the three young females who are draped around his table. It's raining heavily outside and the boss man tells me he has a free room for me, so I bring in all my belongings. After a fun evening the girl who brought me the note follows me to my room.

'I am eighteen,' she informs me. She looks it, but I doubt it. I give her a couple of pounds and she goes back to work.

I take a roundabout route so that I can arrive in Bangkok on my flight departure day, and I find myself once again at the bridge over the River Kwai. It's over two years since I last stood on the bridge and after three months of eating rice, I could possibly pass for one of the poor souls who built it.

Headquarters at a wat again with the monks clamouring for photographs. Good humour at breakfast with local people and off I jolly well go, for today I will reach the sea. Blistering hot, but I still reach Samut Songkhram. I appear to be the only visitor at the resort so camping space is no problem. I settle near a posh hotel. It's an upmarket resort and I have a great spot facing the Gulf of Thailand.

I treat myself to an expensive meal in the hotel and I'm surprised to find I'm actually far from being the only visitor. The dining room is full of Hooray Henrys, the sort who don't speak to below stairs people like me. A lah-de-dah English couple are none too pleased when the head waiter asks them to let me share their table. They speak not a single word to me throughout the meal and don't acknowledge my efforts to converse. The man orders a bottle of red wine after much deliberation, but half a bottle remains when they leave. Thanks very much, soon there's none left.

I have an interesting second day strolling round chatting with locals and in the evening I find myself placed on the table with Lord and Lady Muck again. When Lord Muck asks for his bottle of wine the waiter replies, 'You finished it last night, sir.'

Lord Muck speaks to me. 'The thieving bastards! The staff have drunk my wine!'

Well, how's a back street kid supposed to know how the other half lives?

I renew friendship with the couple that run the information centre at Damnoen Saduak floating market. They proudly produce the visitors' book containing my photo and the few words I wrote two and a half years ago.

I'm anxious to see another country. I'm not eating well, the many food outlets offer only cow pats or noodles. On the road today I had stale doughnuts for breakfast, two ice lollies for elevenses, a cow pat for lunch and eight fairy cakes for dinner. A Thai Army colonel invites me to his house, his batman at his beck and call. The colonel tells me that fighting continues at the Burmese border. I recall that when I crossed over to renew my Thai visa I was told to leave the country by five pm. The colonel has to leave but invites me to stay on as long as I like, his batman will look after me. I refuse politely and enter the death trap road system in Bangkok. I must be the only person mad enough to ride a bike on the approach roads to the airport, and several times I think I'm not going to make it.

The airport is thronged with hundreds of travellers, mostly Asian. I note the many restaurants with satisfaction, McDonalds, KFC, Pizza Hut, and Dunkin Donuts, none of them selling rice. I have a long wait for my flight to Bangladesh and I manage a few hours' sleep on the floor.

CHAPTER 84

Welcome to Bangladesh

Lift off to Bangladesh. My bike was taken care of perfectly at Bangkok but at the arrival airport the treatment of luggage is criminal. The handlers seem intent on causing as much damage as possible, throwing all the packages from a great height or any distance, especially those marked fragile. A clear window at the start of the carousel allows a full view of the baggage handlers' couldn't-care-less attitude. They ask for money all the time, just for handing over a case. I fear for the bicycle.

An immigration officer tries to convince me he's helping me through arrivals, all the time muttering, 'Money you give.' He's done nothing, but I give him a dollar to shut him up. With a sigh of relief I collect my undamaged chariot. My luggage is only slightly damaged. I have to pay a staggering £40 for a visa, but at least I didn't have to get it in advance.

Emerging from the airport I encounter hundreds and hundreds of people standing behind a barrier awaiting arrivals, or maybe the Beatles. I throw my arms in the air and shout, 'Here I am!' The multitude bursts into cheers and welcomes me to Bangladesh. Having no reason to stay in Dhaka I set off in search of new experiences. Only yards from the airport poor souls are living on rubbish tips and constantly raking them for anything useful.

Abdul comes alongside, cyclist and soldier. He proves useful as a guide and a pacemaker. Back at the barracks I'm allowed in only because Abdul's father is Commanding Officer. He introduces me to the army cycling team and they all cringe at the weight of my transport. I'm not allowed to sleep at the barracks and although Abdul insists I'll reach the next town before nightfall I know I won't.

I am getting a good response from the people and I approach a collection of houses in a forest clearing. At first they're puzzled, but soon they're all smiles.

'Follow us,' and within a few hundred yards is a timber house, their forest rest home. 'You can stay here,' are their welcome words. So on my very first night I'm being treated with great kindness. When I describe my travels to these eager to listen people one asks me, 'But what benefit does this bring?'

'People like you are the benefit,' I reply.

An ever-growing audience of men watches me swallow my soup and coffee before I enter my tent (the bed in the cabin is more than rough). I fall asleep, but at midnight two men disturb me. One is the officer in charge of Chandra Sal Forest and the other is Chief Forest Ranger.

'We come to speak to you, but you are sleeping,' they complain. Friendships are formed and the question I am so often asked is prominent again. 'Why do you cycle the world?'

'Because it's an achievement and the best way to meet people,' I explain.

'How can you meet people if you are asleep?' they ask.

I decide not to point out that it's one in the morning.

Finally I sleep, then next morning I accept last night's invitation to breakfast with the forestry men. I tell them how in less than one day I have been swamped with friendship.

'We don't think a Bangladeshi in England would get such a response,' they say quite rightly.

According to Abdul the road I'm riding is the best surfaced in Bangladesh. I don't want to try the others. Mixing with kamikaze road users and hardly able to see for the choking dust I stop at Mirzapur and I'm immediately invited to the home of politician Akram Hussain. The family gives me tea and a permanent invitation to be their house guest at any time.

Dust-covered I call a halt at Tangail. Curious villagers surround me. Student Reza takes charge and finds me a hotel for £1. I've already turned down one for 60p. If I carry on this extravagant way I'll get to be a red wine drinker. Not that there's any chance of a drink in Bangladesh, yes, I was aware beforehand. People pack the street to watch me having a haircut. Westerners are probably only seen at the coast, although I've never heard of anybody coming to Bangladesh for a holiday. Reza takes me to a café where curtains conceal several tables. These are the tables set aside for women, since to eat they must take off their face covering and no man but their husband must see their face. What a pity so many beautiful faces are unadmired for the majority of the time.

News comes that an Englishman has been captured and is being held in the mountains near Burma.

Bangladesh-India border

Akram Hussein and family

CHAPTER 85

Forrest Gump and his Followers

Reza the student turns up and I join his family for breakfast. He tells me in his best English that his father is a solicitor and his mother is a woman. I presume he means a housewife. They update me on the hostage situation, hill tribesmen are holding three men. Reza guides me out of Tangail with its hordes of pedal rickshaws. Bangladesh has thousands of these, illustrating how flat the country is. At least they are quieter than motorbikes.

After twelve miles a huge bridge halts my progress. It's among the top twenty largest bridges in the world. 'You can't ride over the bridge. But I will help you,' says a police officer. He stops what seems to be an empty lorry. The rather nervous driver leaves his cab, climbs into the back and lifts my bike up after him. I scramble up to find twenty men lying flat to keep well below the sides. The driver puts his finger to his lips and I stay silent. We drive away and I get pulled down amongst this collection of human derelicts. At the entry checkpoint nobody stops the truck and nobody checks the guard post as we exit. Several miles clear I wave goodbye to the driver. The men still stay out of sight. Was it a rehearsal for an illegal immigrant run?

The squalor and the poverty would be unbelievable if I hadn't seen it all before. How women use their hands to form blocks of manure to use as fuel. How they constantly collect dry leaves and forage for branches, again for fuel. How they wash clothes, cattle, children and themselves in filthy pools and rivers.

It's impossible to stop even for ten minutes, because when I stop everybody stops. They stand as close as they can and watch every movement I make. A shout goes out when I produce my camera (a little disposable one that I use in case of theft) and cyclists, pedestrians and rickshaw operators turn back if they have passed, all eager to have their photograph taken. The subject I am interested in photographing is obscured.

The menu at Bagra Hotel is impressive and so it should be at £5 a night. Staff place the menu in my hands and afterwards inform me that nothing on it is actually available. I can't recognise or eat the rubbish they put in front of me.

I'm out of there and rolling along, although I need nerves of steel to cope with the manic driving. Welcome calls ring out all day and throngs of locals on battered bikes tag along. They argue whose turn it is to ride alongside me. Dare I say the last twinge of pain in my shoulder and ribs has gone? What a great feeling to stretch, swing my arms above my head, twist my body, fasten my shoelaces, cough, sneeze, breathe deeply, laugh and fart without a stab of pain.

The pack behind me gets bigger. Forrest Gump walking across America with his band of followers had nothing on this. I'm going to lose them, I pile on the speed and I'm sure I'll burn them off. We fly down a country road and reach a village. They stop and hand their bikes over to people who haven't got one. I'm racing a fresh pack and I can't win. The practice carries on at village after village. It's one hell of a ride.

At Rangpur Motel I pay £7, but during the day I spend very little. It is whispered to me that I could have a small can of beer brought to my room for £3. I order a large pot of tea.

My mind wanders back to the landmine victims in Cambodia. I remember a ten-year old boy with only one and a half legs. He rode a bike by pushing the pedal between his flip-flop and the sole of his good foot, his flip-flop pulling up the pedal after every downward push. He rode as fast as any of the others who wanted to race me, and he had the biggest smile.

I recall how annoyed I was when my shoes were stolen in Thailand and I'm ashamed how quickly I forgot how many in Cambodia had lost their feet.

At eight in the evening I wander round the hotel. Guests sit in the lounge twiddling their thumbs. It must be a boring life being a Muslim, can't have a drink, can't stand on the corner watching the girls go by. Is it true that at a Muslim striptease the men shout, 'Show us your face'? A Muslim called to me today, 'Pray to your god for me.' Five times a day all his life seemingly have produced nothing so far.

CHAPTER 86

Bangladesh is Part of the World

Every village is a scattering of hovels and every town the same as the last. The eating-houses are filthy corrugated iron shacks, but like it or not this is where I must eat. The choice is rice with several meats and different sorts of sweet things, sounds better than it looks or tastes.

As I ride I marvel at how hard people work. They carry colossal loads on rickshaws and on their heads. They smash millions of defective bricks to be used in making concrete. Time and again I see holes being dug by hand, holes as big as football pitches, yards deep. I imagine they are being formed to help lower the water level on the surface in times of flooding. Practically all the country seems to be flat, the mountainous high ground is along the Burmese border.

At the moment the border is the scene of military activity. Fourteen days ago three men were taken hostage and held in some remote village. The British Prime Minister instructed the SAS to secure the release of what must have been some high-ranking people. The SAS have been successful and I wonder if they would be dispatched to rescue an old man on a bike. I hope I don't have to find out, but I'm confident that if the situation arose the children in the remote village would be clamouring for a balloon and I would be on my way.

At Thakurgaon the hotel is full and I am directed to an imposing building. Was it George Bernard Shaw who said, 'It's the kind of house God would buy if he had enough money?' Two serious men approach me. They don't speak English, so they phone Sir. The conversation goes

Sir: 'Please identify yourself.'

Me: 'I'm an Englishman cycling the world.'

Sir: 'What are you doing in Bangladesh?'

Me: 'Bangladesh is part of the world.'

Sir: Has the government sent you?'

Me: 'I am simply a tourist who needs a room.'

Sir: 'I will give you permission.'

Puzzled by the cross-examination, I take possession of the room. After an excursion into town, where I am delighted to find a cake shop, I return to what I think is a hotel. This isn't the case, it's a government house used by high-ranking officials involved in political business. Sir turns out to be Deputy Commissioner of the District, who directed the relief operation in the devastating floods of 1998 and earned praise from all over the world for his handling of food, fuel and shelter. We spend a good hour together talking about the structure of the family, how Muslim marriages are made and how nothing can break the strength of the family.

And so to bed. Tomorrow I should reach India.

I get rather annoyed at the border. 'This is not an immigration checkpoint. You must go to Burimari,' I am ordered.

I produce the business card given to me by the Deputy Commissioner and the officials are suitably impressed. They still send me away but they speak more politely. I've been checking every day that I could enter India at this spot, but it's not the case. Burimari is 210 miles away, it makes a good ride but the problem is where to sleep. From the attention I am getting from people I can tell camping will be a nightmare. I am steaming along, my legs part of the machine.

I see four people by a river. 'Yes, sleep here,' they indicate.

However, by the time Thrifty is erected a hundred locals have gathered. Traffic on the road has halted, buses are disgorging their passengers, a mass of people scramble to see this strange man. They all press nearer and nearer while I make some coffee and heat a can of stew. These people lead simple lives, without even television, and they are happy I'm here.

Some young women (not entirely covered in garments) make obvious suggestions and then have a fit of giggling. I do my regular balloon act and sing a few silly songs so they can hear a strange voice. I wonder if I crawl into my tent they'll get the idea and go away. Among the mass are mischievous elements who start smacking the tent with sticks, then rocks, then opening the tent flaps and grabbing my ankles. I've got to get out of here, so I drag my gear into the open and refit my wheels (a frame without wheels is a less attractive item to steal).

It's a nightmare getting packed up. Arguments break out around me as the majority who welcome me reprimand the troublemakers. Fist fights break out and spread like wildfire until I'm in the middle of a huge brawl. My bike is loaded. Have I forgotten anything? My supporters clear a path and I'm away. Many shout, 'We're sorry,' and the flirtatious maidens are crying. I stand on the bridge a minute and watch the battle continuing.

Darkness is fast approaching. 'It's going to be a grim night,' I think as I dodge the rickshaws, even in the dark they keep on working without one light between them. My front wheel plunges into a deep hole that I couldn't see. I can't risk damage to my transport, it's madness to continue tonight. I sit on a bench just off the road, 7.30 pm and getting cold. A rickshaw looms up, they can carry up to six passengers. It stops and a semicircle forms in front of me. Another one stops and in no time, even in the dark, I have thirty Bangladeshis standing silently staring.

My bare legs are the give-away, easily spotted in the dark. Fed-up I hit the road again.

'Do you speak English?' says a voice in the dark and Akbar befriends me. 'I am a Christian, not a Muslim. Are you a Christian?' he asks.

I'm ready to admit to being Jack the Ripper. 'I travel the world. I am a missionary.'

Liar! Liar! Pants on fire!

Akbar lets me sleep at his house.

Christian Akbar (in middle)

Akbar's friends wanted balloons

CHAPTER 87

Bangladesh – India – Nepal

I leave Akbar and his three male friends each possessively holding a balloon animal. I am determined to access India today, but following the border soldiers' written instructions I find that few of the towns they mention are on my useless map, not even the border town I'm looking for.

No motor traffic, but I'm riding on roads choked with bicycles and rickshaws. I go eleven hours at high speed with hordes racing after me. At every village a fresh bunch takes over. When I pause for a drink the people insist I meet the headman. I want to move on, but they block the road and like it or not I must sit with the man. An audience gathers round and I can't understand a word. I notice that too many people are fiddling with my bike, so I shoulder my way through the mass to grab my machine. People scatter as I surge forward. I pedal away like mad. I break free, the few chasing me give up now after a short distance. I have covered 120 miles on a lot of loose sand, not even knowing if I am going the right way.

A man on a motorbike gives me hope, yes, I am right for Burimari. The light fades and when I enter Patgram ten miles on its pitch dark. Schoolteacher Matthew steps forward. He takes me to Paradise Hotel. Paradise it ain't, but it is shelter. Half the town followed us as we walked here and they stand outside hoping to catch a glimpse of me. The hotel owner gives this important man a 25% discount and the local political leaders assemble for photos in my disgusting room. I'm starving so I eat a banana and glance round the room for a waste bin for the skin. 'Throw it on the floor,' advises the owner so the banana skin joins the other rubbish already taking root there.

Matthew takes me sightseeing in the town. Every square inch of ground is covered with desperate people. Any motor vehicle can only move a few inches at a time because there are no spaces for the people to move into. In the local hospital we have tea with the doctors and then the sister takes me a tour of the wards. Appalling squalor: no staff, no equipment, groaning patients two to each tumbledown bed, no nothing.

Elevated in the eyes of the townsfolk by claiming me as his friend Matthew insists on seeing me off at the border. He gets a lift and is waiting for me when I arrive.

'I am looking forward to receiving a letter from England every week, now I have met you,' he tells me hopefully. (He eventually received a letter.)

On both sides of the border the immigration office is a shed. On the Bangladeshi side everybody who can walk swamps the office. Those who can cram inside watch the official adopt an air of importance as he stamps my passport. Outside, minor scuffles break out as they argue who will wheel my bike to the Indian border. The proud and jubilant winner lords it over the others who follow enviously behind.

I take it easy now with a gentle ride to Siliguri. The Welcome Guest House run by an ex-Gurkha is a good choice, especially when I am served roast chicken, fried egg and chips, ice cream and at last, a bottle of beer.

In the morning I soon give up scouring the shops for maps. Everybody is friendly, many speak English and shop signs are in English too. I don't get swamped by people. This part of India is only a narrow stretch and before long I enter Nepal (Never-Ending Peace and Love). After a meal at the border I still have enough time to mop up the few miles to Chandragadhi. I find to my delight that two ex-Gurkha soldiers have built a pub here that is a replica of the one they used when stationed in England.

The Hotel Friendship lives up to its name. It's a boys' night out and I join six Nepalese on a booze-up. They drink whisky like water, but I stick to beer as always (unless somebody leaves half a bottle of red wine on my table). Only one of the six drinkers surfaces in the morning and he looks a bit green. Kamal the owner advises me to stay because a nationwide strike means nowhere is open. His staff are so impressed with my travels that they return to work just to prepare my food, I am the only guest.

Passing into another day I wake to find the hotel deserted, not a soul in the building. All the doors and windows are securely padlocked and fixed with iron bars. I am locked in. For seven hours I pace every landing, try every window and door. I am going to be known as the Mosquito Man of Nepal. Finally I find myself talking through the bars to Benjamin and Ann. They work for the American Peace Corps and they speak Nepalese.

I am granted a pardon.

Kids watch television

Breakfast

CHAPTER 88

A Holy Mess

On a construction site next to my hotel women carry a stack of bricks or a basket of cement on their head. The men also toil away, 50p for eight hours' work. Twelve hotel staff sleep on the floor of the room above mine and their wages are similar.

Twenty-eight-year-old Rezla cleans my bike. She has been watching me scribbling notes and has spent some of her precious pennies on a gift for me, a notepad and two ballpoint pens. I take her arm and we head for the few shops in this backwater. I buy her some shoes and other bits and bobs.

'Yes, of course I will come back,' I reassure her, feeling my nose growing longer as I speak.

An easy ride down to Itahari. Today is International Women's Day. I pause to watch a procession of placard-carrying women marching down the street. I decide not to shout 'Get back to the ironing'. I linger a bit longer, but they don't start burning their bras, so I move on.

I am riding the Mahendra Highway, which stretches East-West across Nepal. Just now it is flat. It will be some time before I start to climb the Himalayas.

'I've done it before,' I smugly tell myself, choosing to forget how whacked I was last time when I reached Kathmandu.

At Hotel Akash I am advised to remain another night. Tomorrow is a holy festival and the practice is for men to get blind drunk and pelt each other and everybody else with eggs, tomatoes, old motor oil, soot, and anything else that will make a mess. A tourist on a bicycle will be a prime target.

Fool that I am I choose to ignore the advice.

All this makes me think about the Water Festival in Thailand, the Songkran. Thousands of tourists flock to take part. They cannot be aware of the number of deaths and injuries that occur during this long event. All over the country huge drums of water are set up along the roads and well before the actual day of celebration men, women and children shower every passing thing. They even put chemicals in the water that stain the cars and obliterate the windscreens. People block the roads to ensure that nobody escapes a drenching. Motorcyclists and bike riders are the most vulnerable, many are brought to the ground or caused to enter the path of lorries and cars. Excited children run across the roads to throw water on approaching motorbikes, they often end up under a car. Gangs of people drive round the countryside in open trucks and drench everybody they can. Try riding a bike when buckets of water are being thrown on you from above, many a cyclist goes under the truck wheels. Some people use large water pistols that shoot ice cubes regardless of the pain inflicted on the victim. Every year the death toll is in the hundreds, and thousands are injured. When two hundred people were killed in a fire in Lima, Peru, the president there called for a day of national mourning. The same year in Thailand around seven hundred were killed during Songkran. Was a day of mourning called for? Of course not, this death toll seems acceptable and normal in Thailand.

So today I ride the gauntlet of a similar festival in Nepal. Groups of drunks already smothered from head to foot lie in wait armed with a variety of gadgets that propel assorted substances. Violence between them is always a hair's breadth away as one drunk manages to pour more oil or paint over a fellow drunk than he himself received.

A polythene bag filled with red paint bursts as it comes into contact with my head. I'm in a sorry state. Yesterday and today, have been precarious with swarms of young men drinking themselves stupid. The noise they make means it's impossible to sleep. Great camping country, but too risky. The celebration is tenuously linked to some story about an evil man destroyed by God. I find a shack hotel. I can't understand a word in the registration book, but I fill in the twelve columns anyway, Pluto, Goofy, Donald, Mickey etc. Instead of sleeping on the bed I put my tent up on it to avoid the dirt and the mosquitoes.

A Mars bar that I buy is three years out of date, but the shopkeeper refuses to give my money back and is astonished that I even ask. Obtaining food here is as hard as it gets. Everywhere is filthy; cleaning has never been introduced to the place. I'm living on biscuits and fruit. When I order some rice the staff member spends a few minutes picking bugs out of the plate she has just placed in front of me. I get used to a moving meal.

I've ridden 250 miles in Nepal and I approach Hetauda, the first reasonably sized town I've spent time in. On the outskirts of the town I find a pathetic family. The man and woman, hardly more than skeletons, try to make a shelter from sheets of cardboard they've managed to scavenge. Five barefoot children clothed in the minimum of rags. They can't all be hers; they're too close in age. In answer to my questioning eyes she puts her hand on three little heads then touches her chest. She manages to indicate that she takes care of the other two for a friend or a sister who has died. The little hope in her eyes fades as I ride away. At the first general store I fill one bag with fruit, another with two bottles of milk, a large bag of rice, sugar, flour and bread. Oh, there are some cornflakes, how about some toffees for the kids and a tub of ice cream?

Back at cardboard house with supplies that will still only last a short time, the family are beside themselves. I don't want the reception I receive. The mother speaks to the children and they drop to the floor to try and kiss my feet. So do the mother and father. I want to cry, so I cry.

CHAPTER 89

An Aston Villa Fan in Nepal

The Hotel Lido in Hetauda is clean, clean. It even has a television, but I won't be watching it. I've wasted too much time watching TV in the past. Tomorrow I'll reach Royal Chitwan Park and renew my friendship with Vishal Kumal. It's a friendship that began more than two years ago and we've maintained it by post.

Today involves a little climbing as the road flirts with the mountains. These are the first hills I've encountered for a few weeks, but there are lots more to come. Now the road hugs the mountain and the river hugs the road. It makes for lovely scenery. At a café stop, two five-year-olds keep me amused with non-stop chatter. I've experienced this a lot, adults quickly realise I can't speak the language, but young children aren't aware that other languages exist. Finally the five-year-olds stop babbling and speak to the woman. They almost certainly say, 'This old goat is too miserable even to speak to us.'

An English couple sit down at a table and we exchange hellos. The woman screams and jumps to her feet shouting, 'Snake!'

The man produces a camera and takes several shots of a snake hanging from the branch of a nearby tree, the woman shouting, 'Don't go any nearer'.

He goes down on one knee to take a better picture, stands on a chair, moves to other positions. Two boys are splitting their sides laughing, it's a rubber snake they've hung there, and not for the first time.

I wrote to Vishal over five months ago to tell him I would be starting in Vietnam. So what an amazing coincidence when he comes riding towards me on a motorbike.

Before long I'm riding into Sauraha and no less than six shopkeepers call out, 'Welcome, Bob.'

Vishal lays on a great meal with his family present. They try to use a knife and fork for the first time. Two and a half years ago Vishal asked me to send him an Aston Villa football shirt when I got home. A Villa fan in my local not only gave me a shirt, but said he was very involved with the club and if Vishal sent back a photo he would get it printed in the club magazine, boasting that they even had supporters in Nepal. I despatched the coveted shirt to Vishal and explained that he could have his picture in the magazine. He sent me a photo of himself in a white T-shirt.

Sauraha is a lovely spot. I have splendid digs and after a rest day we set off for several days trekking and canoeing. We reach the river by motorbike. What uncomfortable machines they are, after fourteen miles of rough track I dismount with cramped legs and backache. We ride through a ramshackle village and Vishal tells me that a few weeks ago a lorry tore through these scattered dwellings at reckless speed and killed a man on a bike. Villagers dragged the driver from his cab and beat him to death. Body and lorry disposed of, things returned to normal. The police put in an appearance several days later. They had been tracing the driver's route, but had no idea which way he'd passed. Nobody knew anything.

We spend two hours in a dugout canoe on the Rapti River. The two men managing the vessel have paddled three hours against the current to pick us up. For their five hours' labour they charge £1 and they don't conceal their delight at earning this sum. Working in the fields from dawn to dusk they normally earn 35p a day if they're lucky. The boat leaks badly and needs constant baling out. One of the boatmen uses his flip-flop to scoop out the unwanted water.

Nothing could be more peaceful than this journey down the river watching local people going about their necessary chores. They carry back-breaking loads of wood, illegally taken from the forest (fine 60p if caught), men catch fish using a spear made from a stick and a sharpened bicycle spoke, children swim, men and women wash themselves, women wash clothes, buffaloes wallow in the water and wash off the dung they've been lying in. Regardless of all this the boatmen drink frequently from the river as they have done all their lives.

The glorious river trip culminates at Vishal's village. Two and a half years since I was last here and the village remains absolutely traffic free. The villagers are so poor that there's no farm machinery and only two or three motorbikes. The hovels they live in are fifteen kilometres from the main road and the authorities have recently started to make a proper surface, one kilometre a year, so the road will take fifteen years to reach here. Electricity has been laid on in the last two years and Vishal's family has a small black and white television. Local children press their faces against the flimsy timber walls to glimpse a very poor picture through gaps in the planks.

The baskets contain other snakes

Threshing rice

Wash day

Vishal's in-laws

CHAPTER 90

Biscuits for Rhinos

A good many people in Vishal's village have tapped illegally into an electricity supply that they can't afford to have properly connected. The village also has a telephone that was installed seven months ago. A far cry from Britain where people aren't dressed unless they have a mobile phone.

Vishal has built a better restaurant since my last visit. 'Two Hungry Eyes' serves excellent food.

'It should do,' says Vishal. 'The chef is very expensive.'

The chef earns £20 for a seven-day week.

Vishal has done well when you understand that the majority of people here are illiterate. His education was nearly brought to a halt at fourteen because he didn't have the 60p enrolment fee for the next school term. His father told him to get married and work in the fields.

'What good is school to anyone?'

An understanding uncle gave him 60p and his schooling continued.

Vishal, his father-in-law and I set off to trek in the Chitwan jungle. The heat is becoming intolerable. We set up camp on the edge of the Rapti River in the hope of seeing rhinoceroses when they come to drink at night or in the early morning. Vishal circles the tent at some distance with a rope fixed a few feet above the ground. He hangs our footwear and a few articles of clothing on it.

'If a tiger comes along he will smell humans and move away,' he explains.

I hope he's right. The two other men take turns to keep vigil all night, but the rhinos obviously aren't thirsty. Not even a mosquito shows itself.

We are supposed to be visiting Tiger Tops, the world famous resort for Hooray Henrys. We've obtained the necessary permission, but it is withdrawn at the last minute. Perhaps they don't want a below stairs person like me helping himself to the red wine. We trek miles in search of rhino but we are not short of wildlife, crocodiles, lemur monkeys, deer, peacocks and plentiful other exotic birds.

A tremendous roaring and crashing. Vishal shouts, 'Run! Run!'

I catch sight of two rhinos head to head and then I am running for my life. We stop for breath. Vishal won't let me go back and give them a few biscuits. On the trek back we are lucky enough to see another rhino, at a safe distance.

At the Kumal village mother-in-law continues to provide a variety of food to suit my difficult taste. The advent of electricity means the little shop now has a fridge. Much effort has been made to obtain beer. With five bottles inside me I confess to staggering. The area is so peaceful and beautiful that any traveller reaching here would be delighted with the surroundings and the friendliness of these lovely people. They are thrilled with one tourist, so they'd be well pleased to see their first backpackers. I visit 31-year-old Vishal's old school. His headmaster considers my friend his star pupil. The five hundred or so children here are currently the lucky ones, but even so the headmaster says many will have to leave at a young age to help scratch out a living from the soil.

I am introduced to Kopil, a waiter at a posh hotel in Sauraha. Despite being married with three children he still enjoys the attention of many female guests. One of his western lady friends gave him £1,500 to build himself a stone house in the village of straw roofed hovels. Her only stipulation was that he should call the house by her name.

'This afternoon I am going to paint her name above the door and I would like you to take a photograph for me to send to her,' he requests. 'Her name is Christine and she is from England.'

In the late afternoon Vishal and I present ourselves at the house. Above the door is painted 'Margreet'.

'You said the girl was Christine,' I point out.

Kopil scratches his head. 'Did I? This was Margreet from Holland.'

He admits he has so many girlfriends that he doesn't even remember which one gave him such a huge sum of money. His unconcerned wife smiles in the background. Another hair-raising canoe ride in wilderness splendour, this time including my friend's ten-year-old splendid nephew Biggyan. Now the leaky dugout negotiates the rushing waters of Narayani. Nine rivers join this water to make it Nepal's biggest river. The dugout is far from stable and the sides are only inches above the water. Whirlpools form where rivers meet. Water rushes over the side to increase the pond that the boatman scoops out with his flip-flop. No lifejackets and the instruction I am given is if the boat sinks don't try to swim, the river is too deep and the current too strong. Wait for the canoe to re-surface and hang on. Time and again the dugout is within fractions of capsizing, but we break out into calm water.

The only way Bob can speak, balloons for the kids

CHAPTER 91

Language Problems

In this most peaceful of locations violent death occurs twice during my visit. A rhino savages a fourteen-year-old boy on a school jungle trip and at a separate location another rhino kills a farmer working alone on his mustard crop. This rhino afterwards takes a dip in the village pond, injures two more locals and ambles back to its forest retreat. It is forty-two degrees and rising, cattle are dying in the fields.

Vishal has laid on a cultural dance for me, the only tourist here. Thirteen musicians plus three dancers.

'They will have to charge you,' I am told. The fee is £2.

The dancers are all men, two dressed as women.

'Why can't there be women dancers?' I ask.

'Because the dance goes on for an hour and women can't do that. The men can do it because they've been drinking all day,' is the crazy reply.

It's Vishal's turn to have too much to drink and he's glad to take over my abode and sleep for the first time in a tent. In the morning I amuse the family by collapsing the canvas onto the still-sleeping man. With his hangover he thinks the sky has fallen on him.

Since being in Nepal I have made one of my classic blunders. In every country there are essential survival words to learn, such as 'hot', 'cold', 'water' etc. In the quest for a cold drink I learned the word for cold, pronounced something like 'cheese-o'. So I was riding along ordering beer cheese-o. Mostly a waste of time because few places have electricity therefore no fridges. Gradually I forgot the correct pronunciation, but I knew the word sounded something like a sneeze and racking my brains I decided the word was 'tishy'. Not noticing the odd looks I got, I have been asking for a beer tishy.

Now at Kumal village the family shop has a fridge so at least four times a day I ask Biggyan to fetch me a beer tishy. Each time he runs and speaks to his mother. She just shrugs her shoulders and he completes the task. Vishal finally tells me to stop using that word – 'tishy' is the slang word for a womb. They have me tagged as an alcoholic sex maniac.

Nine of us take part in a family outing to an old Hindu temple. We use motorbikes, rickshaws, buses, lorries and finally a frightening cable car ride to Manakamana Temple. Tourists have to pay considerably more to ride the cable car unless they work for a charity. I tell the ticket seller that I work for Care Towards Children and when he asks for proof I show him my Cyclist Touring Club membership card, but it doesn't work. At the tea house along the road I take a handkerchief from my pocket to hold the glass of scalding hot tea. Vishal asks what it is, so I explain I use it to wipe my nose. He is disgusted.

'You then put it back in your pocket?'

The Nepalese pinch their nose with two fingers and blow hard. On the way to the temple I sit in the seat behind the driver, whose constant attempts to eject phlegm out of the window fail frequently. My handkerchief comes in useful for wiping my face. Only Hindus are allowed to enter the temple and a queue of hundreds has formed. Each carries a creature to be slaughtered, goats and chickens. A waterfall of blood must run from this holy place. Another outing with Vishal to a memorial near Hetauda is marred by having to push the punctured motorbike three miles in furnace heat. Sculpted effigies of men who died for Nepal surround a beautifully laid out garden. On the way back we encounter two coaches that have crashed head on. Three are dead and many injured. They didn't die for Nepal, but they died because of the stupid Nepalese overtaking and crazy driving. I would use up many rolls of film if I took a photograph of every wreck I see.

With my tanned skin I am often taken for Nepalese and as I stand outside a farmyard looking at the animals three soldiers approach me. One of them speaks to me and is taken aback when I reply in English.

When the Kumal family stop laughing they tell me he said, 'Hey, old man, can you sell us a goat?'

Travelling always means saying goodbye and so I leave another family of people who have taken me into their home and their hearts.

'I'll be back,' says the old goatherd. But how much sand have I got left at the top of the hourglass?

CHAPTER 92

Hanging on the Back of a Lorry

In the last ten days I've travelled by motorbike, rickshaw, buffalo cart, dugout canoe, bus, lorry and cable car. Now I'm back astride the best transport of all. It's raining and within half a mile a van driver offers me a lift to Pokhara, 125 miles away. It's a kind offer, but I shall savour this long-awaited ride.

The cheap tent I bought in Thailand needs attention before I can use it again so I bed down in Mugling. Back on the road to Pokhara I ride slowly with the sun sapping my strength. I pause at the spot where I camped two and a half years ago to look at the glorious snow-capped peaks of the Himalayas. It's getting dark and then the back tyre bursts.

Time to pamper myself so I book a posh room at the Lakeside Hotel at £3 a night. Television, phone, ensuite bathroom with hot water, towels, soap and toilet paper, who do I think I am?

Now where shall I head for? The Everest Steak House, stuff all that rice. I relax after a delicious steak meal, watching from the elevated deck hundreds of back packers swarming the streets, as usual all clutching the Lonely Planet Guide. A poor little rich boy taking a gap year (never done a stroke of work and he's having a year off) sits at my table and pours scorn on me for riding a bike.

'So how did you get here?' I counter.

'On a coach from Kathmandu with dozens of other travellers,' says the seasoned explorer.

'Well, I've come thousands of miles on a bike and had adventures you wouldn't dream of. Look at the seething mass on the road, not one single cyclist. Do you really think you're finding the lonely planet?'

He thinks for a minute. 'Yes, you're right,' he admits. 'We're carried everywhere. I wish you good luck.'

I stay here five days and have the pleasure of meeting twenty-eight-year-old Elaine. We meet up and dine and drink together a couple of evenings. She is eager to hear my stories.

'Bob, you're the most fascinating man I've ever met. I wish you were younger.'

'You're pretty fascinating yourself and I wish you were older,' I reply. We don't let the age difference interfere with our mutual fascination when it's time for sleepy-bo-bo.

Heading for Kathmandu in unrelenting heat. I could roast a turkey on my back carrier. I can manage only twenty-five miles. I'd be a fool to carry on and risk death from heat exhaustion. I abandon my plan to ride back into India, across Pakistan, Iran, Turkey and onwards. I take shelter at Hotel Navaratna in Damauli, then at a grubby highway motel, leaving me forty-five miles to the capital. This is the toughest stretch, with a rise of twelve miles as the city draws nearer. I make two of the toughest climbs hanging on the back of a lorry.

Kathmandu seethes with people and assorted traffic either stationary or moving at one mile an hour.

CHAPTER 93

Welcome to Greece (Not)

I plan to fly to Greece and continue my journey back to England, so I purchase a ticket and leave Nepal on 3rd April. The aircraft stops at Abu Dhabi and there's an eight-hour delay at Bahrain, making for a long drawn out journey. A well-informed Brazilian informs me that the length of delay entitles passengers to a hotel room, although the airline doesn't broadcast this and hundreds slouch around as best they can. I stick close to Mr Brazil and after many arguments eight of us are shepherded onto a bus and whisked away. We have on board a splendid sprightly eighty-four-year-old Englishwoman who keeps shouting, 'You're not going to kidnap me!'

With all the airport fuss we only get three hours' comfortable rest before being transported back through immaculate Bahrain, I think they wash the dust before it's allowed to settle.

I'm in Athens but my bike isn't. I've entered a lovely country (not). I was previously unaware what miserable people Greeks are. They don't even smile at their own babies. Of all the countries I've experienced Greece stands out as the most unsociable.

The guy in charge of missing luggage can't locate my bike on his computer and he couldn't care less. This is my first sample of Greek behaviour. I'm told to go to a particular hotel in Athens, phone Mr Luggage in the morning for an update. If the bike has arrived it will be delivered to the hotel. I find the hotel after an effort and the manageress says there is a room for me. I'm putting my details in the book when a Greek woman comes into reception. The two women engage in conversation. The manageress says she's sorry, but she had forgotten that the newcomer had booked the last room. My second sample of Greek behaviour.

It takes more effort to find another hotel, this time close to the Acropolis. Morning dawns. I phone Mr Luggage, but it's his day off. I get put through to a series of people with limited English who don't want to understand the problem. Finally I am told that the bike still hasn't been located. I recall that in Brazil when my bike went missing it was located within seconds in Spain and delivered to me next day.

A worried man prowls the streets. Coupled with the bike problem is the shock of European prices. Astronomical prices for food mean that every time I eat I ask for the cheapest thing on the menu. Amazingly all the lowest priced meals have been sold. I decide to send a postcard home. I buy the card and go to another stall to purchase the stamp. The attendant pulls out a tray of stamps from under the counter, but he can't change the note I offer. I step to the next stall and buy an ice cream, it only takes a minute. Back at stamp stall a different man is behind the counter, having entered by the back door.

'We have no stamps,' he tells me.

'You have stamps under the counter. I've seen them,' I say.

He flies into a rage and bangs the counter with the side of his fist. 'We have-a no stampas. If-a we have-a stampas we sell-a stampas.'

I find stampas elsewhere.

After three days the bike is located in Bahrain. I ask the airline to deliver it, but I'm told that because the bike is coming from a non-European country I must come to the airport for an interview concerning possible non-payment of VAT.

A very fed-up Bob has to talk a taxi driver into taking him twenty-five miles to the airport. He complains that the roads are too busy. When I get there I walk miles from one desk to another – chaos – and finally a uniformed officer questions me in an office. I am able to show him the receipt that proves I bought the bike in England and paid the VAT.

The officer is pleased to see that the bike cost £1,100 because it means he can claim more VAT than he thought. He won't listen to my arguments, 'You will go with the security guard to collect the bike and bring it here.'

I walk with the guard who doesn't speak a word of English. I drag the bike out of a huge pile of unclaimed articles. It's in a sorry state. It's obviously been beaten and tortured. One arm of the handlebars has been bent to touch the scarred frame. There's worse damage still, but I don't spot it straight away. I pump up the tyres and replace the pedals.

We start the long walk back to the officer and it dawns on me that the guard isn't aware of the situation. As far as he's concerned he only had to escort me through a secure area. As we pass an exit door I say, 'Cheerio'. I'm through that door in a flash. Riding is awkward with warped handlebars but I'm away like the wind. I'm up till the early hours working on my machine. I bend the bars into reasonable shape with the help of a chair and eagerly await morning.

A quick check to see if Interpol are staked outside and I'm back on the road again. I feel so good riding past the heap of hardcore called the Acropolis and heading for the countryside. Ten miles out I realise that all is not well with the back wheel. Inspection shows the rim is cracked and crushed. The section breaks off when I try to straighten it. I don't want to go back to Athens and enquiries tell me a bike shop is eight miles away, so riding slowly I make the distance.

The bike shop staff are not at all helpful. 'Come back in three days,' they tell me.

I plead with them although none of us can speak the other's language. Reluctantly a young man builds me another wheel. It takes him less than thirty minutes, why so much fuss? A relieved man takes to the road again and enjoys the scenery, but not people's attitude. They'd rather tell me to piss off than help with directions. They don't just say no to a request, they fly into a rage and tell me off for asking.

Tonight my tent occupies a hilltop with splendid views of the valley. I sleep well knowing I'm sleeping free.

All set for a good day though the wind is so strong I even have to pedal downhill. The sun shines and I'm riding through impressive scenery of snow-capped mountains, verdant valleys, fields awash with poppies and trees laden with spring blossom. That night another hillside becomes my base. I can see a farmhouse in the distance, where dogs sense me and create a racket, but nobody comes to investigate. I wake up in pouring rain and realise the Thai tent isn't suitable. Pools of water have formed inside and constant dripping though the canvas has soaked everything. I can't move off in this downpour so I sit it out till one o'clock then pack my sodden equipment and head for the nearest town.

Arachova is the chief ski resort in Greece and it's a lovely town full of upmarket hotels and restaurants. My room at Hotel Apollo soon looks like a jumble sale as I hang my clothing everywhere. Food is an urgent priority. I nearly choke on the price, a cup of tea (3p in Nepal) here is £1.50. A television wakes me blaring away at one in the morning in the guest lounge next to my room. I open the door to find a surly young Greek standing in front of the TV set. I signal my disapproval and he switches it off. I consider that while I'm up I might as well visit the bathroom. Returning to my room I'm unconcerned that he is standing closer to my door. I sleep. In the morning my wallet is missing. Plenty of surly young Greeks are about but not the one in question. Nobody is interested; all at once nobody speaks English.

I'm not happy but I've learned not to carry much money in my wallet. Most of my money is spread around my body in the hope that when I'm robbed (as I have been several times) my money won't all be found. The slender screw-top water bottle on my bike holds water plus a tight roll of high denomination notes in plastic. I live in hope that the highway robbers don't think of it. Of course it doesn't work if the bike gets stolen.

CHAPTER 94

Moussaka or Beer?

Thinking about it, I bet Surly Greek used that stunt with the loud TV regularly. He probably worked out that most people roused in the early hours will use the bathroom.

The rain that brought me to Apollo Hotel changed to snow in the night. Now the morning is dry, but cold and gloomy, the valleys below obscured by cloud. Wearing three shirts and a jacket I move on. As I descend the weather improves. A glorious road all downhill to the coast and the town of Itea. I pass Delphi, another historical site. At least sixty coaches are parked on the road and hordes of tourists gazing in raptures at a pile of builders' rubble nod wisely at each other.

I am on the coastal road, heading north to a ferry port where I can cross to Italy. I'll be on this road for several days, so far with sparkling sea one side and rugged country the other. After a day of mixed weather the sun has gone by 4.30 in the afternoon and a deluge puts paid to my camping plans. At a seaside village a little west of Eratini I manage to rent an apartment. The village is a lovely spot, my accommodation looks out at brightly coloured fishing boats bobbing on a glittering sea against a backdrop of green hillsides and grey mountains.

In a restaurant today I somehow managed to amuse the staff. As I perused the menu a hovering waiter intervened, 'Perhaps sir would like some moussaka?'

'No, thank you. I'll have a beer. I don't drink wine.'

The waiter walked away convulsed with laughter and began an animated conversation with the other staff. I fail to see what's funny about a man preferring beer to wine.

I did a stupid thing the other day. A handkerchief worked its way out of my pocket and fell onto the chain. It got carried into the jockey wheels on the rear hanger. My chain jammed. The handkerchief was firmly wedged and knotted. I hacked away with my knife, cutting my finger to make things more interesting, but I couldn't free the obstruction. Actually I only needed to use an allen key to remove the cog but no, this fool decided to burn the offending material. Too late I realised the cogs are plastic. I blew out the flames, but I had already melted two teeth. Still possible to ride although constant clicks reminded me what a dope I am. It was two days before I found a bike shop and replaced the mutilated cog.

This is a tremendous road, passing through lovely villages. I've achieved seventy miles today, my best distance for a long time. The weather is good enough to camp out and a meal of lamb chops, chips and two pots of tea sets me up for the night.

I must still be half asleep when I set off. After three miles I realise I'm going back the way I came. The sun tells me I'm wrong, it's early morning and the sun is on my left shoulder. That means I'm heading south. I turn round so the sun is on my right shoulder, north is the required direction. Having to use so many poor maps I use the sun many times to reassure me.

Greece is a country where water has to be crossed many times or long distances travelled round bays. A deluge means I'm thoroughly soaked when I catch a ferry at Aktion for the short route to Preveza. Dripping wet I take a room at Hotel Minos.

Nine days now and I haven't seen a single smile, apart from the laughing waiter. Some people help me, but with blank expressions and no display of friendship. If I see a smiling Greek odds are it's not a Greek. I'm a much-travelled man and the people here are the sourest I've ever met. Mind you, the women all have luxuriant black hair cascading to their waists, it grows from under their arms.

This is my last day in Greece with scenery even more splendid. It's raining, but not heavily. My clothes are wet. In Asia if you get wet you are dry again within minutes of the rain stopping. Not so in Europe, and information tells me it's going to get colder the further north I go. To keep warm I'm wearing practically everything I carry. More clothes are on my shopping list.

After riding six hours I arrive at the port of Igoumenitsa. From here the ferry will take me overnight to Brindisi, Italy. I won't be sorry to leave Greece. The country is beautiful, but there's no warmth in the people, even Ken Dodd couldn't make them laugh.

CHAPTER 95

Easter Goes On and On

On board ship I slip up by paying £48 for a cabin, when it's only £20 to sleep on deck. The cabin has four berths and I'm sharing it with one Turk. After the ship sails the Turk brings another Turk to the cabin. New Turk explains he has paid for deck space, but will I permit him to use the cabin and bathroom facilities.

'Of course,' I say, 'even if you were a Greek.'

New Turk and I sleep not a wink. Old Turk snores loudly all night.

New Turk is addicted to smothering himself with eau de cologne, he reeks to high heaven. He has a pint bottle of the stuff and douses himself ALL OVER before going to bed and again in the morning.

I remark that the only thing that smells worse than a dead Turk is a live one.

'English humour,' he growls.

Yes, I could have saved £28 and got some sleep if I'd stayed on deck.

Arrival at Brindisi and the day starts well. The police are friendly and I get a good breakfast. I wonder about illegal immigrants, because the Greek port where I boarded isn't far from troubled Albania yet I pushed my bike on board with no passport check. I've disembarked in Italy and been just waved away.

The weather decides this isn't sunny Italy and I'm cold and wet through again. At the largish town of Cisternino the locals insist there are no guesthouses so I'm obliged to pay £28 for a night's B&B in a luxury hotel, mixing with the kind of people who don't really want the likes of me staying here. Even the receptionist can't keep the sneer off his face.

The weather isn't just bad, it's horrendous. Water cascades down. The hotel bathroom is equipped with a hairdryer that I use for two hours to dry my clothes, including my sorry-looking Adidas shoes. They haven't been dry for a long time.

Dry but bitterly cold with the wind full in my face. Strong pedalling keeps my body warm, but my hands and feet suffer. Less than two weeks ago I could hardly move for the heat. I find a cheap boarding house at £11 a night. I've covered seventy-five miles in two days, not good, but also not bad considering the weather.

Easter Monday and for the last three days most of the shops have been shut and very few restaurants open. Those that are open get packed to capacity and a non-Italian speaker is somewhat of a nuisance. On the whole the Italians are being helpful and friendly, but as in all modern countries the car rules. I ride miles and never see anybody on foot or on a bike. Today is the best weather so far, less wind and weak sunshine, although riding hard I find I can still achieve only sixty-two miles.

Mountains loom ahead covered in cold white stuff with more falling. I think I can camp if I find a suitable spot. I ride on and on. Disused farms and factories all made inaccessible with high razor wire or snarling guard dogs. No forests just open cultivated land. Something will turn up, it always does. A disused stone quarry attracts my eye, set in wasteland used by picnickers and dog walkers, so I push my bike over rough ground to reach the top of a hill. I'm out of sight of the road and well removed from traffic noise. A concrete shelter, where workmen take cover while blasting is an ideal place, in the dry and out of the wind. As darkness falls it gets a bit spooky, but I sleep well.

Away early, but trouble with the bike means poor mileage. Pouring rain forces me into a hotel in San Severo. I'm pleased I bought a longer, thicker jacket yesterday, word is it's snowing heavily in Austria. As for the bike I'm plagued with punctures and of course everything is wearing out. Today I replaced the chain and that won't be the last thing.

Easter goes on and on here. Still only a few shops open. I sit close to the window in a bar near the hotel, bars in Italy are also cake shops, sweet shops and toy shops. There are many cake shops and the cakes are all delicate, feminine things, tiny with cherries and cream, all right for women to eat, but a man would have to be that way inclined to eat one. Two young boys with grinning faces full of devilment press a picture against the window where I'm sitting. The picture torn from a magazine is of a naked lady. The barman chases the boys away. Spoilsport, I was enjoying that picture.

At last a day when I can take off my jacket. I eventually join the coast road but at five in the evening I haven't reached my destination of Pescara. I'm not far short, but enough is enough. Plenty of campsites along the coast road, but never one when you need it. The spot I find is a lovers' hangout, I don't notice the contraceptives thrown about until I've erected (no pun intended) the tent. The problem now is, should I tell the Pope?

CHAPTER 96

Pedalling Like Mad

Looking back at the events of the last couple of weeks there's precious little excitement or adventure, nothing unusual, typical of modern countries. I want the element of danger, the curiosity of people who have never seen a white man, the prospect of the unexpected round the next bend. In our state of the art world the friendship, hospitality and generosity experienced in the third world are missing. Most times it's impossible to speak to western people, to do so means interrupting their mobile phone call. After a night in the woodland lovers' corner (several cars pulled in but drove off in search of a more private spot) I sleep on the beach, a perfect site except that my head is a few feet from a railway line.

In the town of Cesenatico where the famous cyclist Marco Pantani was born, two German cyclists Christie and Wolfgang encourage me to stay at their hotel. A hundred cyclists from all over Germany make me welcome. It's great to be in the company of people with the same interest.

Today as I was riding in heavy traffic a passenger in a car lobbed a bottle at me. It fell in front of my face and shattered on the crossbar. Fragments flew everywhere, but I received no cuts and the scar on the frame blends in with the others. This is the kind of thing cyclists have to put up with. In England and America I've often been targeted by bottle or beer can throwers, plus shouts of 'Get off the road, you stupid **** They've invented cars now!'

I notice a building site and take a meal while waiting for the workers to finish for the day. Site clear I set up tent in rainfall. A couple of workers return before it gets dark to trowel off the concrete they've not long laid. They express surprise, but raise no objections. They soon leave but one returns shortly with 'Hey, Inglis! My wife say you want food?' So hospitality can be found here after all. It was good of them to offer me food, but I had already eaten, pizza, of course. The Italians live on it. They even built a monument to it, the Leaning Tower of Pizza. It's okay if you like stale bread with tomatoes squashed in.

The last three days have produced good mileage, two days of ninety-five and one of seventy-five miles. I'm drawing nearer to Austria and the Alps. Hannibal crossed on an elephant, but he didn't have to pedal the beast.

I leave the building site early, only a little damp. I reach the point on the east coast where I am to head off north-west, entering the mountains where I'm pleased with the scenery. I turn in at 3.30pm and settle in a hotel in Ala. Not much more than a day's ride to the border now, depending on how tough it gets.

On a glorious day, with weather and scenery just as glorious too, I pass through beautiful Trento and other lovely towns. In Merano I stop for the night in my canvas house, but fully clothed and in my sleeping bag I'm still cold.

I had a run-in with the police today. They objected to me riding on the motorway, something I've done a few times. I ignored the horns of various vehicles, but I couldn't ignore the one with flashing lights. The young policeman was stern and spoke Oxford English. 'Why did you ignore the sign that said no bikes?'

'Never saw it,' I lied.

The policeman opened a gate in a fence and put me on a service road that led to the road I was looking for.

'Thank you, young man,' I grinned. After all, he's not long been potty trained.

I don't want to ride on motorways, but sometimes signs are confusing and the choice is between going back miles or taking a chance, so I usually take a chance. Then there are times when a road suddenly becomes a no-cycling road. This happened two days ago. For eight days I rode SS16 up the east coast. At a mile-long tunnel a sign suddenly said no bikes.

What was I supposed to do? Disappear up my own saddle stem? I went on. That was the longest, most nerve-racking mile of my life, pedalling like mad up a dimly lit passage where items have fallen off lorries and can hardly be seen. Traffic thunders through like an express train, not expecting to encounter a slow-moving vehicle that shouldn't be there, noise reverberates and echoes back from the walls. My hair would have turned white if it wasn't already.

But why isn't provision made? A sidewalk would suffice, but no alternative is offered.

Road SS12 runs parallel with the forbidden motorway and it's a great road. Each side of the valley is lined with mountains green or white covered. I am somewhat shocked to find prostitutes plying their trade. These women are all black, I don't think I've ever seen people so black and they are all beautiful with exquisite bodies. They obviously don't feel the cold; they're dressed in micro skirts, high heels, halter tops displaying a cleavage you could get lost in. They could all feature in the centrefold of Playboy magazine. Sometimes these women stand alone at the side of the road, sometimes in groups. Their main targets are long-distance lorry drivers; some laugh and shout comments as I pass – 'We've never tried it on a saddle.'

Now and then I stop and have a good-humoured chat with the girls, but when a British driver offers me the use of his lorry while he has a coffee I decline. Every time a lorry pulls into a lay-by another pair of legs that go on forever disappears into its cab. Many GB trucks are parked in the bays. The drivers tell me this is the longest catwalk in Europe.

CHAPTER 97

Ups and Downs in Austria

Twenty-five miles from Austria I ride hard for eight hours yet I'm still in Italy. Now the border is fifteen miles, but that doesn't mean I've only travelled ten miles, it means the pass I took is blocked with snow.

Leaving Merano the road immediately rises and continues to rise sixteen miles to Saint Leonhard. It gets steeper as it approaches the pass, a 13% gradient according to the map. I ride over twenty miles of this road, only to be told at a roadside café that it's not possible to go further.

'The road ahead is under four metres of snow. You must go back to Merano and take the Reschen Pass.'

At least it's downhill to Merano, though I've wasted four hours of tough climbing for nothing. But nobody could spend four hours in such wonderful scenery and say it was wasted. Countryside like this beats all the Inca ruins and the Roman ruins, and it's free. Waterfalls tumble down the rock faces, in Thailand they tried to charge me £3 to look at a trickle of water.

Off early to scale the Reschen Pass where the road rises at 15% and goes on to 18%. I reach an unlit tunnel 485 metres long with a sign at the entrance 'No Cyclists'. Who is the idiot that prohibits cyclists, but doesn't provide an alternative route?

I ride the tunnel and thank goodness I stay dry. I would be in a fix if the snow fell as it did two days ago, because I don't think I could get through that stuff. Hard going, but I slog on, occasionally walking a stretch. When I'm almost at the summit a car travelling in the opposite direction stops and a man jumps out.

He turns excitedly to his wife in the car. 'It is him! It's Bob the Bike! Hey Bob you crazy man, where have you come from this time?' The man is a builder's merchant I have used regularly in my work in England. He and his wife definitely didn't expect to see me on their holiday, and when I tell them I'm on my way from Vietnam they drive off shaking their heads.

I reach the town of Reschen alongside the lake without fully grasping that I have reached the summit. In seconds I've forgotten the struggle to the top when I race downhill mile after mile into Austria where the sheer loveliness of the countryside continues. I bed down in Telfs west of Innsbruck. I work out how the Austrians have found a novel way of getting rid of the water surplus from their rushing rivers, surging streams and wonderful waterfalls, they sell it in the bars and call it beer. I compliment the bar waiter on the beauty of his home town. 'I'm not from here. I'm from Monchengladbach in Germany.'

'Well, what a coincidence. I served two years military service there forty-seven years ago. I even had a girlfriend,' I respond.

'I am forty-six. My mother brought me up in Humboldtstrasse,' says the waiter.

I don't ask his name. My girl lived in Humboldtstrasse. I pay up and take my leave before he starts singing O, Mein Papa.

An easy ride takes me into Zirl, then a 15% gradient has me walking a long way. Out of breath I reach the top for a great swoop into Germany. Lunch in Garmisch, what a splendid town, something to shout about. The snag is the weather with six months of winter every year.

A man calls on me to stop. His clothes of many colours make him look as if he has escaped from Disneyland. He proudly proclaims himself a fellow cyclist. His bike is decorated like a Christmas tree. We talk awhile and I am pleased I can still remember fragments of German.

My friend advises, 'Sleep at the monastery at Ettal. You sleep free and they feed you.'

I take his advice and present myself to the monks at the Benedictine Abbey. No fuss, I get a fine room with ensuite. A firm voice informs me, 'Evensong at six pm.' And here I am singing for my supper.

CHAPTER 98

One Beer in a Brewery

At evensong in Ettal Monastery are thirty monks with a congregation of thirteen, four other male guests included. The monks all sing sitting down, but every so often they and the audience stand up, arch their bodies and sing while looking at the floor. Another way of contacting God?

The monastery is also a brewery and the meal includes a pint of beer. The food is good, but nobody speaks during the entire meal. One monk sits in the pulpit reading what sounds like the history of the Benedictines. At one point all the monks have to pull their hoods over their heads. Religion baffles me.

A senior monk asks if I am coming to mass.

'No.'

'Are you an atheist?' and at my answer 'Yes' he strides away with a look of contempt.

After breakfast I leave with the thought that nobody will believe I slept in a brewery and only drank one pint of beer. It's a lovely day and I gradually leave behind the snowy peaks, riding through Oberammergau where the famous passion play is staged. For good measure I also ride through Unterammergau. A helpful man puts me onto little used country roads and encourages me to ride the last ten miles to Augsburg on the cycle path that runs alongside the River Lech. With the weather so good I decide to camp, but first I must eat.

I find food and drink at a riverside restaurant that gives an excellent view of a canal built to train canoeists. The participants entertain me as they hurtle from one obstacle to another. I complain about the practice of smothering every meal in salad cream and my German is just good enough to understand the waitress's reply, 'Hold your meal under the tap.'

A crowd of tourists disembarks from a coach. A reporter from the local paper is present to collect their opinions. When it's my turn I shyly produce my brag book of stories of my exploits. The reporter abandons the other tourists and spends half an hour with camera and pen interviewing me instead. The common or garden tourists look a little peeved and I get to feature in the Augsburg newspaper.

A few miles on I set up my portable home close to the river. The weather stays warm, but with many heavy showers during the night, so that in the morning I have the unpleasant task of removing scores of slugs that are clinging to the tent. I continue in the rain, taking Route Two, but not for long since this is another non-cyclist road. When the police stop me, I hold out my wrists for the handcuffs and the good-natured bobbies laugh, amused that an old man is flouting the law.

'You must ride in front,' they instruct me, so I ride a few miles followed by flashing lights until they put me on a cycle path and I find my way back to country roads.

I had hoped to reach Herzogenaurach today but it's too far and I move into a room just north of Dinkelsburg. Two friends live in Herzogenaurach whom I met in Costa Rica and spent time with in Panama over three years ago. Dorothee and Norman were good to me and I think highly of them. They don't know I'm going to knock on their door. I hope they are at home.

Norman - Dentist's Assistant and husband of Dorothee

They are not at home. I take a room in Hotel Krone and at hourly intervals until ten pm I check the house. I try again in the morning but Dorothee and Norman are still not at home so I ride away disappointed.

Monday 30th April is the first day in three weeks that I can start my ride without a jacket. The sun shines from seven in the morning. Within an hour I can also rid myself of one of the three shirts I've been wearing twenty-four hours a day since landing in Greece. (I would still refuse to use Smelly Turk's eau-de-cologne.)

The day's ride is superb with lovely countryside. Top marks to the planners who installed so many cycle paths. What a marvellous secure feeling to ride on a cyclists-only road. In England and many other countries a rider is conscious that death is at his elbow, but here if the road isn't wide enough for a cycle path a line down the middle of the pavement separates cyclists and walkers. How easily and cheaply this could be done in England. The result here is that thousands of people ride bicycles for pleasure, economy and fitness.

I camp alongside the River Main at Miltenburg. Heading for Frankfurt I realise it's May Day, it seems all Germans ride bikes on this day. I have never seen so many people riding for pleasure. Throughout Germany there must be millions on bikes, all riding safely along cycle paths. How great it would be to see this in England.

The Main joins the mighty Rhine and the cycle paths become confusing. I pitch tent close to Koblenz and woods next to Koln provide my next night's location.

Time to leave the river and not until I try to buy something with German money I realise I am in Holland (pre-euro times). I have ridden here from Greece with no borders.

CHAPTER 99

The Green Green Grass of Home

Towards the end of a day's riding in Holland I have the good fortune to meet Gert.

'You sleep at my house,' she invites and I gratefully accept the offer. She and her husband Les introduce me to their family and allow me to spend the night in their splendid house. Their daughter shows me the balloon animals she has learned to make and the family is amused and pleased when I slip up to my allotted bedroom, shape a few balloons and present them to her.

Leaving these lovely people I head off in bitter cold with a strong wind blowing against me all day. Flat countries don't mean easy riding. I am concerned about lack of accommodation and places to camp. At Café Het Maasdijk Veen I am told there is nowhere to camp until I produce my brag book, interest is shown and following a few phone calls a camping place is secured. It's going to be cold, but I can wrap myself in my now clean clothes that Gert has kindly washed.

An amusing thing keeps happening as I ride through Europe. People don't believe I'm English. They look at my brown skin and say, 'Yes, but where do your parents come from?' They only believe me when I pull up the leg of my shorts and show them where the brown ends.

I'm closing in on the Hook of Holland and I'll board a ship there for the green green grass of home. Oh, to be in England. With another bitter cold start and all the shops closed on Sunday I get no breakfast, but I'm about to enter the last lap of my journey.

Vietnam is a long way behind. I didn't complete the full journey, the heat was too much, but I've pedalled two-thirds of the distance. This trip adds up to over nine thousand miles, bringing my world miles total to in excess of 33,000. I haven't touched every country, but I've cycled more than the circumference of the world, now aged sixty-six and keeping in contact with nobody.

A chat with a young couple in Rotterdam produces coffee and apple pie followed by a meal. Now it's the Hook of Holland. I've got to wait all night for the 7.40 am sailing. I can stay warm in a Dutch pub until one am. My brag book brings me celebrity status and ensures I don't buy my own beer.

A shocking state of affairs at the Stena Ferry dock, locked with no waiting room. I erect my tent on the railway station platform and cope with the cold. A group of English youths is looking very much the worse for wear huddled together in a corner. They've come over for a stag party and from the looks of them it included a punch-up.

The crossing is rough, the noise of the waves hitting the ship is frightening. Passengers are heaving their hearts up on all sides. Samuel Johnson said, 'Being in a ship is being in a jail, with the chance of being drowned.'

I'm the first person off in Harwich and soon I am enjoying the country lanes and all the familiar things. A village cemetery looks cosy enough and after a pub meal I set up headquarters for the night. The nearest headstone reads, 'As you are so once was I. As I am so will you be.'

For my second night I choose to sleep beside a canal, very peaceful. I'm packing up in the morning when Mr Busybody walks by with his dog and comments, 'I don't know what the bye-laws say about camping on the towpath.'

'Stuff the bye-laws and stuff you,' I answer, or something like that. He quickens his pace and hurries off. Using many back lanes I cover 110 miles in eight and a half hours. I enter my house to be greeted by my grandsons.

A letter is waiting for me from the woman who nursed me after I was injured by a motorcycle – Chiamchit.

Good Dutch friends Gert and Ies

The tent pitched on the platform at the Hook of Holland railway station

CHAPTER 100

Epilogue – Sirima

That letter has brought me back to Bangkok. At least five hundred miles on main roads to Chiang Mai, where Chaimchit runs a restaurant. The Burmese shelled Fang, killing several people and scaring off the tourists, which meant the closure of her business.

She doesn't know I'm here. Sophocles said, 'To reach the age when you lose the sexual urge is like being unchained from a madman.' I haven't reached that age.

Five days later I am at Lampang, about sixty miles from Chiang Mai. I make contact and Chiamchit arrives in Lampang. Three honeymoon weeks blighted by her son, who constantly insults me, argues with his mother and collapses in tears for no particular reason.

It's inevitable, I listen to the same words I heard many months ago. 'I am devoted to my son. I can't let anything spoil our relationship.'

As Roy Orbison sang, 'It's Over, It's Over.'

I'm more than a little down in the mouth, but the ride from Bangkok has made me dream of carrying on to Laos, China, Mongolia…

In Chang Mai I've paid two months' rent at Hotel SP and they won't refund my money. I think I'll just hang out here until it expires and then take off.

I make friends with rich American Jerry, who for some reason wants to open a massage parlour in America. Most days he attends college to learn the trade and after classes he practises at Tip Top Massage. Every day I ride out and afterwards return to poke fun at Jerry as he lies on a mat amongst other out of condition guys. The shop is wide open to passers-by.

Sirima is one of the women who encourage tourists to be customers. It becomes my regular habit to try to talk with Sirima when I call at Tip Top and tease Jerry. The usual language difficulties persist. I don't know it yet, but I've met my match.

'I am thirty-seven,' she tells me, which translates as forty-three. Her husband died ten years ago, leaving her with a four-year-old daughter and a nine-year-old son. Amongst other menial jobs she has worked twenty-four years on a sewing machine in a sweat shop for less than £3 a day, falling asleep over the machine when required to work overtime twenty-four hours at a stretch.

She has taken a six-month massage course and hopes to do better. The big prize is maybe to net a Western husband.

I have not fallen for Sirima but as the days pass I begin to feel protective towards her and help her out a little. She sees me walk past several times with a woman on my arm. At times I go into an internet café where the owner sends a message for me to one of 'Bobby's Angels'. She tells me much later that she got the café owner to tell her what messages I had sent.

I go away for four days. 'You no come back,' she says, but I know I will because I have already paid for weeks more accommodation at the hotel.

After a miserable four days I am back in the city. Tidy myself up, why not go and see Sirima? She has gone. The female boss has complained to her that I never spend money, but just take up Sirima's time and Sirima has walked out. I feel responsible. Where is she? I reason she will try to get work in a similar establishment. I comb the streets. I find her at Tina's Beauty Shop. The boss is an arrogant American. Well, being an American he's got no choice.

She's more than a little pleased to see me. She shows me the floor she sleeps on above the shop. She thinks it's a huge improvement on the downstairs floor she slept on at the previous shop. 'Here I have some coat hooks on the wall.'

I take her for a meal for the first time and afterwards return her to her address. She keeps her distance. We carry on like this for a week or more and I'm not even allowed to kiss her cheek. I point out the availability of women, Bob, what a nasty piece of blackmail. She calls out to me as I walk away, 'You go hotel. You sleep alone.' I sleep alone.

Three weeks pass. With a rented motorbike we have picnicked in the country, visited tourist spots, walked side by side at the zoo, two feet apart. I have kissed her fingers and touched her forehead, the only physical contact she has allowed. Sirima invites me to her home village, a lovely backwater thirty miles from the city in a valley surrounded by mountains. The family gathers in the shack house, father, mother, three brothers, aunts, uncles, cousins. Oh dear, oh dear.

Looking anxious Sirima sits behind her father while an English-speaking cousin fires off a lot of questions and translates my answers for the others. Finally the cousin says, 'Yes, it's okay. You can marry his daughter.' Sirima jumps to her feet and runs to put her arms around me. I am dumbstruck, I haven't even asked her.

CHAPTER 101

Wanderlust Returns

On the way back to Chiang Mai Sirima says, 'Now my father says it's okay I will come to your room.'

My mind is working overtime. I have a few weeks left at the hotel. I can have my cake and eat it and be on my way. Sirima plays her master stroke. She turns up at nine pm and brings all her worldly goods with her, two supermarket bags contain all she possesses. She is not going to be a one-nighter, a notch on the bedpost. She hangs her clothes in the wardrobe, she washes all my clothes and tidies the room. I get to kiss her cheek.

The weeks pass. Sirima goes off to work every morning. My day to check out draws near and I plan my departure. I will check out while she is at work and reception will hand over her things to her.

My conscience speaks. 'You can't do that. She'll be devastated.'

I answer my conscience. No, I can't hurt her. So I don't. Instead I go to Tina's Beauty Shop. Arrogant American tells me not to take her away. 'She is my best masseuse and she features in my plans.'

'Plan your own life, not someone else's,' I reply. I take her hand and lead her from the shop. 'She's out of here.' Sirima skips delighted down the road.

We spend a week at her brother's house. He and his wife have to go to work each day. We don't, but we manage to occupy ourselves. I decide to give it a try. I don't promise marriage, but I rent a three-bedroom, two-bathroom bungalow for £50 a month in the small town of San Kamphaeng. I'm not confident it will work out, something will come up that I can't live with and I'll be away, maybe religion, maybe objections to me going off on my bike or having a regular beer. There will be something...

She doesn't put a foot wrong. She's a marvellous housekeeper, she tends the garden, she's an excellent cook and dressmaker and she's always so cheerful. Daily my affection grows. However, after a few months the novelty begins to wear off. Time marches on, it's become boring. No newspapers, no television, no Western food. When will she do something wrong? The wanderlust is strong.

We live on a small estate of bungalows where I am the only English speaker so three times a week I ride into Chiang Mai to talk with tourists in the bars and eat fish and chips, apple pie and so on. A forty-year-old Australian asks me to help find him a village wife and he comes to my home. 'No problem,' says Sirima and we all go to the sweatshop where she spent so many years.

'This Australian is looking for a wife,' announces my woman. Thirty women stand up.

The care she takes of me is amazing, but I am itching to resume travelling. I break the news. 'I am touring Laos.' She knows I'm not coming back. I pay three months rent and leave some money, but she won't be able to pay the rent next time it becomes due. It will be back to her parents, back to the rice fields, the sewing machine or massage.

CHAPTER 102

What About Sirima?

I ride north into the Golden Triangle and cross the mighty Mekong River at Chiang Khong, heading for Luang Namtha on one of the worst surfaces I've ever ridden. I doubt if a goat would try this. The guys in search of the lonely planet take a boat down to Luang Prabang. I expect it's an interesting trip, but I prefer to enter wilderness country. I frequently fall to the ground as my wheels slip sideways on loose rocks.

The hill tribe people make me welcome. They have nothing, but they would give away their last mouthful of food. I accept a chunk of roasted rat, it tastes like beef. Wide-eyed naked children mob me and once again I make balloon animals to give them. I sleep under a roof of banana leaves.

It takes me three days to reach Luang Namtha. The only traffic I've seen was a couple of battered motorbikes. The riders must have spread the word that a man on a bike is coming because people throng the streets and cheer as I stumble in.

After a couple of days I head for China on what is classed as a main road. From the opposite direction four Austrian cyclists in their forties approach.

'We're getting out of Laos, It's too dangerous,' they tell me. 'Have you heard about the killings?'

I have heard about them. It seems that two Swiss cyclists, man and wife, were riding behind a bus when bandits attacked it with machine guns. Off-target bullets killed the cyclists.

The Austrians call 'You must be mad,' as I carry on.

A frightened man hears every rustle.

Needing to obtain a visa to enter China I turn around and head for Cambodia. By now I have been on the road a month, indulging in what I love most, adrenaline flowing as I get my kick out of living rough. My conscience speaks to me. 'What about Sirima? You told yourself you'd leave when something occurred that you couldn't live with. Nothing occurred. She excelled every day.'

I want to go back. So I do.

I am back. I kiss two fingers and touch her forehead. 'Shall we get married?' She is over the moon.

After the ordeal of getting a visa we are finally in England, getting a frosty reception from my son and his chosen one who are living in my house. I set about arranging the wedding at Birmingham Register Office. An unhelpful man deals with me, demanding three visits before he is satisfied with the paperwork.

'Where are you from?' I enquire.

'Afghanistan,' he replies.

'Aren't you worried about your family?' (The height of the troubles.)

'No, they are all here.'

The authorities tell me we need a translator for Sirima, since both of us can only speak a few words of each other's language. I am stumped until only three hundred yards from my house I spot a mobile café: 'Authentic Thai Food,' parked outside a house. I knock on the house door. Yes, the man has a Thai wife. She can hardly speak English. He tells me there is a Thai temple in Birmingham and the monks do an interpreter service.

We get married with Thai monks in orange robes as witnesses and translators.

My money is almost exhausted so I sell my house in England and build a bungalow in my wife's home village. It's in a country lane with a small piece of woodland alongside and a stream running through. We have superb mountain views. It cost £8,000.

I'm still the only white man for miles, but my Thai improves. The years go by and luck stays with me. I take my wife and daughter to Phuket for a holiday, but after a few days we are homesick for our village and we cut the holiday short. The tsunami strikes Phuket the day after we leave.

I put my stepdaughter through university. Sirima attended school only between the ages of six and ten, then she had to leave to steer a buffalo across the rice fields.

Our lovely daughter, my stepdaughter, is now twenty-five. She was married in January 2013 in a traditional Thai wedding that put Princess Kate in the shade. My wife is dancing at the prospect of maybe being a grandmother in the future. In Thailand 2013 is 2556, and Sirima and I have been together eleven years. She's a wonderful woman. I'm glad she outsmarted me.

On a sad note, my son, his wife and my two grandsons don't speak to me since I remarried. They didn't want to share their inheritance. I don't even know where they live. It hurts.

I continue to cycle and will do so as long as I am able.

From young and green to old and grey.

All the best

Bob the Bike

http://arkpublishing.co.uk

Made in the USA
Charleston, SC
21 June 2015